The Flow of Funds in Britain

The Flow of Funds in Britain

An introduction to financial markets

SANDRA MASON

 Paul Elek   London

© Sandra Mason 1976

First published in 1976 by
Elek Books Ltd
54–58 Caledonian Road
London N1 9RN

ISBN 0 236 40016 9

Printed in Great Britain by
Jolly & Barber Ltd,
Rugby   Warwickshire

Contents

Figures

Tables

Acknowledgements

No book is the product of one person alone and this is no exception. I have gained immeasurably from discussions with many people both in and out of the financial system, especially my colleagues first in merchant banking and then at the London Business School. I owe a special debt to the organizers of the *Financial Times*-City course, and to Basil Taylor in particular, for the initial opportunity to develop some of these ideas and the suggestion that they might be developed for a wider audience; support by the Institute of Finance at the London Business School provided me with the opportunity to complete this book. I am especially grateful to Jack Revell, Harold Rose, Bill Martin, Michael Noble and Basil Taylor who read the draft and provided valuable advice on many sections. None of them is responsible for any remaining errors. Special thanks are also due to Hilary Andersen who typed the manuscript, and to my publishers Elek, who put up with several deferrals of the completion date.

Finally I should acknowledge the great debt I owe to the official statisticians and to all those who have worked on financial data-gathering at the Cambridge University, Department of Applied Economics. Without their work, quite literally this book could not have been written. Naturally, they bear no responsibility for the way I have handled their figures.

August 1975

Introduction

Half a pound of tuppenny rice
Half a pound of treacle
That's the way the money goes
Pop goes the weasel

Up and down the City Road
In and out the Eagle
That's the way the money goes
Pop goes the weasel.

The old nursery rhyme provides an apt summary of what the financial system is all about. It is a 'money-go-round', a process by which money, and the power it gives to buy goods and services, is passed from hand to hand. Those who have more money than they need for the moment lend this to others who want to spend more than they have. Over the years, a wide variety of financial institutions and markets has developed with the aim of easing this transfer process. As a result, in the money-go-round of the UK today there are many channels through which money passes and the financial system appears to be very complex.

This book has been written in the belief that what goes on in the financial system can best be seen by looking at the way money actually flows through the financial markets and institutions, identifying in whose hands it starts and where it ends up as well as the channels used. To show this, statistics are required and, in this sense, the book is an introduction to the use of financial statistics as well as to the British financial system. The tables and figures are integral parts of the text and need to be studied closely. No prior knowledge of the financial world is assumed. Thus I hope that the book will be useful to students who are beginning to investigate the functions of the financial system as well as to those already involved with the system, who wish to gain a better perspective of the role of different markets and institutions.

PLAN OF THE BOOK

There are three main parts to the book. Chapter 1 provides an introduction to both the nature of the financial system generally and the method subsequently used to analyse it. Anyone with a good appreciation of the character of financial transactions may find some sections of the chapter redundant, but all readers would be advised to check on the technical aspects of the analysis of financial statistics. The basic analysis of the financial system is in Chapters 2–7. Most of this is in the form of a study of fund flows and institutions in the UK financial system, with an emphasis on the period between 1963 and 1973, a time of many changes in the way the financial system operated. Inevitably the changes have continued since then, but the structural characteristics of the financial system remain largely unaltered; the comment takes account of the major developments up to the middle of 1975. In Chapter 7, the structure of the UK financial system is compared with a number of foreign financial markets.

The last two chapters move away from the detailed study of fund flows and institutions to consider briefly why the financial system is as it is, and how one tries to judge whether the way the system operates is in any sense ideal. Inevitably the discussion of whether the UK system meets the demands made of it is inconclusive. One can point to certain areas where things might be improved and to others where the system appears to be quite effective. But in many cases no conclusions can be reached. In part this is due to inadequate data; as always more research is required. In addition, a firm conclusion about the system's effectiveness often requires that certain value judgements be made; conflicting objectives, like social and economic aims, have to be weighed up against each other. How this is done is a matter for personal choice; so are the conclusions about whether the system operates well or badly. What the analysis shows is the nature of some of the conflicting objectives that need to be reconciled.

In writing I have tried to avoid the use of jargon, though some technical terms have to be employed. These are defined in the glossary at the beginning of the book. Since there is a lack of standard terminology in this field, all readers are advised to look at the glossary and to note particularly the general definitions given to the words 'borrowing' and 'lending'. In view of the importance of statistical data to the analysis, the comments on sources in Chapter 1 have been supplemented in an Appendix on the data used. There is also a bibliography of further reading, based on the main material used as background to the book. Because of the very wide-ranging character of the analysis, no attempt has been made to provide detailed references on every item in the text. References are included only where direct use has been made of a particular piece of analysis.

Glossary

The definitions below are for some general terms that are used frequently in the book. They have been given an exact meaning which does not always correspond precisely with the normal everyday interpretation. For more detailed information on, for example, types of financial instrument or particular institutions, use the subject index.

Assets—*see* Financial assets and Physical assets.

Banking system—that part of the financial system that involves dealings with the banks (q.v.).

Banks—all banking institutions, i.e. including deposit banks, overseas banks, merchant banks and discount houses. Contrasts with the 'other' financial institutions (q.v.).

Bills and deposits—a general group of short-term financial instruments including cash, treasury and commercial bills, bank and building society deposits (see p. 61).

Borrowing—here used as a general term to describe all kinds of financial transactions where one group is *obtaining* money from another without the corresponding exchange of goods and services. It includes money raised by new issues of securities and increases in deposits as well as borrowing in the form of loans which is the more colloquial meaning. The converse of lending (q.v.).

Capital spending—the purchase of all kinds of physical assets (q.v.).

Companies—one of the main economic groupings, comprising all limited companies in the UK, including foreign-owned companies, but excluding nationalized industries. Divided into industrial and commercial companies (which includes property companies) and financial companies (see financial institutions).

Current spending—the purchase of all goods and services that are not defined as physical assets (q.v.).

Financial assets—all types of financial instrument when seen from the point of view of the lender.

Financial institutions—all organizations that specialize in handling financial transactions whether as principals, agents or consultants. Also described as financial companies. Divided into banks and 'other' financial institutions (q.v.).

Financial instruments—the tokens (piece of paper, entry in a ledger or the equivalent) that are created and exchanged in the course of financial transactions. They represent claims to payment and ultimately claims to goods and services (see p. 7).

Financial markets—the market in a particular instrument consists of all those who are involved with that instrument either as holders of outstanding amounts, new borrowers or lenders or as specialist agents or consultants. Markets may be formal or informal, with or without a physical location, well developed or rudimentary (see p. 11).

Financial surplus or deficit—the difference between a group's saving and its capital spending allowing for capital transfers.

Financial system—the totality of all financial transactions that take place and the financial instruments that they give rise to. Covers all formal financial markets and institutions including the payments system, plus the financial dealings that take place without the intervention of the formal system (see p. 5).

Financial transactions—a financial transaction takes place both when goods and services are exchanged for a financial instrument (e.g. money) and when one financial instrument is exchanged for another (see p. 5). They include the use of money as a means of payment as well as borrowing and lending (q.v.).

Funds—a term used as a synonym for money, especially in the context of money flows, e.g. flows of funds. (Not to be confused with life funds (q.v.).)

Government—one of the main economic groupings, comprising all the public sector including central government, local authorities and nationalized industries.

Gross—when applied to any item, as in gross sales or gross borrowings, indicates that this is measured before deducting any contra items, e.g. before deducting purchases or lending. Contrasts with net (q.v.).

Investment—a synonym for capital spending (q.v.). (Not to be confused with lending (q.v.), which is one colloquial use of this word.)

Lending—here used as a general term to describe all kinds of financial transactions in which one group is *handing over* money to another without the corresponding exchange of goods and services. It includes increases in deposits and the purchase of new securities as well as the granting of loans, which is the more colloquial meaning. The converse of borrowing (q.v.).

Liabilities—all types of financial instruments when seen from the point of view of the borrower.

Life funds—the group of financial instruments created when people enter into life assurance or pension contracts. Technically the present value of the liabilities taken on by the institution concerned.

Loans—a general group of financial instruments including bank advances, mortgages, hire purchase and instalment credit (see p. 69).

Money—a particular group of financial instruments used as a means of payment as well as a store of value. Comprises notes and coin and certain bank deposits.

Net—when applied to any item, as in net purchases or net lending, indicates that this is the difference between two contra items, e.g. purchases less sales, lending less borrowing. Contrasts with gross (q.v.).

Net worth—the difference between the total of a group's holdings of physical and financial assets and its liabilities (q.v.). Represents the true wealth of the group (see p. 8).

Other financial institutions—all financial institutions apart from banks (q.v.), i.e. including building societies, finance houses, life assurance companies and pension funds, investment and unit trusts.

Other instruments—all financial instruments not classified as bills and deposits, loans, securities or life funds (q.v.). Includes trade credit, a variety of official financing instruments and unidentified financial transactions (q.v.). In the statistical analysis, also covers most local authority debt owing to identification problems (see p. 85).

Overseas—one of the main economic groupings, comprising all foreign persons, companies and governments that have dealings with the UK.

Persons—one of the main economic groupings, comprising private individuals in the UK, unincorporated businesses and certain non-profit-making organizations.

Physical assets—in principle, all kinds of goods. Here confined to land, buildings, plant and equipment, stock and work in progress and the like. Consumer durables are excluded.

Saving—the difference between current income and current spending (q.v.).

Securities—a general group of financial instruments including British government stocks, company debentures, preference and ordinary shares and unit trust units (see p. 74).

Transfers—payments between groups or individuals that do not involve a corresponding exchange of goods and services or financial instruments. Divided into current transfers (taxes on income, social security, etc.) and capital transfers (investment grants, capital taxes, etc.).

Unidentified transactions—those forms of borrowing and lending that are known to take place but are not identified in the statistics. Their extent is normally measured on a net basis as the difference between the identified financial surplus or deficit (q.v.) and identified net borrowing or lending (q.v.) (see p. 90).

Notes on figures and tables

The following conventions have been used for the figures and tables:

   £m. is £ millions
   £b. is £1,000 millions
   n/a is not available
   — is either nil or less than half the
      final digit shown

Owing to rounding, the percentages in the figures and tables do not always add to 100.

Unless otherwise stated, the sources of the figures and tables are those given in the Appendix.

1 Analysing the financial system

1.1 ALL FINANCIERS NOW

Virtually everyone in the UK today has some dealings with the network of financial markets and institutions that make up the financial system. For, whether young or old, rich or poor, working or unemployed, most people make use of money. And once money is involved, so is the financial system.

Monetary transactions are an integral part of our everyday world. Many result from our daily activities; income is received in the form of money which is then used to buy the food, clothing and other goods and services needed to maintain our existence. But more complex financial activities have also entered normal life. As people have become more affluent, large numbers have contracted to pay regular sums for life assurance policies or to create holdings in unit trusts. Spare cash has been placed on deposit with a bank or a building society rather than in the teapot or the box under the bed. And a substantial proportion of wages and salaries is now paid in the form of contributions to pension funds.

At the same time, the greater sense of security produced by relatively full employment has enabled more people to anticipate their future income by borrowing. Loans to purchase large items such as cars and other consumer durables, or in the form of house mortgages, have become commonplace. Even for such ephemeral items as holidays, deferred payment schemes are quite widespread.

All these individual borrowing and saving activities involve dealings with the financial system. In a similar way, the many organizations that go to make up the business world, the government and the social structure of the country are closely linked to the financial system. Quite apart from their extensive day-to-day monetary transactions such as buying raw materials, selling finished products and paying wages, many businesses borrow money to finance expansion. Others may have a temporary surplus of cash which they will probably hold on deposit with the bank. The government is also a heavy borrower of funds to finance its spending on housing, schools, hospitals and the like. And the requirements of economic management have caused the authorities to become increasingly involved with the financial markets and institutions in other ways.

1.2 THE 'BLACK BOX' VIEW

Financial transactions of many kinds are thus commonplace today. Both as private individuals and as part of organizations, most of us are accustomed to dealing with certain sections of the financial system. Some types of financial institution are widely known. They include the big commercial banks, like Barclays and National Westminster, the building societies, like Nationwide and the Halifax, and insurance companies like the Prudential. All of these have extensive business with the public and have branch offices scattered across the country. Most people are also aware of certain of the formal financial markets: notable among these is the Stock Exchange, which can make headline news at times.

But most of us tend generally to be very single-minded in our financial dealings. As long as we can obtain the financial service we want on acceptable terms with apparently adequate security, little attention is paid to how this service is provided. The way in which the particular institution or market concerned functions, and fits in with, and is influenced by, the rest of the financial system, is not seen as an important matter. Those parts of the system that do not deal with the public are largely ignored.

A similar attitude can exist even among people who are closely involved with one part of the financial system. While fully appreciating what goes on in that one area, they may ignore much of what is happening elsewhere; their mental map of the financial system is dominated by one aspect of the system only and may thus bear little resemblance to reality.

In effect, many people view the financial system, or parts of it, as a 'black box'; like the motorcar or the computer, you may know what you put into it and what it can do for you, but how it does it remains a mystery. Some would add that there is little need to try to unravel the mystery; provided the system works and produces the service that is required of it, that is all that matters.

The proviso indicates some of the dangers associated with this 'black box' view of the financial system. Without at least some understanding of how the system works, it can be very difficult to see whether it is really doing a good job. It can also be hard to tell the true character of the financial service being bought. Indeed, surveys indicate that, while many people are today borrowers or lenders, few of them are fully aware of the terms on which the transactions are concluded or the precise nature of the contract that has been entered into. This is particularly the case with longer-term contracts such as life assurance or pension provision, where relatively few people have any idea of what they expect to receive for their contributions. It has also been true of both private and business transactions with second-tier banks and finance houses, where many depositors and borrowers have clearly failed to recognize the risky nature of the business they transacted.

There are therefore two main reasons why a deeper understanding of the way the financial system works is desirable. The first has to do with personal protection. Assessing the quality of the financial service being offered is a far cry from testing fruit and vegetables in the market or trying on clothes before a purchase. Many financial transactions involve the future; money is either being borrowed with a commitment to repay in the future or is being saved for future use. It thus becomes necessary to examine not only the overt terms of the contract being offered, but also the likelihood of their being fulfilled. Will money deposited with a secondary bank be repaid, what is likely to be the actual bonus rate paid on a life assurance policy in twenty years' time, how will the mortgage rate vary over the life of the loan, and will it be possible to keep up the payments?

These sorts of questions are of course extremely difficult to answer. Yet self interest requires that some attempt be made to find an answer; otherwise there is the risk of undertaking financial transactions that do not turn out as expected, something that can produce very uncomfortable conditions at a later date. Understanding how the system works is the only protection. Understanding, that is, both how particular financial institutions and markets operate and how they relate to the rest of the financial system, how the terms of a loan are arrived at and whether they are fair. This makes it possible to see, for example, why payment of a given assurance premium produces a certain sum of money in due course, and what are the differences in risk involved in depositing funds with different institutions at varying interest rates.

The second reason for seeking deeper understanding of the financial system is a more general one. As the importance of financial transactions has grown, so what is happening in the financial system has come to have a greater impact on other aspects of people's lives. It thus matters more whether the system is doing its job properly. In recent years there have been many criticisms of the way the financial system operates, complaints coming both from private individuals and from the business world. The former have been dissatisfied, for instance, with the restrictions placed on their borrowing capacity or the lack of protection against inflation in long-term contracts like life assurance policies. Companies have argued that financial institutions have been unduly loath to put money into industrial projects, preferring instead short-term opportunities in the Stock Exchange or the security of real property.

Some of the issues raised by these and other criticisms of the financial system are examined in the concluding chapter. But no criticism can be assessed fairly without a clear idea of what goes on in the financial system and the role that it is designed to fulfil. This involves not only knowledge of financial markets and institutions, and how they operate and relate to each other, but also an understanding of how the different kinds of financial transactions fit in with all the other activities, economic and social, that people and organizations are undertaking. For the financial system is but part of the wider economic and social structure; like other services it exists to improve our capacity to attain more fundamental aims, and it is on its ability to fulfil this role that the financial system stands or falls.

1.3 THE NEED FOR SIMPLIFICATION

In certain respects the UK financial system today resembles a tangled ball of string. There are many threads going in all different directions in a manner that is difficult to sort out. Or, perhaps more suitably, it is like the mass of wires of many colours that appears when one looks inside a sophisticated piece of electrical equipment such as a television set or a computer. The system is highly complex with a large number of intricate networks. There are many hundreds of financial institutions, each operating in a variety of financial markets. They handle most of the financial transactions emanating from the 56 million people in the UK together with those of hundreds of thousands of UK businesses and other private organizations, scores of government bodies and innumerable foreign people and organizations.

Over the years financial institutions and markets have become surrounded with much mystique. But basically the system is not difficult to understand. Much of the apparent complexity is a result of the fine degree of specialization that has been developed. And, in the same way as it is not necessary to know in detail the layout of every kind of computer in order to understand generally how computers work and what makes them operate well or badly, so detailed knowledge of the intricacies of every type of financial deal is not required. What is essential is an appreciation of the principles underlying the operations of institutions and markets. These are in fact relatively simple.

In order to see what is really going on, it is necessary to simplify the system down to its essentials; to look only at the batches of coloured wires in the computer rather than at each wire separately. The individual financial institutions, their users and the types of transaction being carried out need to be grouped so that the broad lines of activity can be discerned. To change the analogy, the skeleton of the financial system needs to be identified; once this has been seen and the nature of the bone structure has been understood, then the complexity that is the flesh and blood of the system can be reintroduced.

The rest of this chapter is concerned with the key categories and concepts that are required for the analysis of the financial system. The definition of each of these needs to be clearly understood if confusion is to be avoided subsequently. Three general areas are involved; the character of the financial system itself, the nature of the individuals and organizations that deal with the system, and the methods by which the many financial transactions that are carried out can be analysed in a meaningful way. In addition the data to be used to describe the financial system are discussed.

1.4 THE NATURE OF FINANCIAL TRANSACTIONS

The financial system can be viewed from three standpoints. It can be seen as a set of formal and informal financial *markets,* where certain financial transactions are carried out. Alternatively the system comprises a network of *institutions* specializing in such transactions, together with the people and organizations who deal with them. But, more comprehensively, the financial system consists of the totality of the financial *transactions* that take place and the financial *instruments* that are created as a result.

In any given period, each of us may make a number of different kinds of financial transactions. Wages are received, food bought, taxes paid, money banked, loans arranged and so forth. Similarly, a business will purchase materials, pay wages, receive sales income and raise new capital to buy plant and machinery. These transactions actually occur in a very higgledy-piggledy manner. But, at the end of the day, month or year, it is possible to sit down and analyse the nature of the transactions that have been carried out, grouping them under various headings.

For an individual, such an analysis might contain the following items.

A. Current transactions
    1. Income received
    2. Current spending on goods and services (food, clothing etc.) and other payments (taxes, interest etc.)
B. Capital transactions
    3. Income saved = (1) − (2)
    4. Capital spending (on land, houses, etc.)
    5. Income available for lending = (3) − (4)
C. Lending and borrowing

6. Total new lending (deposits with banks and building societies, life assurance funds etc.)

7. Total new borrowing (loans from banks, finance houses, building societies etc.)

8. Net lending or borrowing = (6) − (7) = (5)

More detailed analyses for different groups are illustrated in Tables 2.2 and 2.4–2.7 in the next chapter. It should be noted that the presentation for companies in Table 2.4 differs from that in a normal profit and loss account in that it relates to actual receipts and payments during the period rather than the expected out-turn. Thus, for example, there is no allowance for depreciation, but payments for maintenance and replacement of existing plant are included in capital spending. In a similar fashion, all tax items are payments made in the period, rather than the amounts due to be paid on the income received.

The various kinds of financial transactions that people undertake can be closely related. Borrowing may be associated with current spending on cars, or raw materials, as well as the purchase of capital items like houses and plant and equipment; in the form of retailer credit it may even finance spending on very perishable items. Surplus income that is saved and used to lend to financial institutions or others will normally in a later period produce current income. Existing capital may be sold to finance both current spending and lending. Nonetheless it is helpful to make a broad distinction between current financial transactions, items (1) and (2) above, and capital transactions, which include the remainder of the items shown. The reason for this is that the nature of the financial service required in the two cases is somewhat different.

In the case of current transactions, which form the bulk of most people's financial activity, what is needed is an efficient exchange and payments system, a mechanism by which income received can be turned into a variety of goods and services with the minimum of effort. The financial system provides this through the use of money, either in the traditional form of notes and coin, which are accepted as a means of exchange and passed from hand to hand in payment, or in more sophisticated guises such as bank and giro deposits with their associated transfer systems.

There are many historical examples of systems of exchange and payment that are not financially based; these include both straight barter and the use of what we would call money substitutes like beads or cowrie shells. But the modern financial system offers a means of carrying out current transactions that greatly eases the process of everyday life. One has only to think of the problems that would occur if all payments, however large, had to be made in notes or coin, to realize how important this financial service is. The impossibility of organizing a complex economic system like ours using nothing but barter or payment in kind is obvious. This does not mean that barter or payment in kind are unknown in society today; indeed, far from it. But their use is provoked primarily by the wish to avoid taxation rather than by their convenience as a way of doing business.

For capital transactions an efficient payment system is also important. But additional financial services are required. A major role of the financial system today is to provide opportunities for people to make use of their surplus income by lending or to borrow to supplement their spending capacity. It is this ability to act as middle-man between those with money and those without that provides the fundamental justification for the existence of much of the financial system. For in this way, productive use is being made of money that might otherwise remain idle.

Indeed, the growth of the financial system has both reflected and encouraged a split between the savers and the spenders in the economy. This split is important, for the existence of spare income on the one hand and opportunities for productive spending on the other does not of itself either require or justify the development of an extensive financial system. It is perfectly possible, for example, that those with the spare income will use it themselves for capital spending on physical assets of various kinds; in this case there will be no lenders and consequently no borrowers and no channelling function for the financial system. But, increasingly, many of the individuals who have some spare money have not chosen to use this for capital spending, other than perhaps on houses for their own occupation. Most other capital spending projects have grown too large or too risky for the small savers to undertake them directly. However, the opportunities for productive spending attract other people and organizations to spend, if possible, well beyond either their own resources or the retained profit of the organization. With many people and organizations thus potentially in financial surplus or deficit, lending and borrowing opportunities abound, and the financial system flourishes.

1.5 FINANCIAL INSTRUMENTS

In a financial transaction, the holder of goods or services may exchange them for a piece of paper, or its equivalent, which gives him a claim either on those goods or services or on something of equivalent value to him. Alternatively, the financial transactions may involve the exchange of one such claim for another. Either way, the token or 'piece of paper' used to indicate the claim is the financial instrument.

The instrument most frequently used in financial transactions is, of course, money, which can be exchanged directly for most types of goods and services, indeed by definition for anything that can be bought. Certain other financial instruments, trade credit for example, may also be used directly to obtain goods and services. But it is more common for money to be used as an intermediate holding; other financial instruments are first exchanged for money, which is then used to buy food, drink or whatever, or to acquire substitute financial instruments.

Some illustrations will clarify the process. A building society provides money in exchange for the financial instrument, a house mortgage; this money is then used to pay for the house that secures the mortgage. A bank granting a loan to someone wishing to buy, say, a car, gives him the money to pay for the car, not the car itself; in exchange the bank receives a conditional title either to the car or, more likely, to part of the person's future income. The holder of a share in a company that gives him a claim on a slice of the company's assets sells this claim for 'cash' in the bank; he may then use the money to buy other shares.

In each case the financial instruments, the house mortgage, the bank loan and the share, provide a record of who has the ultimate claim on goods and services; they help to indicate how the pattern of wealth ownership is changing. In this sense it has been well said that the financial system is society's scoring mechanism.[7] As claims to resources pass from one person to another, either a new financial instrument is created or an existing one changes hands. The person who gains the claim has acquired a financial asset in the form of the instrument; the one handing over a claim in exchange for actual use of goods and services acquires a liability like a loan or a security, or loses an asset in the form of money.

A statement of the wealth owned by a person or organization needs therefore to include details of the financial assets and liabilities held as well as of any property or equipment that may have been accumulated. Such a statement might look like the following:

1. Assets   Physical assets (land, property, equipment, stocks, etc.)
                 Financial assets (deposits, loans made, securities, life assurance policies, etc.)
2. Liabilities   (Loans received, hire purchase borrowing, trade and other credit, securities issued, etc.)
3. Net worth   (= Assets less Liabilities)

Net worth represents the true wealth owned by the individual or group concerned. The statement indicates whether this ownership is direct, or indirect via the use of financial instruments; it also shows how far other people have claims on the assets held and the income they produce.

The amount of net worth, or wealth, owned changes either when the value of existing physical assets or financial instruments alters in response to changing circumstances, or when new assets or instruments are obtained as a result of capital transactions. Capital spending involves additions to the amount of physical assets held. New financial instruments are created in the process of borrowing and lending; here money changes hands without any exchange of goods and services, the counterpart being instead the new financial instrument and the claims it represents.

Thus, if someone buys a house with his own earnings he adds to his physical assets; no new financial instrument is created, for he does not make a loan to himself. Initially, he accumulates the financial asset of money, then parts with this in exchange for the house. But if he lends a friend the money to buy a house, or anything else, a financial instrument in the form of the loan is effectively created. This ties in with the earlier discussion of the importance of people who wish to borrow and those who wish to lend to the development of the financial system. If there is little demand for borrowing and lending, few financial instruments other than money will be created, and the financial system will be correspondingly small.

Since the opposite is true of the UK today, it is not surprising that there is a wide variety of financial instruments in existence. The main types are listed in Table 1.1, together with certain of their key characteristics. In some cases the instrument actually consists of a real piece of paper, like money in the form of notes, treasury and commercial bills or stocks and shares. In others, like many bank deposits and most loans, the existence of the instrument is marked, primarily, by an entry in a register or a computer file.

The table also indicates broadly how instruments differ according to their length of life and the terms of the contract they represent, that is the form and amount of any repayment required and the extent of any interest payments involved. Of particular importance is the degree to which the terms of payment may be varied either by the borrower or the lender. For instance, the company raising money by an issue of ordinary shares incurs no formal contract either to repay the money or to pay any dividend, though there will undoubtedly be informal expectations about the latter; equally, a building society is free to alter both the interest rate and, in certain respects, the period of the loan that it grants. But the terms on which money is put into national savings instruments or is lent in the form of a company debenture are fixed; even though the day-to-day market price of the latter may vary.

Table 1.1.   Main types of financial instruments

Financial instruments	Some key characteristics [a]			
	Physical form [b]	Length of life [c]	Terms of payment [d]	Market-ability
1. Bills and deposits				
Notes and coin	Paper	Short	Fixed	Good
Treasury bills	Paper	Short	Fixed	Good
Commercial bills	Paper	Short	Fixed	Good
National savings	Paper and entry	Short/medium	Fixed	Poor
Bank deposits	Paper and entry	Short/medium	Variable or fixed	Mixed [e]
Deposits with other financial institutions (building societies, savings banks, etc.)	Paper and entry	Short/medium	Variable or fixed	Poor
2. Loans				
Bank loans	Entry	Short/medium	Variable or fixed	Poor
Hire purchase and other instalment credit	Entry	Short/medium	Fixed	Poor
House purchase loans	Entry	Medium/long	Variable	Poor
Other loans and mortgages	Entry	Medium/long	Variable	Poor
3. Securities				
British government stocks	Paper	All periods	Fixed	Good
Local authority securities	Paper	Short/medium	Fixed	Good
Overseas government securities	Paper	Medium/long	Fixed	Fair
Overseas company securities	Paper	Long	Variable or fixed	Fair
UK company securities:				
Quoted cos: Debentures	Paper	Long	Fixed	Good
Preference shares	Paper	Long	Variable or fixed	Good
Ordinary shares	Paper	Long	Variable	Good
Unquoted cos: Debentures	Paper	Long	Fixed	Poor
Preference shares	Paper	Long	Variable or fixed	Poor
Ordinary shares	Paper	Long	Variable	Poor
Unit trust units	Paper	Long	Variable	Good
4. Life funds				
Life assurance policies	Paper and entry	Medium/long	Variable or fixed	Poor
Pension rights	Entry	Long	Variable or fixed	Poor
5. Other				
Trade credit	Entry	Short/medium	Variable or fixed	Poor
Reserves of foreign currencies	Paper and entry	Short	Variable	Good
Inter-government loans	Entry	All periods	Variable or fixed	Poor

[a] The classifications are intended to give a broad indication only. See Chapter 3 for more detailed discussion.
[b] 'Paper' indicates that instrument normally involves the creation of an actual piece of paper (or metal), 'entry' that it is essentially an entry in a register or computer file.
[c] The length of time for which an instrument is normally outstanding. Short = up to two years, medium = 2–12 years, long = over 12 years.
[d] This refers both to the repayment terms (period and amount) and the interest/dividend payments.
[e] Some are good, e.g. certificates of deposits, others poor.

1.6 THE NATURE OF FINANCIAL MARKETS

The final column in Table 1.1 indicates the extent to which particular financial instruments are, or are not, marketable. This refers to the ease with which existing instruments in that class can be bought or sold; in particular, how readily a holder can turn his claim to future payment into money and so into the actual use of goods or services if he so wishes.

As can be seen, the marketability of financial instruments varies a great deal, in practice from the very good to the very poor rather than the good and poor shown. The actual market in which dealings take place may be formal or informal. It may have a real location, as has the Stock Exchange, the main market in securities. But it may also consist of nothing more than a group of dealers, each on the end of several telephone lines, as with the foreign exchange market and that in certificates of deposit. For some financial instruments the market is so informal as to be non-existent. It can be difficult to buy, and even more difficult to sell, shares in unquoted companies, while there are few dealings in house mortgages or bank loans.

Markets in outstanding financial instruments are normally called secondary markets. Their extent is closely related to the characteristics of the instrument involved. For their purpose is to enable the holder of the instrument, whether as an asset or a liability, to adjust his holdings without extinguishing the instrument. This makes it possible for long-term borrowers to be financed by lenders who may need their money in a short while and vice versa. But if the lenders are to be prepared to undertake such a potentially risky contract they must be able to see an active market with plenty of actual and potential buyers or sellers of the instrument. This in turn means that the title that the instrument represents must be in a form that can easily be passed on; usually there must be a piece of paper involved and the units of ownership must be of reasonable size. In addition the nature of the contract needs to be such that the buyer or seller of the instrument can readily see what he is dealing in.

Relatively few financial instruments actually have all the necessary characteristics to justify a secondary market of any size. Either the quality of the contract is too uncertain, as with loans to individuals or the shares of small companies, or the instrument itself is not in a suitable form, which applies to most bank loans and deposits and to many trade debts. But where a demand for greater flexibility develops sufficiently among the holders of a certain instrument, its characteristics may be changed to enable a secondary market to develop. The form may be altered, as happened with the introduction of the negotiable certificate of deposit in recent years, or the problem of uncertain quality may be handled by spreading the risk, as is done with the factoring of business debts.

In addition to secondary markets in existing financial instruments, there are primary or new issue markets. These are concerned with the creation of financial instruments. They are not usually formal market places or trading centres in the conventional sense, but are established networks which handle applications by people who wish to borrow or lend in a particular manner. The institutions forming part of the network have information about where to find lenders to satisfy the specified borrowing needs, these lenders being sometimes but not always the institutions themselves; the latter are also fully conversant with the legal and other regulations that must be complied with if a particular instrument is to be created or issued.

The best known market of this kind is the 'new issue market', the extensive network that handles the issue of new securities by companies and public authorities. Here the merchant banks and brokers involved are not normally themselves the lenders; they act on behalf of insurance companies and other investors who actually provide the money. The market is closely regulated by the Stock Exchange, which operates the secondary market in the same securities. The 'money market' is a similar network, linking those who want to obtain money for short but varying periods and those who have spare money available for lending. Each time money is deposited, a new financial instrument is created; hence this is essentially a new issue market except for dealings in the certificates of deposits already mentioned. But, since the people involved are, in another sense, dealing in the right to hold an existing financial instrument, money, the name 'money market' has developed.

1.7 WHERE FINANCIAL INSTITUTIONS FIT IN

Financial institutions are involved in most of the established financial markets, both the secondary markets in existing instruments and the primary ones dealing with new borrowing and lending. Indeed, the institutions have been largely responsible for the development of many of the major markets that exist today. They are organizations who specialize in handling money and other types of financial instrument, dealing either on their own account or on behalf of other people. The justification for their existence lies in the fact that they can, by putting themselves in between those with spare income and those wanting to borrow, ease the transfer of funds from one to another, so, in principle, benefiting all concerned.

Sometimes this function is carried out simply by ensuring that all the parties wishing to borrow and lend in a particular manner are aware of each other's existence; this is the broker's or agent's method. But the more important role of the institutions lies in their ability to ease the exchange of funds by themselves creating new kinds of financial instrument which are more attractive to the borrower or lender than those the other party could himself offer. Bank or building society deposits represent a more acceptable home for the lending of the small saver than would the loans to companies or private individuals that are made by these institutions with the saver's money.

The reasons why the financial institutions are able to carry out this role are considered in Chapter 4. Of course not all financial transactions between borrowers and lenders involve the services of a financial institution. Many still take place directly between individuals or organizations, like the granting of new trade or retail credit and the financing of many small businesses. But the intermediating role of the institutions has grown to such an extent that a substantial proportion of the financial instruments in existence today are those issued by groups like the banks, the building societies and the life assurance companies. This is evident just in the names of the instruments listed in Table 1.1; bank deposits, building society deposits and life assurance policies stand alongside instruments like treasury and commercial bills, British government and company securities, each named after the borrower that is involved.

The range of financial institutions in existence and the instruments they deal in is a wide one. Table 1.2 shows the main types of institution in the UK and the form in which they primarily borrow and lend. Broking firms who specialize in putting people and institutions in touch with each other rather than themselves borrowing or lending are also included.

The institutions are divided into two broad groups, the banks and the other financial institutions. This is a conventional distinction that will be useful for subsequent analysis. It is based primarily on the idea that the banks are those institutions whose liabilities (deposits) are treated as money, that is used as a means of payment, while the other institutions are more concerned with longer-term borrowing and lending. In practice the split is a somewhat arbitrary one these days, illustrated by the fact that the liabilities of finance houses, building societies and national savings banks are also deposits, and are in many respects similar to those of the institutions conventionally defined as banks. The characteristics of the different institutions are discussed in depth in Chapters 4 and 5.

Table 1.2. Main types of financial institutions

Financial institutions	Main form of Borrowing (Liabilities)	Main form of Lending (Assets)
1. Banks		
Commercial banks	Deposits	Loans
Discount houses	Deposits	Bills and govt securities
Money and foreign exchange brokers	—— [a]	—— [a]
British banks operating overseas	Deposits	Deposits and loans
Foreign banks in London	Deposits	Deposits and loans
Merchant banks	Deposits [a]	Deposits and loans [a]
2. Other financial institutions		
Finance houses	Deposits and loans	Loans (HP, etc.)
Building societies	Deposits	House purchase loans
National and Trustee Savings banks	Deposits	Govt and LA securities
Life assurance companies	Funds from premiums [b]	Securities, property and loans
Pension funds	Funds from premiums	Securities, property and loans
Non-life insurance companies [c]	—— [b]	Securities, property and loans
Insurance brokers	—— [a]	—— [a]
Investment trusts	Securities	Securities
Unit trusts	Securities (units)	Securities
Stockbrokers and jobbers	—— [a]	—— [a]

[a] The business of these institutions does not primarily involve borrowing and lending, but bringing borrower and lender together. This is true to a lesser extent of much of merchant banking. See Chapters 4 and 5.

[b] Non-life insurance companies are not seen as *borrowing* from their policy-holders, since the latter will only in the rare circumstances of a claim receive any money back; this is also true of certain life assurance policies. But non-life companies are viewed as financial institutions since they have substantial reserves to lend out. See Chapter 5.

[c] Including Lloyds underwriters.

1.8 WHO USES THE FINANCIAL SYSTEM?

An important part of the study of the financial system consists of examining the relative importance of the different kinds of financial instruments, markets and institutions, seeing how they relate to each other, how far certain institutions and markets dominate the system and how the structure has changed over the years. But, as has already been stressed, it is of equal importance to know who uses the system, what is the nature of the use made and how this fits in with the rest of economic and social activity.

To do this in practice, it is necessary to divide the large number of individuals and organizations dealing with the financial system into some fairly clearly differentiated groups. The most useful classification is one reflecting the nature of the person or organization concerned and the underlying purpose of the transactions being carried out. Thus persons undertaking private transactions on their own behalf need to be distinguished from the same people when they are acting in a business capacity. Industrial and commercial businesses should be separated from the financial institutions, and government-controlled bodies like nationalized industries require setting apart from similar but privately owned businesses. Overseas individuals and organizations are also usually segregated because the impact of their activities differs from that of their home-based equivalents.

In all cases, the ideal groupings inevitably have to be modified by the practical problems of obtaining information. The main groups to be used in the later analysis are summarized in Table 1.3. The definitions are those of the official statisticians.[42] Five main categories are identified, including all financial institutions under the heading 'financial companies'.

As the name implies, the group 'Persons' includes all private individuals in the UK. Everyone is potentially covered, whatever their age, wealth or status, though the data to be analysed deal only with readily measurable financial transactions and so ignore activity where no money passes hands, like housework by wives (or husbands) and voluntary work of many kinds. But, 'persons' also includes unincorporated businesses, i.e. small private businesses that are not companies but are run and owned by individuals or as partnerships; this approach is adopted in the UK for reasons of statistical convenience, since it can, in practice, be very difficult to separate the transactions of the business from those of the owner as a private individual. Certain other organizations that are not companies, like charities or friendly societies, also come under this heading. So too do the current transactions of life assurance companies which are treated at this stage as though they were owned by their policy holders (see Section 3.6, p. 82).

Most of the privately owned businesses of any size in the UK are included in the 'Industrial and commercial companies' group; UK subsidiaries of foreign companies are covered as well as UK-owned businesses, and both private and publicly quoted companies come under this heading. Financial institutions are in a separate category,

Table 1.3. How people and organizations are grouped

Name of group	Main categories included [a]
1. Persons (Personal sector) [d]	Private individuals Unincorporated businesses (partnerships, sole traders etc.) Charities Friendly societies Life assurance companies (current transactions) Trade unions
2. Industrial and commercial companies	Public quoted UK companies Public unquoted UK companies Private unquoted UK companies
3. Financial companies	Banks [b] Other financial institutions [b c] Bank of England Banking Department
4. Government (Public sector) [d]	Central government Local authorities Nationalized industries National Insurance Fund Bank of England Issue Department Other miscellaneous government agencies
5. Overseas	Foreign individuals Foreign companies Foreign governments Foreign financial institutions (except their London-based operations)

[a] For full details see reference 42 in Bibliography.
[b] See Table 1.2 for detailed list.
[c] Includes capital transactions of life assurance companies.
[d] Name in official statistics.

but property companies are classified as industrial and commercial. However, nationalized industries are incorporated into the 'Government' group, together with central and local government authorities and a variety of other official entities like the National Insurance Fund and the Exchange Equalization Account.

All the foreign people and organizations (including governments) with which the UK has financial transactions are brought together under the heading 'Overseas'. The different groups within this category, for example foreign persons or foreign companies, are not normally separated out owing to problems of identifying their financial transactions. But, occasionally, a more detailed analysis can be made.

1.9 THE PRESENTATION OF FINANCIAL TRANSACTIONS

The use of wide groupings comprising large numbers of different units is essential if the analysis of the financial system and its inter-relationships is not to become too complex. But in the process of aggregation there is an inevitable loss of information. Varying sets of people or organizations with different patterns of behaviour have to be put together. What results is a kind of average picture and, while this is useful, it is not the whole story. Groups of the size used, with thousands or millions of units, can never be homogeneous enough for the average picture to be representative of individual behaviour. What is depicted is how the group as a whole relates to the rest of the system being studied. If the data permit, sub-groups of particular interest can be examined in more detail.

In the area of financial transactions, grouping produces some special problems. Certain transactions, like receiving income or buying goods and services, can by definition be in only one direction; wages or spending may be low, they may even be nil, but wages are always something that is *received* by an individual just as spending always represents an *outflow* of money. But, for capital transactions, and all transactions in financial instruments, this is not the case. Current income may be either greater or smaller than current spending; thus saving may be positive or negative, a person may be a net borrower or a net lender. Similarly, in any period, a person may be a buyer or a seller of a particular financial instrument. He may take out a loan, or be repaying one; he may build up his bank deposit or run it down; he may increase his holdings of securities or reduce them.

This means that adding up individual financial transactions may produce a result less representative of individual behaviour than might normally be expected from grouping. For the net figure of transactions by a group in a particular kind of financial instrument combines a great many positive and negative items into a final total. This can be either positive or negative but it cannot be both. The same is true for the group's saving or net borrowing or lending. The overall pattern of financial transactions may therefore look very different from that of the individuals concerned, unless the latter form a very homogeneous group. The aggregate figures still represent fairly the net transaction of the group as a whole. But they need careful interpretation.

A further difficulty arises where the individuals and organizations being grouped are not only dealing in the same financial instruments but are in fact borrowing and lending directly with one another, the instruments being issued by one individual to the other. This occurs with direct personal loans, with trade credit and the buying and selling of securities by businesses, and with the deposits by one bank with another. In this case not only does the net picture not show the full extent of the financial transactions, it shows no transactions in that instrument at all; the borrowing and lending directly cancel out in the process of aggregation.

A similar problem arises from the fact that the financial transactions for any individual have to be aggregated over a period of time. For any period as a whole a person can be a net borrower or a net lender, but not both. However, for shorter periods within the total, he may well change from one to the other; he may also successively buy and sell a particular financial instrument. In this case, the net figures mask the true extent of his dealings with the financial system.

In practice, the problem of interpretation is only serious either when a person's or a group's financial circumstances alters greatly in successive periods, or for certain financial instruments where holdings are frequently increased and reduced. Among the latter, the most important are cash in the form of notes and coin, bank deposits and very marketable instruments like Stock Exchange securities. A clearer picture can be obtained by subdividing the overall length of time being examined; looking, for instance, at quarters individually as well as the year as a whole. This approach is especially important in

Table 1.4.   Alternative presentations of financial transactions [a]

Type of financial instrument	Gross transactions [b]		Net trans- actions [c]	Presentation 1. [d]		Presentation 2. [e]	
£m.	−	+		Sources	Uses	Sources	Uses
Deposits	−100	+200	+100	—	+100	—	+100
Loans	−200	+50	−150	−150	—	−150	—
Securities	−200	—	−200	−200	—	—	−200
Life funds	—	+250	+250	—	+250	—	+250
Total	−500	+500	nil	−350	+350	−150	+150

[a] The figures illustrate the position of an imaginary group carrying out no *net* borrowing or lending, to whom only loans are a primary source of funds. The group does not acquire loans as assets but it can, of course, repay outstanding borrowings.
[b] These two columns show the actual, total, transactions that took place.
[c] This is the presentation used for the UK flow of funds data.
[d] Used in chapters 2 to 6. It assumes that only net transactions data are available. If gross figures were used the position would be as in the first two columns of the table.
[e] Used in chapter 7. It is similar to the presentation employed by OECD (see Appendix).

the case of the regular variations produced by seasonal changes, both climatic ones and those induced by the annual cycle of tax and other payments.

The way in which a 'net' presentation of financial transactions can obscure the actual pattern of dealings in financial instruments is illustrated in Table 1.4. The net picture is of course much simpler, but there is a corresponding loss of information. The table also shows two other ways of presenting the net figures, separating them into the sources and uses of funds to the group or person concerned. In the first case, any transaction bringing in funds during the period is classified under sources. Such transactions are conventionally shown with a minus sign, whether they be an increase in liabilities (for example new loans for an individual, security issue for a company) or a sale of assets already held. All transactions involving outflows of funds, conventionally shown with a plus sign, are classified as uses. In the second presentation all changes in liabilities are put in the sources column, while all those in assets are defined as uses.

In both cases, the actual figures are the same, but the pattern of sources and uses shown and the total of transactions differ. Each approach is designed to serve a different purpose, the first giving a clearer picture of money flows in the period, the second a view of how asset and liability holdings are changing. Both forms of presentation have their uses. The first is the one employed in the main analysis of the UK system, especially in Chapter 2. The second is used for the comparative analysis of overseas financial markets in Chapter 7.

1.10 THE OVERALL FLOW OF FUNDS

To see the operations of the financial system as a whole, information on the groups in the system needs to be brought together to show not only the form of the financial transactions being undertaken, but also the other group or groups that are party to these dealings. For there are always two participants in each transaction, the borrower and the lender, the seller and the buyer, the person who pays and the one who receives. To understand fully how the financial system works, they must both be identified.

This is done by putting the analyses of the financial transactions of the groups in the system down alongside each other, to form what is known as a flow of funds table. The categories used in each analysis need to be the same, and all types of financial transactions have to be identified. If this is done properly, then the figures for each type of transaction will balance out to zero, showing precisely who is dealing with whom.

While fund flow tables can be constructed to cover current as well as capital transactions, they are in practice normally used for the latter, especially for borrowing and lending. Table 6.1 is an example of such a table for UK borrowing and lending in 1973. Table 2.9 shows a simplified picture of the same data, but this time divided into sources and uses of funds and including saving and capital spending.

In both tables, the total of all the transactions by the different groups in any one type of financial instrument is zero. What one group is borrowing the others must be lending. The same is obviously true for the net borrowing or lending undertaken by each group. However the total of all the saving in the system is not zero, but is equal to the total of the capital spending being undertaken by the groups.

It is important to understand why this must be so. All income not spent on current or capital items by the person or group who receives it is lent out; eventually it will be spent by someone else, if not by the original borrower, then by whoever borrows in turn from him. Hence the total of all incomes in a period must equal the total of all spending. Looked at another way, all revenue received by producers as a result of current and capital spending must be allocated to one group or another in the form of income; for example, a company's sales revenue is either paid out in wages or interest, transferred to the government in the form of taxes or retained as profit. Furthermore, just as spending is divided into current and capital items, so income can be divided into that currently spent and that saved. From this it follows that the total flow of savings in the system in any period must equal the total of capital spending, even though this is seldom true for any one individual or group. Put in terms of symbols, if Y is total income, E is total expenditure, C current spending, I capital spending (investment) and S saving, then

$$Y \equiv E$$

and since $Y = C + S$ and $E = C + I$, therefore

$$C + S \equiv C + I$$

and

$$S \equiv I.$$

1.11 WHAT SORT OF INFORMATION

Last, but certainly not least, in order to understand what is going on in the financial system, it is necessary to have information; real figures have to be put into the analysis, not just examples. The analytical framework can show what the basic functions of the system are and how they can best be examined. But, on its own, it says nothing about what is actually happening here and now.

For this purpose statistical data are needed, data that enumerate the financial transactions that are taking place and the holdings of financial instruments that exist. Individual observation of what is going on is inadequate. No one person or group of people can hope to see clearly all the intricacies of something like the financial system, let alone attempt to assess correctly the relative importance of some among the millions of individual financial transactions that occur each day. Expert observation is invaluable as a complement to the statistics, helping to interpret the picture that they present. But, if a full view of the system is to be obtained, it must be mapped out in figures.

In the UK, the main source of the necessary data is the official statistics prepared by the Central Statistical Office with the Bank of England and published in such periodicals as the annual *Blue Book on National Income and Expenditure,* the monthly *Financial Statistics* and the *Bank of England Quarterly Bulletin.* These figures are based on a wide variety of returns made by individuals and organizations, both directly, to the two bodies mentioned and to other government organizations.[42]

These official figures have improved greatly in recent years; the initial promptings of the Radcliffe Committee in the late 1950s[8] have been reinforced by the growing attention being paid to financial matters both in government and elsewhere. But there are still gaps. In part these reflect the way that the figures are collected. For instance, quite full information is obtained from financial institutions; hence most transactions where they are involved are well documented. But financial transactions not involving these institutions, particularly those transactions directly between persons and companies and within these two groups, are much less well identified. There are significant 'balancing' items in the flows between groups and these represent only the net result of unidentified transactions. In consequence, published figures almost certainly understate the extent to which financial transactions are carried out outside the formal financial system.

Another area where official information is less than complete is that relating to holdings of financial assets and liabilities. Once again, data on financial institutions are reasonably good, with the important qualification that holdings are not always given at their current market value, but at cost or book value or some other figure. However, comprehensive data for other sectors are not available from official sources. Such data have been estimated for earlier years by a team at the Department of Applied Economics at Cambridge led by Professor Jack Revell, the latest year available being 1966.[48-50] Further work to bring the figures up to date is being undertaken at the

Bank of England, but only limited results have been published so far.[52, 53]

Since up-to-date information on asset and liability holdings is important if a full picture of the financial system is to be obtained, an attempt has been made, for the purpose of subsequent analysis, to carry the Cambridge figures forward to 1973. The bases for these rough estimates are given in the Appendix, together with some more technical details about the sources and definitions of the other figures being used. But one technical point requires some comment here.

This concerns how far the effects of grouping, discussed earlier, are present in the published figures. The official flow of funds statements are virtually all presented net; that is they show only the net change in each group's holdings of different types of financial instruments, not the total turnover involved. In the case of company securities, borrowings in the form of new issues are separated from dealings in existing securities; but this is done for companies and the overseas group alone, not for other groups. In addition, transactions in individual types of financial instrument are not always separately identified; a notable case is that of company securities which are shown only in total, and this is also true of most transactions in the different kinds of local authority debt. Furthermore, the transactions taking place within groups are all netted out; thus the important dealings between banks, within the government or among companies are all *prima facie* ignored.

The latter effect is partly a deliberate choice by the official statisticians who are aiming to avoid complicating the overall picture with transactions relevant only to a single group. But, more generally, this 'net' presentation reflects the fact that many figures are derived not directly from inquiries about the flows themselves but indirectly from the changes taking place in holdings of assets and liabilities; the latter approach can produce only a net figure. Fortunately, for certain dealings that are important to the understanding of the financial system, such as those between the banks and among other financial institutions, additional data are available to supplement the flows of funds statements. It is also possible to see how much certain financial institutions turn over their holdings of some types of financial instruments. But, as the subsequent analysis will show, the picture for other groups is much less clear.

Overall, therefore, the published data that will be used to study the UK financial system in practice must be handled with care. But despite the various problems mentioned, it is more than adequate to provide a broad picture of what is happening. To this, we now turn.

2. The users of the financial system

2.1 GETTING THE FACTS: THE FIRST STAGE

What actually goes on in the UK financial system today? All those banks, insurance companies, building societies and financial markets of many kinds: what are they doing, who are they serving, what functions do they really fulfil? The aim of the next few chapters is to answer these and many related questions. But because the analysis of a complex system is involved, the questions have to be answered in stages; different aspects of the system need to be considered separately. The first stage will be to try to answer the question, how do we, all of us in the UK, use the facilities offered by the financial system?

This question will be approached by looking at the financial transactions of the five main groups defined in the previous chapter, namely persons, companies divided into industrial and commercial and financial, government and overseas. All of us, as individuals, are involved in one or more of these groups. The financing needs of each group will be studied to see the way it employs the payments mechanism, the extent to which it takes advantage of borrowing and lending opportunities and the general form of its borrowing and lending activities. In addition a preliminary picture will be given of how the financial transactions of the different groups relate to each other; this will provide a broad indication of the role played by the financial markets and institutions, a role that will be examined in more detail in subsequent chapters.

The emphasis in this section of the book is on finding out the facts about what happens in the financial system rather than explaining why things are as they are; some comments are given on the reasons behind developments in recent years, but the main discussion of the factors determining the way the system works comes later. Much of the present analysis is presented in the form of tables and diagrams. The text describes the main features of these but inevitably it is possible only to highlight parts of the complex picture; considerable attention needs thus to be given to the figures shown as well as to the verbal comments.

To simplify matters, the presentation in this chapter focuses on the main classes of borrowing and lending only, on the five broad categories of financial instruments already mentioned, bills and deposits, loans, securities, life funds and 'other' instruments. The main constituents of each of these categories was listed in Table 1.1, and a more detailed analysis of transactions in particular types of financial instruments is given in Chapter 3. Since the figures used for the broad categories are derived from this more detailed analysis, transactions in different instruments within a group, like simultaneous purchases of company securities and sales of government stock, or additions to building society deposits and withdrawals from banks, are not netted out; hence the simplified analysis with which we start still gives a full view of the extent of the borrowing and lending transactions being carried out, in so far as this is possible from the available data.

2.2 THE IMPORTANCE OF DIFFERENT GROUPS

Before looking at the transactions of the individual groups, it is useful to have some idea of their relative importance, how significant each of them is in the UK today and how their position has changed over the years. A straight count of numbers is no use for this purpose since one cannot in any meaningful way compare 56 million individuals with around half a million industrial and commercial companies or less than a thousand different government bodies. Instead one needs to look at their role in different kinds of activity, at how large a share they have as producers and consumers, as income receivers and as spenders and savers.

Table 2.1 summarizes the situation in 1973, the latest year for which full figures are available, and compares it with that in 1957. Shares in production, incomes and the total of current and capital spending are shown here; saving and capital spending alone are examined later. The figures illustrate clearly the varying roles that the groups have in the UK economy. Nearly half the value added to raw materials in the process of producing the goods and services used in the UK is contributed by the activities of companies; these figures include financial companies, but the contribution of the latter is only small. The remainder of value added is fairly evenly divided between government, here mainly the nationalized industries and local authorities, the unincorporated businesses in the personal sector and the imports provided by the overseas sector. But both companies and government take a much smaller share of the incomes created in the course of production; a large part of these is paid out in the form of wages and salaries to workers in the 'persons' group.

Persons therefore receive by far the largest slice of total incomes, both before and after transfer payments like national insurance contributions and benefits and taxes; they also account for over half the total of final spending, that is current and capital spending on

Table 2.1. The size of the groups compared

	Group shares: % in			
		Total incomes		
	Total production (value added)[b]	Before transfers	After transfers	Final spending[c]
1957				
Persons	15	64	65	57
Companies[a]	46	13	7	6
Government	19	3	9	19
Overseas	20	20	19	18
	100	100	100	100
1973				
Persons	16	64	62	53
Companies[a]	40	8	6	7
Government	21	5	9	21
Overseas	23	23	23	19
	100	100	100	100

[a] Includes financial companies as well as industrial and commercial.
[b] i.e., sales less cost of materials used.
[c] Current and capital spending on finished goods.

finished goods and services. The government's direct income from production, mainly the profits of nationalized industries, is much smaller, but this is supplemented by substantial receipts from taxes and other transfers; hence government now makes over a fifth of all final purchases. However, the relatively small share of income retained by companies in the form of profits is further eroded both by taxes and by other transfers, like the payment of interest and dividends mainly to persons. This means that the companies' role in spending on finished goods is very small. But they are of course the major buyers of the materials and services that are used in production; if this intermediate spending were added to final spending, their share of the total would be much higher. The overseas group is little affected by transfer payments, and their revenue from our imports is broadly balanced by their spending on our exports; this gives them comparable shares of both production and final spending.

The basic roles of the groups have changed relatively little since 1957. Government has grown slightly in importance and companies have declined. Meanwhile, the share of incomes taken by persons has been eroded by increased transfer payments. The position of the overseas group has varied from year to year reflecting our rapidly fluctuating balance of payments experience; the group was slightly more important in 1973 than in 1957.

2.3 PERSONS—SPENDERS AND LENDERS

The many private individuals and unincorporated businesses that make up the 'persons' group are each insignificant in the total. But together they comprise one of the most important users of the UK financial system. The major use they make of the payments system for receiving income and spending has already to some degree been indicated. In addition they are substantial borrowers and lenders, particularly the latter.

The financial transactions of the group are analysed in Table 2.2 where the figures for 1973 are contrasted with those of ten years earlier. There have been few changes in the pattern of current transactions. Most income is received in the form of wages and salaries earned in the course of employment. Transfer payments, both national insurance benefits received as income and contributions and taxes paid, have increased in importance. The bulk of income of all kinds is used for current spending leaving only a small amount surplus in the form of saving. In 1973, the latter represented 8% of all income received and 10% of disposable income, that is income after all prior commitments.

Together, persons spend less than two-thirds of their savings on the purchase of physical assets in the form of houses, land and the like. They thus choose to accumulate a significant part of their wealth in the form of financial instruments by lending their spare income to other groups. In fact, they lend far more in total than their savings, 16% of income being lent in 1973 compared with 8% saved. This disparity between saving and lending has increased since 1963 and reflects the growing amount of borrowing being undertaken by some members of the group. In 1973 borrowing by the group as a whole was 13% of income against 8% in 1963.

It is helpful to remember the situation that underlies this general picture. In any one year, some people will be borrowing heavily to finance the purchase of physical assets like a home, while others will be repaying borrowing, or saving in the form of bank or building society deposits, life assurance premiums and in other ways. The

Table 2.2.   Persons: summary of financial transactions

Type of financial transaction		1963		1973	
		£m.	%	£m.	%
A. Current transactions					
1. Income received					
Wages and salaries, etc.[a]	+	18,195	71	42,890	69
Income of self-employed	+	2,207	9	6,244	10
Rent, dividends and interest (net)[b]	+	2,998	12	6,339	10
National insurance benefits, etc.[c]	+	2,152	8	6,497	11
Total income	=	25,552	100	61,970	100
2. Prior commitments					
National insurance contributions	−	1,303	5	3,926	6
Tax payments, etc.[d]	−	2,507	10	7,920	13
3. Income available for spending	=	21,742	85	50,124	81
4. Current spending	−	20,118	79	44,855	73
B. Capital transactions					
5. Income saved	=	1,624	6	5,269	8
6. Capital spending	−	932	3	2,982	5
7. Capital transfers					
Grants received	+	107	—	419	1
Taxes on capital, etc.	−	311	1	739	1
8. Income available for lending	=	488	2	1,967	3
C. Lending and borrowing					
9. Total lending	+	2,585	10	9,915	16
10. Total borrowing[e]	−	2,097	8	7,948	13
11. Net lending (+) or borrowing (−)	=	488	2	1,967	3

[a] Includes employers' contributions to pension funds and national insurance plus a small amount of income in kind.
[b] Interest received is shown net of interest paid. Rent includes the imputed income from owner-occupied dwellings.
[c] Includes current transfers to charities.
[d] Includes transfers abroad.
[e] Includes unidentified borrowings (net).

overall picture of increased borrowing and lending in relation to income may thus represent either many persons and businesses each borrowing and lending a bit more, or those who borrow and those who lend doing each to a greater extent; or both may be happening at the same time, which is most likely to be the case.

The result of this increase in borrowing and lending activities can be seen in Fig. 2.1, which shows the capital transactions of the group analysed into sources and uses of funds. Despite the increase in borrowing, savings (including capital transfers) remain the major source of funds. They are supplemented in three main ways, by loans and mortgages, by the sale of securities and by 'other' sources, which are largely unidentified. Loans and mortgages are dominated by lending for house purchase, though bank loans for other purposes have been generally growing in importance; they were cut back in 1974 as a result of general restraints on bank lending. The unidentified sources of funds used by persons are believed to be mainly credit of various kinds extended both to individuals and small businesses, particularly that from industrial and commercial companies.

The fact that persons have been continual sellers of certain securities already held reflects both changes in the way some people hold their wealth and the shifting pattern of saving within the group. Company securities are the main instruments involved and, as will be seen shortly, individuals have been important holders of these. But many of the wealthy individuals involved have been forced by high rates of income tax and estate duty to liquidate some of their holdings, both to meet tax payments and to finance current spending. In addition, other holders have chosen to switch their wealth into different forms, either into physical assets, mainly property of various kinds, or into financial assets, like unit trusts or life assurance, that offer additional advantages such as spread of investment or tax relief.

Meanwhile, those people who now have a surplus of income have tended to use this to buy assets other than the company securities being sold. The purchase of land and houses has been an important outlet, together with the working assets required by unincorporated businesses. So also has the acquisition of wealth through regular payments for life assurance policies and pension rights. But, while the total amount of money lent in the latter way has grown substantially, such types of lending have become a less important part of total uses of funds. For there has been an even faster increase in the money lent in more liquid forms, mainly as deposits with banks and building societies. In total, bills and deposits, of which the latter are the main ingredient, accounted in 1973 for over 40% of the uses of funds by persons compared with some 30% in 1963; in contrast the

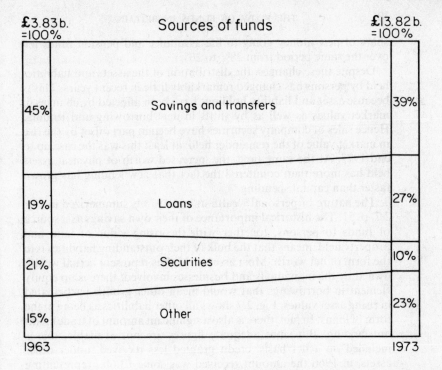

£3.83b.
=100%

£13.82 b.
=100%

Sources of funds

45%	Savings and transfers	39%
19%	Loans	27%
21%	Securities	10%
15%	Other	23%

1963   1973

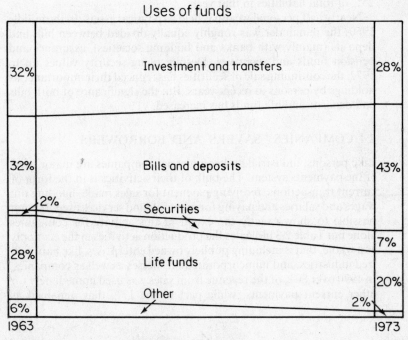

Uses of funds

32%	Investment and transfers	28%
32%	Bills and deposits	43%
2%	Securities	
		7%
28%	Life funds	20%
6%	Other	2%

1963   1973

Fig. 2.1 Persons: sources and uses of funds

share of new money going to life assurance and pension funds fell
over the same period from 28% to 20%.

Despite these changes, the distribution of the assets and liabilities
held by persons has changed remarkably little in recent years. This is
because asset and liability holdings have been affected by changes in
market values as well as by shifts in new borrowing and lending.
Hence sales of company securities have been in part offset by the rise
in market value of the remainder held; at least this was the case up to
end 1973. At the same time, the increased worth of physical assets
held has more than countered the fact that new lending has grown
faster than capital spending.

The nature of personal wealth at end 1973 is summarized in Fig.
2.7, p. 51. The historical importance of their own savings as a source
of funds to persons, together with the rising value of land and
property held, means that the bulk of their outstanding liabilities is in
the form of net worth. Most assets held thus represent actual wealth
owned by the individuals and businesses involved; there is no equity
element in borrowings that would mean other groups participated
in rising asset values. Fig. 2.7 shows all other liabilities as being in the
form of loans. In fact, there is also a significant amount of trade credit
outstanding. But since adequate figures are not available, this is
included on a net basis, credit granted less received, under other
assets; in 1966 the amount received was some £3.6b., representing
25% of total liabilities in that year.

Nearly half personal wealth is held as physical assets. In the middle
1960s the remainder was roughly equally divided between bills and
deposits (mainly with banks and building societies), assurance and
pension funds and securities. Despite rising security values up to
1972, the continuing sale of securities has reduced their importance as
holdings by persons in recent years. But the significance of both bills
and deposits and life funds has increased.

2.4 COMPANIES—SAVERS AND BORROWERS

Like persons, industrial and commercial companies are major users
of the payments system. The bulk of their activities is in the form of
current transactions, receiving payment for sales made, handing out
wages and salaries and paying for materials and services used. It is not
possible to show exactly the extent of this activity for companies
alone but Table 2.3 indicates the production activities in the economy
as a whole, that is including publicly owned enterprises, like nationalized industries, and unincorporated businesses as well as companies.
In 1970 over 80% of the revenue from sales was used immediately for
other current payments, while part of the 17% that remained as

Table 2.3. Operating income and expenditure of UK industry, 1970[b]

	£b.	%
Revenue from sales[a]	75·5	100
Purchases of materials, etc.	32·7	43
Wages and salaries, etc.	30·2	40
Profits and trading income	12·6	17

[a] Net of sales taxes and subsidies.
[b] Including nationalized industries and other public enterprises.
Source: derived from *Economic Trends*, May 1974.

profits was required to meet payments of taxes and to service capital used through the payment of interest and dividends.

Companies have in fact supplementary sources of income, available to meet these and other payments, in the form of income from trading abroad and non-trading income like interest and dividends received. The extent of these in relation to UK trading profits is indicated in Table 2.4. Their importance has increased in recent years, particularly in the case of income from abroad, so that together these two items now represent over one-third of total company income after payment of wages and for materials. The size of interest and dividend payments by companies has fallen in relation to income but the share of taxes and that of the profits earned by foreign-owned companies in the UK (profits 'due abroad') has risen.

None the less, in 1973 companies managed to retain nearly half their profit and non-trading income. This is similar to the situation in 1963 though the position has varied in intervening years. The 47% in 1973 is probably equivalent to around 11% of the total of sales revenue plus non-trading income, little different from the share of savings in the total of personal income. But capital spending by companies is much higher in relation to savings than is the case for 'persons'. Such spending is required to maintain and expand plant and equipment and to sustain increases in stocks and work in progress. As a result, the company group as a whole is rarely a substantial net lender. In some years, like 1963, retained profit does exceed capital spending but frequently the opposite is true; there were large deficits, that is companies were large net borrowers, in 1969/70 and again in 1973 and 1974 (see Fig. 2.8, p. 54).

But, regardless of the extent to which the capital spending of the group is, or is not, financed out of saving, companies as a whole

Table 2.4. Industrial and commercial companies:
summary of financial transactions

Type of financial transaction		1963		1973	
		£m.	%	£m.	%
A. Current transactions					
1. Income received					
Profits from UK trading	+	4,300	77	9,263	65
Rent, interest and dividends	+	261	5	1,021	7
Income from abroad	+	1,006	18	3,890	28
Total income	=	5,567	100	14,174	100
2. Prior commitments					
Interest and dividend payments [a]	−	1,761	32	4,029	28
Taxes on income and profits due abroad	−	1,231	22	3,512	25
B. Capital transactions					
3. Retained profit (Income saved)	=	2,575	46	6,633	47
4. Capital spending					
Spending in UK [b]	−	2,163	39	7,850	56
Spending overseas [b]	−	253	4	1,274	9
Spending by foreigners in UK	+	202	4	882	6
5. Capital transfers					
Grants received	+	14	—	373	3
Taxes on capital etc.	−	5	—	26	—
6. Income available for lending	=	370	7	−1,262	−9
C. Lending and borrowing					
7. Total lending [c]	+	1,475	27	4,536	32
8. Total borrowing	−	1,105	20	5,798	41
9. Net lending (+) or borrowing (−)	=	370	7	−1,262	−9

[a] Includes current transfers to charities.
[b] By UK companies.
[c] Includes unidentified lending (net).

undertake substantial two-way lending and borrowing transactions. Even in 1963, these were equivalent to over a fifth of profit and non-trading income, and by 1973 the proportion had grown to around 40%, equal to some 10% of sales revenue; there was some reduction in 1974, due mainly to the difficult financial climate. The simultaneous borrowing and lending reflects in part the differing positions of individual companies within the group. Some will be investing much more than their retained earnings and so need to borrow additional funds, while others, whose investment programmes are currently low, have spare funds to lend out through the financial system. The moves from surplus to deficit and back again in the figures for the group as a whole imply shifts in the relative numbers of these two groups, as well as a general change in the situation of all companies as monetary conditions in the economy vary.

It is clear from Fig. 2.2 that the growth in company borrowing has been primarily in the form of loans. While savings, plus capital transfers like investment grants, still form the major source of funds, loans, mainly from banks, represented 38% of the money available for capital spending and lending in 1973 compared with less than 20% ten years earlier. The extent of borrowing by means of new issues of securities has declined very sharply; that through commercial bills has fluctuated with a marked resurgence in periods of financial difficulty like 1969–71 and 1974.

The great increase in bank borrowing by companies has been associated with a growth in bank deposits as an outlet for company funds. Though over half of all capital funds were still used to purchase capital assets or to finance increased stocks in 1972 and 1973, more than 20% went into deposits, mostly with banks; the figure was well under 10% during most of the 1960s. This growth in deposits was only to a limited extent the result of companies having more spare cash around; companies had a small surplus for lending in 1971 and a larger one in 1972 but returned to deficit in 1973. What happened also in 1972 and 1973 was that many companies were deliberately borrowing from banks with the intention of depositing the money made available, at one and the same time making sure of their overdraft lines and taking advantage of differentials in interest rates. As will be seen, this is a function more akin to that of a financial institution than an industrial and commercial company, and it illustrates how far the latter companies have become financially more aware in recent years. However, the movement ceased in 1974, partly as a result of official action, but more especially owing to the effect of rapid inflation on the value of stock to be financed.

The remaining uses of company funds are the purchase of securities and 'other' lending. Securities of other companies are bought either

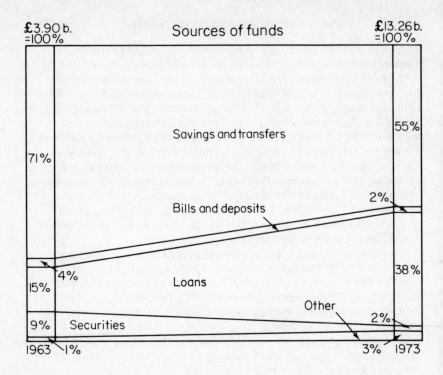

£3.90 b.
=100%

Sources of funds

£13.26 b.
=100%

71%

Savings and transfers

55%

2%

Bills and deposits

2%

15%

4%

Loans

38%

Other

9%

Securities

2%

1963

1%

3%

1973

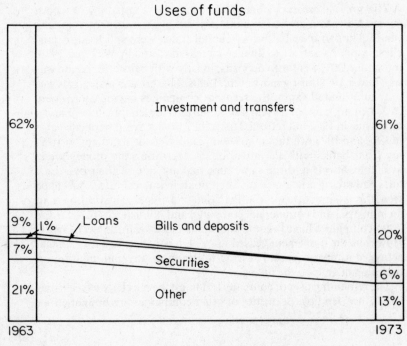

Uses of funds

62%

Investment and transfers

61%

9%

1%

Loans

Bills and deposits

20%

7%

Securities

6%

21%

Other

13%

1963

1973

Fig. 2.2 Industrial and commercial companies: sources and uses of funds

in the course of mergers or complete acquisitions or as trade investments; only purchases for cash are included in the figures. They have formed a steady part of companies' capital transactions in the last decade and have recently exceeded borrowing through new issues of securities by a substantial margin. The 'other' lending is largely unidentified and is thought to be mostly trade credit extended to other sectors, primarily persons, where the contra item of unidentified borrowings has already been noted.

The balance sheet of companies' outstanding assets and liabilities, given in Fig. 2.7, p. 51, presents a somewhat different picture from current capital transactions. Bills and deposits and loans represent much smaller proportions of assets and liabilities respectively. Assets are primarily the physical assets, plant, buildings and stocks, required for business purposes; as with persons, the rise in value of physical assets already held has helped to balance the growing importance of current lending activities. On the liabilities side, securities, which are the traditional form of company financing, have declined in importance; though up to 1973 the decline was less than might be expected from recent year-by-year capital transactions, reflecting a compensating rise in the market value of outstanding equities. The share of loans in total liabilities has risen.

There are two special features in the analysis of companies' wealth in Fig. 2.7. The first is the substantial net worth item shown among corporate liabilities. In principle, companies have no net worth of their own, this being the property of their equity holders. But, in practice, an inconsistency can arise between the market value given to liabilities in the form of ordinary shares and the values placed independently on the physical assets held. This is primarily the result of differing approaches to valuation by the stock market and the accountants and property valuers.

The second feature is the item overseas investment, which is included as a liability of companies. This represents the physical assets in the UK that are directly owned by foreign companies or their subsidiaries. In many cases, for example branches of foreign companies, there are no formal financial instruments giving a claim to the assets involved. Even where these exist, the inclusion of what are straight inter-company transactions would distort the picture of companies' assets and liabilities; all the self-cancelling transactions between UK companies and their subsidiaries are excluded in the presentation. Transactions between overseas companies, in the overseas group, and UK companies are not self-cancelling; hence a pseudo-financial instrument has been created by the statisticians to represent the direct foreign ownership of UK business. It can be seen as a form of net worth that is actually owned by the overseas group.

The capital spending flows that give rise to foreign ownership in the UK were shown separately in Table 2.4, p. 32, along with the spending abroad by UK companies, which gives rise to a similar item in the liabilities of the overseas group.

2.5 FINANCIAL COMPANIES—THE BORROWERS AND LENDERS

The pattern of the transactions carried out by the financial company group is very different from that of other companies. This is, of course, only to be expected since the nature of their business, as financial institutions, is of a totally other character.

The differences can be clearly seen even in current transactions. In the first place, financial companies are, as a group, smaller than the non-financial ones; their total income of £5,215m. in 1973 compares with the equivalent figure of £14.174m. in Table 2.4. Secondly, as Table 2.5 shows, virtually all their income comes in the form of rent, interest and dividends, while the direct profit on UK trading is a negative item, that is a loss, not a profit.

The explanation for the last fact lies in the way that financial companies are remunerated for the services that they provide. Although they receive some income in the form of fees and other charges, comparable to the sales revenue in Table 2.3, this is not sufficient to cover all their direct costs, mainly the payment of wages and salaries to employees. Hence the negative trading profit. The deficiency is made up from the margin between the interest rates at which they borrow money and those at which they lend, the latter being of course higher than the former. This shows up in Table 2.5 in the difference between rent, interest and dividends received and interest and dividends paid. The gap between these two transfer payments is wide enough to absorb the apparent loss on trading and to pay taxes and still leave a significant proportion of total income as retained profit or savings.

The amount saved by financial companies is quite closely matched by their capital spending, which is partly on buildings and equipment required for business purposes and partly more deliberate purchases of property as a means of accumulating wealth. On balance, as a group, they are not net borrowers or lenders on any scale. But, as the nature of their business implies, their total borrowing and lending transactions are vast. Even in 1963, these were over three times the companies' total income, while by 1973 the ratio had expanded to nearly five times despite the fact that their income had increased fivefold in the meantime. Both borrowing and lending declined somewhat in 1974, primarily owing to constraints on banking

Table 2.5. Financial companies: summary of financial transactions

Type of financial transaction		1963		1973	
		£m.	%	£m.	%
A. Current transactions					
1. Income received					
Profits from UK trading	+	−197	−21	−787	−15
Rent, interest and dividends	+	972	106	5,470	105
Income from abroad	+	144	15	532	10
Total income	=	939	100	5,215	100
2. Prior commitments					
Interest and dividend payments [a]	−	521	56	3,335	64
Taxes on income, and profits due abroad	−	248	26	1,056	20
B. Capital transactions					
3. Retained profit (Income saved)	=	170	18	824	16
4. Capital spending					
Spending in UK [b]	−	153	16	971	19
Spending overseas [b]	−	—	—	15	—
Spending by foreigners in UK	+	6	1	49	1
5. Capital transfers					
Grants received	+	—	—	5	—
Taxes on capital, etc.	−	—	—	56	1
6. Income available for lending	=	23	3	−164	−3
C. Lending and borrowing [c]					
7. Total lending	+	3,059	326	25,125	482
8. Total borrowing	−	3,036	323	25,289	485
9. Net lending (+) or borrowing (−)	=	23	3	−164	−3

[a] Includes current transfers to charities.
[b] By UK companies.
[c] Includes unidentified items (net).

business, but the amounts remained well above those of earlier years.

The main form in which financial companies borrow and lend is analysed in Fig. 2.3. To some extent, this analysis in terms of the broad type of financial instrument indicates also the relative importance of the financial institutions that specialize in different instruments. But, as Table 1.2 showed, several groups of institutions may deal in the same type of instrument so only very general implications can be drawn here; the actual position of the various kinds of institution is considered in Chapters 4 and 5.

The insignificance of saving and capital spending in the total capital transactions by financial companies is very evident. So also is the overriding importance of bills and deposits as a source of funds, and of loans as a use. The former are predominantly deposits with the banks and the building societies, those with the banks being by far the largest. Similarly, in the loan category, the banks are pre-eminent. The use of these two groups of financial instruments in the borrowing and lending of financial companies has expanded enormously in the years up to 1973. As will be seen, their growth is intimately connected.

On the sources side, the main group of instruments to suffer a corresponding decline in importance has been borrowing through the creation of life assurance funds and pension rights. Although the amount of money received for this purpose has grown rapidly, its expansion has been much slower than that in deposits. The raising of new money through the issue of securities, which includes the sale of units by unit trusts, continues to be of only marginal importance to financial companies as a whole. A somewhat larger amount of money is normally used to purchase the securities, both newly issued and outstanding, of other companies and of the government; the significance of this use of funds has, however, varied considerably from year to year.

The relative growth in borrowing and lending through deposits and loans is also reflected in the balance sheet of financial companies' outstanding assets and liabilities. Both these groups have expanded to around two-thirds of total assets and liabilities compared with less than 50% in the middle 1960s. The share of life funds in liabilities and of securities in assets has declined, the latter despite an overall upward movement in market values during the period to 1973. Only a small proportion of total assets is held in physical form, while financial companies have very little net worth in their liabilities; the bulk of the assets they control are actually owned by those from whom they borrow their funds. Unlike industrial and commercial companies, they do little saving in relation to their borrowings while a large part of their assets is held in a form that does not change in value. Hence their scope for accumulating net worth is limited.

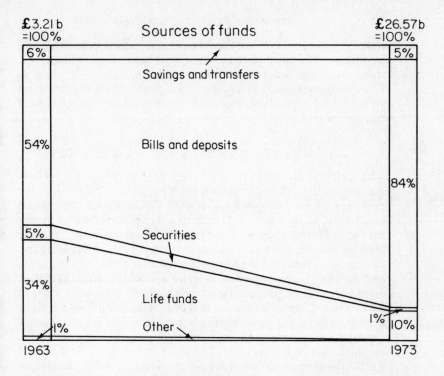

£3.21 b
=100%

Sources of funds

£26.57b
=100%

6% — 5%

Savings and transfers

54% — 84%

Bills and deposits

5%

Securities

34%

Life funds

1% — 1% 10%

Other

1963 — 1973

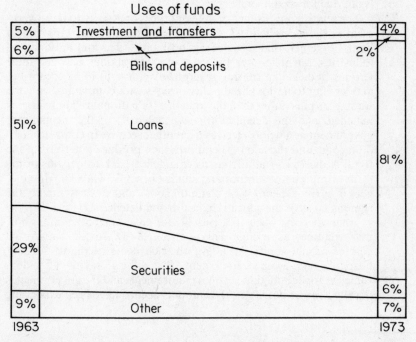

Uses of funds

5% — 4%

Investment and transfers

6% — 2%

Bills and deposits

51% — 81%

Loans

29%

Securities

6%

9% — 7%

Other

1963 — 1973

Fig. 2.3 Financial companies: sources and uses of funds

Indeed, it appears that the great expansion in their borrowing and lending that has taken place in recent years has all but eliminated net worth as a significant liability or outstanding source of funds to financial companies. Put another way, their owned funds (or reserves) have become minuscule in relation to the rest of their financial transactions.

2.6 GOVERNMENT—SPENDERS AND BORROWERS

Although the government undertakes a certain amount of production itself, both in the nationalized industries and through the provision of various common services like education, roads and health care, a major part of its activity is the redistribution of money between different groups of people. This involves raising revenue through taxes and national insurance contributions and passing this income on to others in the form of social security benefits, pensions and the like. In this aspect of its activities, which naturally makes extensive use of the payments mechanism, the government is acting in a way like a financial institution that channels money from lender to borrower. Only the government's action is mostly on current not capital account, no wealth being created in the process except the accumulation of certain rights like those to pensions. And part at least of the government's 'borrowing' in this area is not voluntary and is not due for repayment.

The relative importance of different types of activity to the government is shown in Table 2.6. This gives figures for all government bodies together, that is including local authorities and nationalized industries; but it ignores the extensive transactions between these various bodies, like central government grants to local authorities and lending to nationalized industries. As with companies, only the trading surplus rather than the total sales of nationalized industries is included, and this accounts for less than 10% of the income that government as a whole receives from other sectors. In contrast, taxes on income and those on expenditure each produce one-third of the total. A quarter of all income is channelled back to persons in the form of national insurance and similar benefits, while roughly half goes in current spending on common goods and services, mainly the running costs of the education, health and defence services.

Somewhere between 10% and 20% of government income is normally retained as savings. This contributes towards the substantial cost of official capital spending on such items as roads, schools, hospitals and defence equipment. But, official saving is seldom sufficient to meet all these capital requirements and the government is usually a major borrower; the amounts needed have been expanding

Table 2.6. Government: summary of financial transactions

Type of financial transaction		1963		1973	
		£m.	%	£m.	%
A. Current transactions					
1. Income received					
Taxes on income	+	3,379	33	9,134	33
Taxes on expenditure	+	4,027	38	10,006	37
National insurance contributions	+	1,303	12	3,926	14
Rent, dividends and interest	+	735	8	2,201	8
Trading surplus of public enterprise	+	932	9	2,194	8
Total income	=	10,376	100	27,461	100
2. Current transfer payments					
National insurance benefits, etc.	−	2,260	22	6,802	25
Subsidies	−	569	5	1,456	5
Interest and dividends paid	−	1,286	12	2,902	11
3. Current spending	−	5,176	50	13,270	48
B. Capital transactions					
4. Income saved	=	1,085	11	3,031	11
5. Capital spending	−	2,113	20	5,753	21
6. Capital transfers					
Taxes on capital, etc.	+	316	3	821	3
Capital grants paid	−	121	1	856	3
7. Income available for lending	=	−833	−8	−2,757	−10
C. Lending and borrowing [a]					
8. Total lending	+	424	4	2,720	10
9. Total borrowing	−	1,257	12	5,477	20
10. Net lending (+) or borrowing (−)	=	−833	−8	−2,757	−10

[a] Including unidentified items (net).

rapidly in recent years. In common with other groups, the extent of borrowing has tended to rise in relation to income, here partly in order to finance a greater amount of official lending.

The amount that the government saves in any one year is determined not only by its spending needs, but also by the requirements of general economic policy. Where restraint is called for, the government's action in, for example, raising taxes and/or reducing its spending commitments will enhance its saving and its capacity for lending. The need for re-expansion will correspondingly produce lower saving and higher borrowing. The resulting swings in the government's net borrowing or lending position are clearly seen in Fig. 2.8, p. 54; they were especially marked in the 1968–72 period.

The needs of economic management are also reflected in the pattern of government capital transactions. Here the role of the government in financing the inflows and outflows of foreign exchange consequent upon balance of payments surpluses and deficits is important. These official transactions with the overseas group are included under 'other' sources and uses of funds in Fig. 2.4. They cover changes in the level of the UK gold and dollar reserves, the treasury bills issued as a counterpart of lending by foreign central banks and other official loans and financing. The way in which transactions in this area are linked with changes in the balance of overseas payments is discussed in more detail in the next chapter. But, essentially, an overall deficit in the payments position provides the government with an additional source of funds through the run-down of reserves held and borrowing from abroad. A return to a payments surplus represents a use of funds to build up reserves and repay borrowings.

There are two additional constituents in the other items shown in Fig. 2.4. The first is borrowing by local authorities from sources outside the government and the banks; this is included here because of the difficulties in allocating it correctly among deposits, loans and securities. It forms a regular source of funds to the government group, though, as will be seen, the amounts vary from year to year. The second constituent reflects another aspect of economic management, the transactions between the government and the Bank of England banking department; the latter is included with financial companies. In the official statistics, these transactions are aggregated in one item, the net government indebtedness to the Bank of England banking department. Changes in this item broadly reflect official monetary policy, with borrowing increasing as money tightens through, for example, the special deposits made by the banking system with the Bank of England. The way this occurs is examined further in Chapters 3 and 4.

Taken together, the 'other' items in government capital

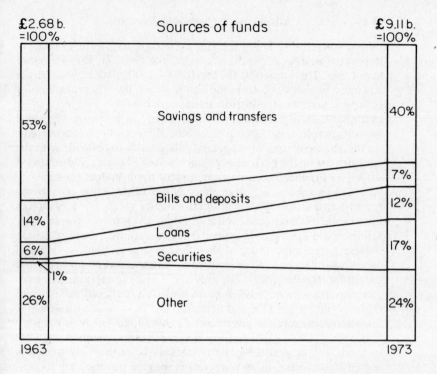

Sources of funds

£2.68 b. =100%

£9.11 b. =100%

53%

Savings and transfers

40%

7%

Bills and deposits

14%

12%

Loans

6%

17%

Securities

1%

26%

Other

24%

1963

1973

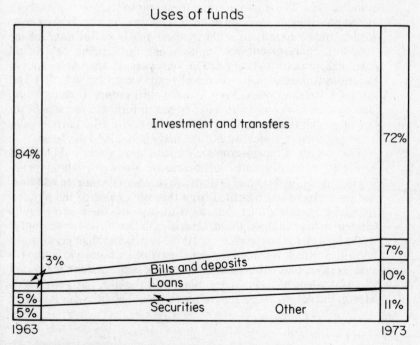

Uses of funds

84%

Investment and transfers

72%

7%

3%

Bills and deposits

Loans

10%

5%

Securities

Other

11%

5%

1963

1973

Fig. 2.4 Government: sources and uses of funds

transactions tend to follow a highly cyclical pattern; at times they are important sources of funds, at others, like 1969–71, they represent major uses. This is not only the result of the cyclical pattern within the economy; it also stems from the way in which the different effects of economic policies on government finances reinforce each other. For example, there is a tendency for borrowing in the form of special deposits to follow the same cycle as official borrowing from overseas; that is, the tightening of monetary policy tends to coincide with the peak deficits on the balance of payments. Added to this, the increased saving and reduced spending consequent upon budget restraints of various kinds frequently take effect as the 'other' items are moving from being a source to a use of funds. Greater saving replaces foreign borrowing, while reduced capital spending leaves money free to repay foreign loans (and special deposits) and to accumulate reserves.

Despite the importance of these 'other' transactions, saving and capital spending are still prominent in the government's sources and uses of funds respectively. The only additional capital transactions of any importance are those in notes and coin, national savings and treasury bills (all in bills and deposits) and those in securities which are almost entirely the government's own. Like 'other' borrowing and lending, these instruments have served both as a source and a use of funds; in one year the government may be raising new money in any of these forms, in another year it may be buying back its outstanding debt. The situation varies from year to year in response both to the government's general financial position, as a net borrower or lender, and to conditions in the financial markets. For much of the 1960s, the government was repurchasing outstanding debt of all kinds except notes and coin and the only periods when new issues of securities formed a major source of funds were 1965–67, 1971 and 1973–74. In recent years, direct loans to other groups, both for house purchase and to companies, have begun to form a more significant use of official funds, while bank loans have formed a fairly regular source of funds for local authorities and nationalized industries.

The pattern of the government's outstanding assets and liabilities in Fig 2.7, p. 51, illustrates the historic importance of capital spending as a use of funds and of savings as a means of finance. In addition, the government has benefited from the rising value of the physical assets held and the fact that, as with persons, there is no equity element in borrowings. Indeed, according to the conventions adopted in the figures, the government had done even better than persons; the securities, which form a substantial part of its borrowings, have a market value that has been declining at the same time as the value of physical assets held, buildings, plant and the like, has been rising. Hence, the net worth element in government liabilities has increased sharply in recent years; the government owns as well as controls an increasing proportion of the physical assets it holds. The remaining liabilities are roughly equally divided between securities, life funds (unfunded pension rights of certain public sector employees) and other (mostly local authority debt outstanding), with a small additional amount of loans. Outstanding lending by the government is relatively unimportant, and the basic infrastructure of the economy plus the productive equipment of the nationalized industries form the vast bulk of all assets held.

2.7 OVERSEAS: MORE AND MORE BORROWING AND LENDING

The current financial transactions of overseas people and organizations with the domestic units in the UK form what is better known as the current account of the balance of overseas payments. The first part of Table 2.7 summarizes these transactions, looked at from the point of view of the overseas group rather than from the domestic standpoint usual in the balance of payments figures. People and organizations abroad receive the bulk of their revenue from the UK as a result of their sale of the goods and services that we import. Most, sometimes all, of this income is spent back in the UK, buying the goods and services that we offer in the form of exports. The balance not spent in, or otherwise transferred to, the UK represents the saving of the overseas group. This is equivalent to the balance of overseas payments on current account, with the sign reversed. When the overseas group receives more income than it spends, the current account is in deficit; when the group spends in the UK more than it gets from the UK, the current account is in surplus.

The second and third sections of Table 2.7 show, in summary, the capital transactions that make up the rest of the balance of overseas payments. Capital spending includes both the purchase of physical assets in the UK by overseas companies and the corresponding spending abroad by UK companies. Both have maintained a steady upward trend over the last decade with the exception of a temporary cut-back in overseas spending in the UK in 1972. This is despite the sharp fluctuations that have taken place in the saving of the overseas sector, reflecting the changing trends in our exports and imports.

The latter fluctuations, corresponding to periods of deterioration and recovery in the balance of payments, have resulted in the overseas group shifting from net lender to net borrower and back again. The official borrowing and lending that is a major counterpart of this has already been discussed. But in addition to the changes in net outcome from year to year, the total borrowing and lending transactions of the overseas group with the rest of the UK have grown enormously in

Table 2.7. Overseas: summary of financial transactions

Type of financial transaction		1963		1973	
		£m.	%	£m.	%
A. Current transactions					
1. Income received					
Sales of foreign goods and services[a] to UK	+	5,946	83	18,338	80
Rent, dividends and interest from UK	+	580	8	1,784	8
Taxes paid abroad by UK	+	430	6	2,169	9
Other current payments abroad by UK	+	250	3	756	3
Total income	=	7,206	100	23,047	100
2. Current transfer payments					
Rent, dividends and interest paid to UK	−	1,272	18	4,721	21
UK taxes paid by foreigners	−	136	2	327	1
Other current payments to UK by foreigners	−	113	2	295	1
3. Current spending					
Spending by foreigners on UK goods[b] and services	−	5,809	80	16,494	72
B. Capital transactions					
4. Income saved[c]	=	−124	−2	1,210	5
5. Capital spending					
Spending by foreigners in UK	−	208	3	931	4
Spending abroad by UK[d]	+	253	4	1,348	6
6. Income available for lending	=	−79	−1	1,627	7
C. Lending and borrowing[e]					
7. Total lending	+	517	7	15,402	67
8. Total borrowing	−	596	8	−13,775	60
9. Net lending (+) or borrowing (−)	=	−79	−1	1,627	7

[a] UK imports.
[b] UK exports.
[c] Equals balance of overseas payments on current account with sign reversed.
[d] Includes £59m. capital transfers in 1973.
[e] Includes unidentified items.

recent years. In 1973 they represented around two-thirds of the group's income compared with under 10% in the early 1960s; there was some reduction in activity in 1974, primarily owing to the effect of the oil crisis on international financial markets.

The underlying trends are seen more clearly in the analysis of the group's capital transactions into sources and uses of funds in Fig. 2.5. As with figures for the government, official borrowing and lending is included in 'other' sources and uses; this is primarily a use of funds in periods of UK balance of payments deficit like 1964–68 and a source at times of surplus, for example 1969–72. In the first period, people and organizations overseas were effectively lending their surplus of funds, which they had gained as a result of our imports exceeding our exports, back to the British government through various official channels, such as the IMF and swap agreements between central banks. In the second period this lending was being repaid, thus providing the overseas group with a source of funds.

It is clear that the great growth in the total of borrowing and lending by the overseas group has been based on an expansion of loans as a source of funds and bills and deposits as a use: the particular financial instruments involved have been bank loans and deposits, and these borrowing and lending transactions have been closely interlinked. They represent the UK's involvement in the development of the Euro-currency markets, which will be discussed in more detail in the next chapter. They tie in with the similar but reverse expansion in loans and deposits already noted in the sources and uses of funds for financial companies.

The growth in transactions in loans and deposits has had a considerable impact on the structure of the assets and liabilities held in the UK by members of the overseas group. Fig. 2.7 shows that these two types of financial instrument accounted for over two-thirds of the liability and asset totals respectively in 1973; this compares with one-third or less only seven years earlier. Both as assets and as liabilities, the outstanding securities held by the group have declined markedly in importance since the middle 1960s; in the former case, the item represents UK securities held by overseas people or organizations; in the latter, it is the securities issued by foreign organizations and held by domestic UK groups.

The physical assets held by the overseas group represents the land, buildings and equipment that they control in the UK. The great expansion in lending means that the importance of such physical assets has declined relatively in recent years, despite the continued flow of new capital spending and a rise in asset values. The far larger amount of foreign land, buildings and the like owned by the overseas group is of course ignored here, but the item 'UK direct investment

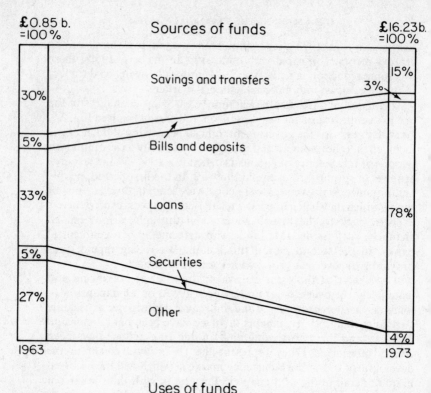

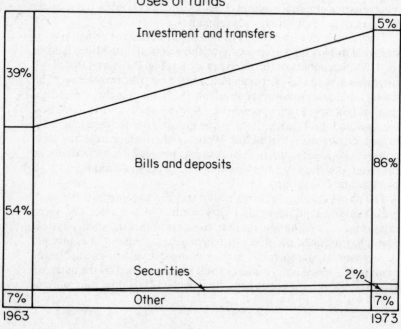

Fig. 2.5 Overseas: sources and uses of funds

abroad' represents the portion of these foreign physical assets that is directly held by UK companies. As with the comparable item in the liabilities of industrial and commercial companies, this is a pseudo-financial instrument introduced to avoid complicating the picture by including inter-company transactions. It shows how far the foreign net worth of the overseas group is in fact owned by UK companies.

In Fig. 2.7, net worth for the overseas group appears as an asset, indicating that, on the basis of the valuations used, the group's liabilities exceed their assets; for other groups the opposite was true. This implies that the domestic groups in the UK own more assets overseas than overseas people and organizations own in the UK. It may be either because the value of foreign assets has risen faster than that of assets in the UK or because historically the overseas group has spent more on current goods and services from the UK than the income it has received and so has been on balance losing wealth to the UK; in other words the balance of payments on current account has historically been in surplus. The latter was of course true for many years, particularly in the nineteenth century, when many of our holdings of foreign assets were being accumulated. But it has not been true in the recent past, a fact that has doubtless contributed to the decline in the proportion of total assets represented by net worth.

2.8 HOW THE GROUPS COMPARE

The broad brush sketches given above of each of the main groups indicate that they differ quite considerably in their financial characteristics. All make a great deal of use of the payments system either for current or capital transactions or both. But the relative importance of these two types of transaction clearly varies; so also does the extent of borrowing and lending in relation to saving and capital spending as well as the forms in which the borrowing and lending takes place. And these differences in the pattern of year-by-year transactions are naturally reflected in holdings of assets and liabilities.

The major role played by capital transactions in the affairs of financial companies and to a lesser extent those of the overseas group has already been mentioned. Borrowing and lending are of far greater importance to them than to the other three groups, both when related to income and when compared with savings as a source of funds and capital spending as a use. Fig. 2.6 indicates the extent of variation between the groups in the latter case; it also highlights the differing patterns of borrowing and lending by putting side by side the distribution of sources and uses of funds of the groups in 1973. Fig. 2.7 performs a comparable function for the distribution of assets and

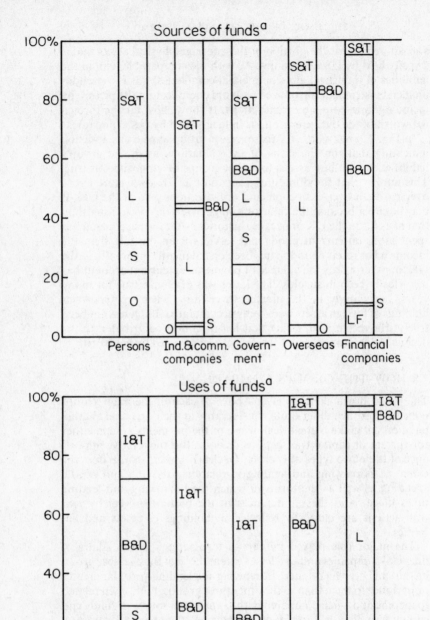

^{a}S&T = savings and transfers I&T = investment and transfers S = securities
L = loans LF = life funds O = other instruments

Fig. 2.6 A comparison of sources and uses of funds, 1973

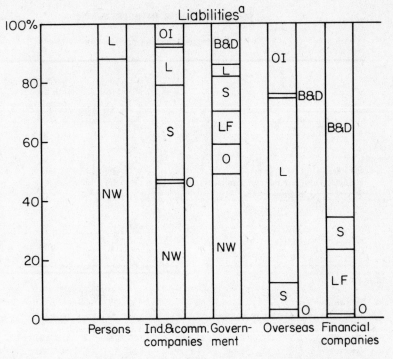

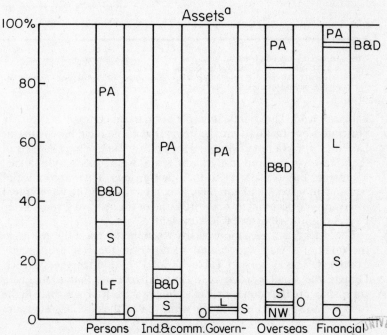

^aPA = physical assets B&D = bills and deposits L = loans S = securities
LF = life funds O = other instruments OI = overseas invest. NW = net worth

Fig. 2.7. A comparison of the distribution of wealth in 1973

Table 2.8. The shares in saving and investment

	Saving	Investment (all capital spending)[a]
	%	%
1963		
Persons	28	16
Industrial and commercial companies	43	41[a]
Financial companies	3	3
Government	19	36
Overseas	2[b]	4
	100	100
1973		
Persons	27	15
Industrial and commercial companies	39	46[a]
Financial companies	5	5
Government	16	29
Overseas	13[b]	5
	100	100

[a] Includes capital spending overseas, mainly by industrial and commercial companies. Their spending overseas was 4% of the total in 1963 and 6% in 1973.
[b] Figures represent the current account of the balance of payment with sign reversed plus receipts from capital spending overseas by UK residents.

liabilities held. The channelling role of financial companies is clearly illustrated by the fact that the items that form their borrowing or liabilities, for example bills and deposits, are the lending or assets of the other groups; conversely loans are a use of funds by financial companies but are sources to the other groups. The importance of persons, industrial and commercial companies and the government as savers who accumulate net worth, and of the last two groups as the buyers of physical assets, is also evident.

The latter fact is seen more clearly when the shares of the groups in the total of saving and capital spending in the UK are directly examined. This is done in Table 2.8 for 1973 and ten years earlier. Despite the small portion of their total revenue that is retained, companies are the main source of saving in the UK. Their share in the total has however been declining, while that of the next largest group, persons, has remained fairly stable. Companies are also the major capital spenders, followed closely by the government. In both functions the role of financial companies is relatively limited.

2.9 WHO IS BORROWING FROM WHOM?

Comparison of each group's share in saving and capital spending shows how far it is on balance a net lender or a net borrower, in financial surplus or financial deficit. In 1973 persons did not spend all they saved, whereas both companies and the government were more important in terms of capital spending than saving. This in turn indicates broadly who has been borrowing from whom in the period concerned; persons and the overseas group must have been lending to companies and the government in some way.

A more precise picture of the situation over the last decade is given in Fig. 2.8 where the annual financial surpluses and deficits of the various groups have been plotted. This summarizes overall net borrowing and lending, the component parts of which have already been examined. It illustrates how persons have in fact been a continual source of funds for other groups. The most important regular borrower of these funds has been the government, which has run a financial deficit in all years but those of extreme monetary stringency like 1969–70. Both industrial and commercial companies and the overseas group have been major borrowers from time to time; the former in years of monetary restraint like 1970 and 1974, the latter more normally in years of expansion. As has already been discussed, the net borrowing and lending of the financial companies is negligible in the total context of these financial flows. But their function in facilitating the borrowing and lending of other groups has been vital.

The true function of financial companies can be seen better in Table 2.9. This is a simplified flow of funds table of the type described in Chapter 1 showing the capital transactions of the groups analysed into their main borrowing and lending categories. It indicates who was borrowing from whom and in what form in 1973. One evident feature is the way financial companies dominate the flows in and out of certain types of financial instruments, especially the taking of money in the form of deposits and borrowing in the form of loans. Indeed, the most important flows in the UK financial system in 1973 were a series of two-way transactions between financial companies and the other groups, notably with the overseas group, persons and industrial and commercial companies.

The precise nature of these flows is the subject of the next chapter. But to complete the summary picture presented here, Table 2.10 gives a simplified analysis of who held what in 1973. Again the importance

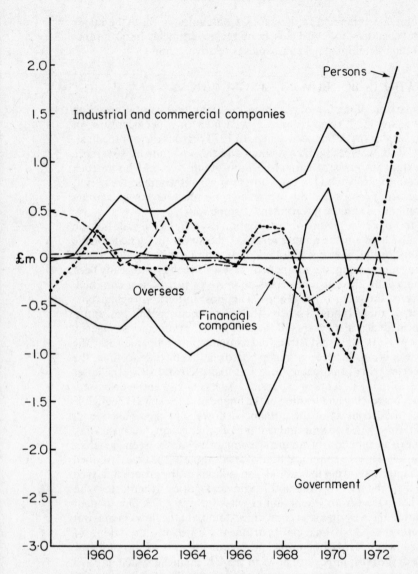

Fig. 2.8 Who borrows and who lends: financial surplus or deficit of main groups
These figures do not tie in exactly with those presented elsewhere
owing to revisions to published data and treatment of investment
overseas. See appendix

Table 2.9. Flow of funds in 1973: a simplified picture[a]

Form of transaction £m.	Persons Sources −	Persons Uses +	Industrial and commercial companies Sources −	Industrial and commercial companies Uses +	Government Sources −	Government Uses +	Overseas Sources −	Overseas Uses +	Financial companies Sources −	Financial companies Uses +	Discrepancy[b]	Total Sources = Uses
1. Savings and investment[c]	5,372	3,903	7,448	8,097	3,636	6,593	2,454	878	1,285	1,122	Source 398	20,593
2. Bills and deposits	97	5,873	70	2,643	682	651	522	13,996	22,214	422	—	23,585
3. Loans	3,767	—	5,050	—	1,091	916	12,621	—	—	21,613	—	22,529
4. Securities	1,450	973	262	744	1,552	8	—	257	279	1,561	—	3,543
5. Life funds	—	2,740	—	—	—	—	—	—	2,740	—	—	2,740
6. Other instruments	3,132	329	426	1,772	2,152	945	632	1,098	56	1,856	Use 398	6,398
7. Total of above	13,818		13,256		9,113		16,229		26,574		398	79,388

[a] The table shows the extent to which the main categories of financial instrument figured as sources and uses of funds to the different groups. The amounts given are based on the net flows in and out of the particular instruments that comprise each category. Thus the presentation is not fully 'gross', as shown in Table 1.4 above. See text for further comments.
[b] Unidentified savings and investment flows (net) are balanced by a corresponding discrepancy in unidentified financial transactions included with 'other instruments'.
[c] These figures do not tie in exactly with those in earlier tables owing to revisions in published data (see Appendix for comment on this).

of financial companies as holders of outstanding financial assets and liabilities is obvious, though their net holdings and net worth are very small. Historically, persons have been lending to industrial and commercial companies and the government, largely through the medium of the financial companies. The latter have also developed a substantial two-way business with the overseas group. Persons are clearly seen to be the prime owners of the country's wealth, lesser shares being held by both industrial and commercial companies and the government.

Table 2.10. The pattern of wealth ownership in 1973: a simplified picture[a]

Type of holding £b.	Persons	Industrial and commercial companies	Government	Overseas	Financial companies	Total for all groups
1. Physical assets held	98·2	97·5	93·0	−5·0	8·0	291·7
2. Financial assets and liabilities						
Bills and deposits	45·1	9·6	−13·8	42·7	−83·6	nil
Loans	−26·4	−16·7	−0·1	−36·8	79·9	nil
Securities	25·9	−31·9	−10·7	−2·7	19·5	nil
Life funds	40·6	—	−11·6	—	−29·0	nil
Other	3·5	−1·0	−6·7	−1·3	5·5	nil
3. Net holdings of financial instruments	88·7	−40·0	−42·9	1·9	−7·7	nil
4. Net worth (= (1) +(3))	186·9	57·5	50·1	−3·1	0·3	291·7

[a] All figures, but especially those for physical assets, are estimates, and the table should be treated as giving broad view only of the pattern of wealth ownership in 1973. For details of how estimates are derived se Appendix.

3. The role of the financial markets

3.1 STAGE TWO: HOW THE FLOWS TAKE PLACE

The broad pattern of financial flows outlined in the previous chapter tells us how financial transactions fit in with the other economic and social activities going on in the UK. It shows the way in which the financial system is integrally linked with the whole process of producing and consuming, investing and saving. But the simple fund flow analysis in Table 2.9 seems a long way from the complexities of the actual financial system. And, while it identifies the main groups of instruments through which the flows take place, it says little about the mechanism that secures these flows.

This mechanism is the set of formal and informal financial markets that makes up the financial system. The term 'market' tends to conjure up a picture of a formal organization of some kind, like a street market or an auction room. Similar formal institutions do of course exist in the financial field, the Stock Exchange being the most obvious example. But much of the market mechanism is of a more informal kind, consisting of groups of people and organizations in some way concerned with a particular financial instrument. Just as the market in, say, bread can be seen as comprising all those who buy, sell or hold bread in one way or another, including the bakers and the people who ultimately eat bread as well as middle-men like retailers and wholesalers, so the market in a financial instrument includes both original borrowers and ultimate lenders, in addition to any specialist market-makers and other organizations who facilitate borrowing and lending transactions.

Hence, to see the role that financial markets of all kinds play in making funds flow from lender to borrower, it is necessary to look in some detail at the transactions that take place in each kind of financial instrument. Both the characteristics of those who operate in each market and the form of the market mechanism need to be examined; the latter includes such questions as the extent to which secondary transactions take place in existing instruments as well as the volume of new borrowing and lending flows and how far dealings are subject to formal rules and regulations. The outcome will be a more detailed picture of how different kinds of financial markets and instruments fit in to the pattern of fund flows through the UK financial system.

3.2 THE SIZE OF THE FINANCIAL MARKETS

As a preliminary to this detailed analysis, a quick overview of the financial markets as a whole is helpful. This puts the main markets in perspective both in relation to each other and to economic activity generally.

The size of a financial market can be measured in a number of different ways. The most useful of these measures, for present purposes, are the amount of the particular financial instrument that is outstanding at any given time, the increase in this total over a period and the extent of buying and selling transactions that are taking place. The first, the amount outstanding, gives some indication of the historic importance of the particular channel for borrowing and lending; though the figure will also be affected by the changes that have occurred in market values where these are used. This figure also shows the potential for dealings in existing instruments; the extent of actual dealings will depend very much on the characteristics of the particular instrument, as discussed in Chapter 1. The present-day importance of new flows in the market is shown by the second measure, that is the new instruments issued during a period. The total of purchases and sales, or turnover, indicates the combined significance of new (or primary) dealings in the instrument plus those in the secondary market for outstanding securities.

Some figures for the UK financial markets in 1973 are given in Table 3.1. Unfortunately, turnover data are not available for many markets. As measured by the amount outstanding at end 1973, the most important group of markets was those in bills and deposits, which account for one-third of the total. This group is followed fairly closely by markets in loans. In both cases, the markets are dominated by instruments issued by financial institutions, mainly the banks. The market in securities came third in importance in terms of outstandings (measured at market values), but was of very little importance as a channel for new borrowing and lending in 1973. New business was also primarily in the form of bills and deposits and loans which together accounted for 86% of all increases in 1973. The market in life funds was relatively unimportant in terms of new transactions, the 5% in 1973 being well below the group's share in total outstandings.

The difference in the relative size of the various markets by the two measures reflects trends in borrowing and lending in recent years, particularly the growing emphasis on bills and deposits and loans which has already been seen in the analysis in Chapter 2. As measured by the total of all new borrowing and lending, the business of financial markets expanded some nine times between 1963 and 1973; the growth was briefly halted in 1966 and 1970, and monetary re-

Table 3.1.   The main groups of financial markets in 1973

Type of instrument [b]	Amount outstanding at end 1973 [a]		Increase during 1973 [a]	
	£b.	%	£b.	%
1. Bills and deposits liabilities of:	106·8	33	23·59	43
Government	13·4	4	0·15	—
Financial institutions	91·1	28	23·20	43
Others	2·3	1	0.24	—
2. Loans made by:	86·5	27	23·27	43
Government	3·5	1	0·90	2
Financial institutions	83·0	26	22·37	41
3. Securities liabilities of:	72·1	23	2·06	4
Government	12·0	4	1·55	3
Financial institutions	15·2	5	0·28	1
Others	44·9	14	0·23	—
4. Life funds liabilities of:	40·6	13	2·74 [d]	5 [d]
Government	11·6	4	[d]	[d]
Financial institutions	29·0	9	2·74	5
5. Other instruments [c]	14·6	5	2·64	5
6. Total [a]	320·6	100	54·30 [d]	100

[a] Figures exclude instruments created as a result of inter-bank and intra-government transactions. Their coverage of trade credit and other direct lending by companies and persons is limited (see Section 3.7 below).
[b] For a more detailed list of the instruments in each group see Table 1.1 above and subsequent tables in this chapter.
[c] Includes all local authority debt, instruments created as a result of certain official transactions and some trade credit (net). See Table 3.14 below.
[d] No estimates have been made of the increase in value of unfunded pension rights during 1973.

straint produced a similar effect in 1974. The markets in bills and deposits and loans have been generally increasing their share of the total business while the market in life funds has declined relatively, though the absolute amount of business in this form has risen. New business in the securities markets has fluctuated substantially during the period, but it too has shown an overall tendency to decline in importance; the level of issues in 1972–74 was in absolute terms little different from that of the middle 1960s.

Table 3.2.   The financial system and the economy

£b.	1966	1973
1. Total of financial instruments [b] outstanding at end year	137·7	320·6
2. Value of physical assets in existence at end year	137·6	291·7 [a]
3. Ratio of financial instruments to physical assets (= (1) ÷ (3))	1·0	1·1
4. Increase in financial instruments [b] during year	7·2 [c]	54·3 [c]
5. Value of gross domestic product for year	33·0	62·2
6. Ratio of increase in financial instruments to GDP ((4) ÷ (6))	0·2	0·9

[a] This figure is a rough estimate only. See Appendix for basis of estimate.
[b] Figures exclude most instruments created as a result of intra-group transactions and cover trade credit on a net basis only. Gross figures, including some intra-group dealings, would give a ratio of outstanding instruments to physical assets of 1.3 in 1966.
[c] Excludes increase in unfunded pension rights.

The total of all financial instruments outstanding at end 1973 is estimated to have been £321b. with an increase during the year of £54b. These figures have little meaning on their own, but they may be compared with measures of the economic wealth and activity that it is the function of the financial system to facilitate.

In Table 3.2, the data on financial instruments are contrasted with the total of all physical assets outstanding (the national wealth) and the annual output of goods and services in the UK, that is the gross domestic product (GDP). Between 1966 and 1973, new financial assets grew at a much faster rate than the value of the economic activity thus being financed. This reflects the increasing role played by the financial system in the process of borrowing and lending, in particular the growing number of institutions being interposed between original lender and final borrower; in 1974, this general trend was temporarily reversed. However, over the period 1966 to 1973 the growing value of financial assets outstanding has probably been largely matched by rises in the value of physical assets, especially of land and building. A substantial proportion of financial assets are expressed in fixed terms and do not therefore rise in value along with the assets whose creation they finance; this effect has already been seen in, for example, the analysis of government assets and liabilities.

3.3 BILLS AND DEPOSITS—THE MONEY MARKET

The main types of financial instrument included in the group bills and deposits were summarized in Table 1.1, and Table 3.3 gives a more detailed list with an indication of the size of individual markets in 1973. The group includes deposits with financial institutions, notably banks and building societies, together with the main short-term borrowings by the government and those by other groups through commercial bills. Bank borrowing is excluded, being classified under loans, and, because of inadequate information, the figures in Table 3.3 do not cover short-term debt of local authorities. Some data on the latter are given in Table 3.4, p. 64, together with an analysis of inter-bank transactions, which are also excluded from the figures.

The markets in bills and deposits are dominated by bank deposits. Even excluding inter-bank transactions, the latter accounted for over two-thirds of the instruments outstanding in this group in 1973 and nearly 90% of new borrowing flows; the proportions were somewhat lower in 1974. Deposits with other financial institutions are much smaller and only those with building societies are of any significance in the total. The latter were of less importance, as a new channel for borrowing and lending in 1973, than they have been historically. The same was true for government short-term borrowing, especially that through national savings.

The extent of the government's short-term borrowing through the issue of new treasury bills and savings deposits has varied greatly in the last decade. In certain years, like 1971, receipts from national savings were of some size, while in 1974 there were substantial additions to the Treasury bill issues. But in other periods, such as 1964–66, the government was repaying its outstanding short-term debt on quite a substantial scale. This illustrates in another context the trends already seen in the analysis of government sources and uses of funds. Bank deposits have been gaining an increasing share of new short-term borrowing and lending, partly at the expense of deposits with other financial institutions. Even so, the absolute amount of new borrowing in the latter form trebled between 1963 and 1973; but total borrowing through bills and deposits increased tenfold.

Underlying these trends are the varying nature and uses of the instruments included in this group. The distinguishing feature that they all have in common is their liquidity, the ease with which their holders can exchange them for cash and so for goods and services or other instruments. In some cases this quality arises directly from the short-term nature of the contract being undertaken; bills are issued or money deposited for a fixed period at the end of which the lender expects to receive his money back, probably with interest. For other

Table 3.3.   The main types of bills and deposits

Type of bills and deposits	Amount outstanding at end 1973		Increase during 1973	
	£b.	%	£b.	%
1. Issued by government[a]	13·4	13	0·15	1
Notes and coin	4·3	4	0·54	2
Treasury bills	1·3	1	−0·33	−1
National savings	7·6	7	0·14	1
Tax reserve certificates	0·2	—	−0·21	−1
2. Issued by financial institutions	91·1	85	23·20	98
Bank notes and deposits[b]	71·7	67	20·85	88
Deposits with other financial institutions	19·4	18	2·35	10
of which:				
Building societies	16·4	15	2·07	9
Savings banks	2·5	2	0·17	1
Finance houses	0·5	1	0·06	—
3. Issued by others	2·3	2	0·24	1
Commercial bills	2·3	2	0·24	1
4. Total[a b]	106·8	100	23·59	100

[a] Excludes local authority short-term debt (see Table 3.15) and government's holdings of its own issues.
[b] Excludes inter-bank dealings.

instruments, like normal bank deposits or national savings, the commitment by the lender may be an open-ended one, but there is a provision enabling the holder of the instrument to regain his money, either immediately or at very short notice; sometimes the provision may include a penalty as with national savings. But, liquidity apart, the individual types of bills and deposits vary considerably, especially in the conditions relating to their issue and the nature of the people and organizations who hold them.

Notes and coin are, of course, the most liquid of all the instruments, being one of the basic forms of money. There is a very free market in such money in the sense that it can easily and quickly be disposed of in exchange for goods and services or other financial instruments. But the market in the other direction is less easy; notes and coin can readily be bought only if the item offered in exchange is either highly liquid itself or is at a price acceptable to the other party involved.

Because of their great liquidity, notes and coin carry no return in the form of interest and there is a relatively small amount of them outstanding, only 4% of the total of bills and deposits in 1973. Most people and organizations need to hold some notes and coin for day-to-day transactions, but extra cash of this kind is usually quickly put to work, either buying goods and services or acquiring interest-bearing assets; at the very least it is normally put into safe-keeping in the form of deposits of some kind. The distribution of outstanding notes and coin between different holders is not known precisely; some 19% was held by the banks at end 1973, but the split of the remainder between other groups is not available. To facilitate the growth in value of day-to-day transactions, the government normally adds a small amount each year to the notes and coin outstanding, but this does not form an important source of official borrowing. In most years, the addition has been taken up largely by persons and companies.

So far bank deposits have been treated as one single type of financial instrument. In the sense that all these deposits represent money lent to a financial institution called a bank for some, usually fairly short, period, the treatment is warranted; bank deposits are clearly different from, for example, treasury bills or national savings or even building society deposits. But, these days, there are many kinds of bank deposits outstanding; money is lent in different amounts, for different periods, under different conditions, to different types of bank. The latter difference will be discussed in the next chapter, but the others now need some elaboration.

The first distinction to be drawn is between the normal deposits on current account and what are confusingly known in the UK as deposits on deposit account or in America as time deposits. The former are usually associated with chequing facilities and are held primarily for the purpose of current day-to-day transactions. They comprise the main source of money in most developed financial systems, and, with a total £9·4m. at the end of 1973, amounted to nearly twice the amount of notes and coin outstanding in the UK. Interest is not normally paid on such deposits, though it has become more common for some banks to do so in recent years. So-called deposit accounts are interest-bearing but are less readily used for current transactions. This is particularly the case where the deposits are for a fixed period; withdrawals from the conventional deposit account in the clearing banks are usually much easier.

Within deposit accounts, a split needs to be made between small- and large-scale deposits; officially the line appears to come at £10,000. As might be expected, small deposits are normally those held by private individuals, while the larger amounts are deposited

Table 3.4.   Growth in money market instruments [a]

Type of instrument	1963	1971	1972	1973	Growth 1963–73
	Amount outstanding at end period (£b.)				1963 = 1
1. Bills					
Treasury bills [b]	3·07	2·18	1·72	1·40	0·5
Commercial bills	0·70 [c]	1·48	1·71	2·30 [c]	3·3 [c]
2. Deposits:					
with UK banks: [a]					
total	11·82	48·86	65·43	95·49	8·1
by UK banks	0·62	8·20	13·20	21·45	34·6
by other UK residents	8·83	15·53	19·56	26·27	3·0
by overseas residents	2·37	18·96	24·67	37·36	15·8
as negotiable CDs	—	4·17	8·00	10·41	[d]
with finance houses	0·39	0·83	0·44 [e]	0·48 [e]	[e]
with discount houses (borrowed funds)	1·23	2·96	2·53	2·57	2·1
with local authorities (temporary debt)	1·35	1·97	2·41	3·39	2·5

[a] Figures include, inextricably, current as well as deposit accounts with banks. See text for comment on their significance.
[b] Figures include bills held by central monetary authorities. If these holdings are excluded, 1973 amount outstanding is 0·4 times that in 1963.
[c] Estimated.
[d] Infinite.
[e] Comparability of figures has been affected by the reclassification of some major finance houses as banks. See p. 72.

either by industrial and commercial companies or by financial institutions, including other banks, at home and abroad. It is this last group of large-scale deposit accounts that has been responsible for most of the rapid growth in bank deposits in recent years. By 1973 deposit accounts, excluding those held by UK banks, represented over 80% of total bank deposits outstanding, compared with under 60% in 1963 and probably around half in the late 1950s.

Large-scale interest-bearing deposits with banks are today the major instruments handled in what are known as the 'money markets'. Other instruments involved are deposits with finance houses and with local authorities, money at call with the discount houses and treasury and commercial bills. But, as Table 3.4 shows, the total of bank deposits far outweighs that of other money market instruments; this would be so even if all personal deposits and current accounts were excluded. It was, however, much less true ten years ago, and the growth in this type of money market activity has been a major feature of the UK financial system in recent years.

As was mentioned in Chapter 1, money markets handle transactions in instruments representing the right to use money for short periods. They are essentially new issue markets and provide outlets for spare cash which enables this money to earn some reward in terms of interest, while at the same time retaining a high degree of security and liquidity. In the past this demand and the corresponding demand for short-term borrowing were relatively limited; only the banks and a few other institutions and companies were concerned to earn interest on their short-term holdings, and the government was the main short-term borrower. This traditional money market operated, and still does today, through the medium of the discount houses. They took deposits (or money at call) from the banks and others and lent this on by buying treasury and commercial bills and short-term government securities. The clearing banks, in particular, thus gained a profitable outlet for the funds that they needed, either because of official requirements or for reasons of commercial prudence, to keep in a secure, liquid form.

Deposit accounts with the banks used to represent the only interest-bearing outlet for short-term funds of comparable security to money at call in the traditional money market. But interest payments on accounts with the major clearing banks were, until 1971, subject to a cartel agreement, which left a wide margin between the rate paid and that which could be earned on loans of various kinds. From the late 1950s onwards, it was increasingly recognized by other banks that it was possible to offer higher rates on deposits, particularly on those of large amounts, and still lend the money on at a profit. At the same time, the holders of such deposits, mainly companies, were becoming aware of the advantages of making profitable use of their short-term money. New borrowers for short-term funds were also arising. Initially they were the local authorities, who were anxious to avoid borrowing long term at what appeared, at the time, to be very high rates of interest, and hire purchase finance houses who were unable to obtain adequate funds in the form of bank loans. Subsequently, in the 1960s, these were joined by many industrial companies wanting to increase their short-term borrowings at a time when lending by the clearing banks was under almost continual official restraints.

As a result, new or parallel money markets developed channelling an increasing volume of short-term funds, usually held by companies, through to various borrowers. Initially the money was often put directly into deposits with the ultimate borrower, the local authority or finance house, using the agency of a specialist money broker. Subsequently, a market also developed for direct short-term lending between companies. But, more and more, the business has been carried out indirectly, the money moving first into a deposit with a bank and then being lent on, either as a further deposit or as a loan, often to an industrial borrower. Table 3.4 illustrates the very different growth in the bank and other deposits as well as in old and new money market instruments. Since the middle 1960s, the clearing banks have themselves participated in the parallel markets and their new-found freedom to compete in 1971 (discussed in more detail in Chapter 8) led to a considerable expansion in interest-bearing deposits.

Along with this expansion of domestic money market activity has come an enormous growth in international transactions in short-term funds. The growth in this international money market, better known as the Euro-dollar or more generally the Euro-currency market, interacted with and stimulated the domestic expansion. Like the expansion of domestic money markets, Euro-dollar business initially arose as a result of official restrictions on interest rates and pressures for more profitable outlets for short-term funds. European holders of dollars were dissatisfied with the rates available to them on deposits in the United States, which were limited under what was called regulation Q. Hence they looked for better opportunities to use their money at home. Such opportunities were provided by banking institutions, many based in the UK, who, having taken the dollar deposits, either lent the money on in this form or converted it into other currencies for the purpose.

The importance of this type of business was evident in the analysis of sources and uses of funds of both the overseas group and financial companies in Chapter 2. Its significance in the UK money market can be seen in the size and rate of growth of deposits with UK banks by overseas residents. The latter now form the largest single group of lenders to the banks and their deposits have grown faster than those of any other group, except the 'other' UK banks.

The great rise in the bank deposits held by UK banks is the product of another extension of money market activities, namely the growth of the inter-bank market. As banks have become more involved in taking deposits and making loans for a wide variety of short-term periods, so their need for greater flexibility in obtaining and lending money has increased; the reasons for this are discussed further in the next chapter. The increasing number of institutions involved in money market business has provided banks with opportunities for balancing their borrowing and lending through transactions with other banks, as well as with final savers and borrowers. This business has grown to such an extent that nearly one-quarter of total bank deposits in the UK came from other UK banks in 1973 compared with 5% in 1963. This excludes deposits from banks overseas and the holdings by UK banks of certificates of deposit.

The introduction of negotiable certificates of deposit (CDs) has been the last major development in the money market in recent years. These instruments were introduced initially in the US domestic market and their use was subsequently extended to Euro-dollar deposits; sterling certificates have been issued since October 1968. As mentioned in Chapter 1 the certificates are 'pieces of paper' issued by the bank taking the deposit, which enable the holder of funds lent for a fixed period to regain his money before the period is up. This he does by selling the certificate, giving its new holder the right to collect the deposited money when it matures. CDs thus make it possible to operate a secondary market in deposits, providing a further degree of flexibility to short-term lenders who wish to adjust their holdings. There were over £10b. of CDs outstanding in the UK at end 1973, 11% of all bank deposits; roughly half of these were denominated in sterling and UK banks are themselves substantial holders of other banks' CDs.

The remaining instruments classified under bills and deposits are the various types of national savings, and deposits with building societies and the National and Trustee Savings banks; in the statistics, only investment accounts with the latter are classified as deposits, ordinary accounts being included with national savings. These instruments do not form part of what is normally defined as the money market owing to a number of special characteristics. Traditionally they have been channels for small-scale personal saving and, as a result of official policies to encourage such savings, they attract a variety of tax advantages. This has led them to be described as privileged circuits[6] and, in order to limit the extent of the privileges, a maximum size of holding has been set for a number of instruments. Hence, these channels are effectively not available to the large-scale holders of short-term money like companies or financial institutions. Nor has any market in the existing instruments or rights to them developed.

Building society deposits have been far the most significant of these outlets for new lending in recent years, and annual increases in deposits outstanding have risen five-fold since 1963. In contrast, people were reducing their holdings of national savings during much of the 1960s. The different trends largely reflect another feature of this group of instruments, namely the fact that the interest rates paid on them have tended to be lower than on money market instruments. This is especially the case for national savings, whereas building

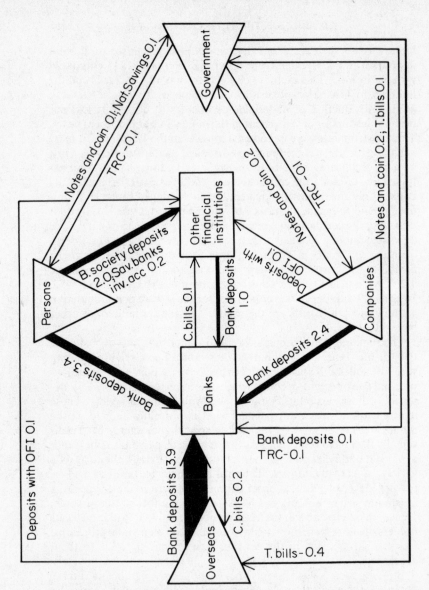

Fig. 3.1 The market for bills and deposits in 1973. Arrows indicate the order of magnitude of flows between groups. The size of the main items involved is shown in £b. Some minor flows are omitted.

society deposit rates have been more competitive. However, in recent years, concern about the level of rates that the societies charge on their loans has led to attempts to keep down the rates paid on the money they themselves borrow in the form of deposits. In 1973 the effect spread to bank deposits with the introduction of a ceiling of $9\frac{1}{2}\%$ on the rate paid on small-scale deposits; this measure was withdrawn in the early part of 1975.

The overall pattern of money flows in the bills and deposits markets is summarized in Fig. 3.1. While all groups are to some degree involved in this part of the financial system, the banks dominate the markets. Their business with the overseas group and with companies is of primary importance. The only other flows of major importance are those between persons and banks and from persons to certain of the other financial institutions. Compared with any of these, the government's involvement in the market is normally small. Turnover in the market is substantially higher than the net flows shown, owing to the short duration of many of the instruments involved. But, with the limited exception of certificates of deposit and treasury and commercial bills, there are virtually no secondary dealings in existing instruments in this group of markets.

3.4 LOANS AND MORTGAGES—HOW WE ALL BORROW

The financial instruments included under the heading of loans and mortgages are distinguished from deposits in that they are usually granted to final borrowers like persons and companies, rather than made by them. They are normally for rather longer periods than most deposits, usually for several years or more, and are not generally liquid assets from the point of view of the lender. Indeed it is often virtually impossible for him to terminate a loan before the stipulated period, though a borrower can mostly repay early; this contrasts with the position of a person (or organization) borrowing in the form of a deposit where the borrowing can seldom be repaid until the term of the deposit is up. Loans are distinguished from securities, also used by final borrowers, in that there is rarely a negotiable instrument created when the loan is made, and there is virtually no secondary market in loan contracts. But the distinctions between the groups of instruments are broad ones only and certain types of loan approach quite close to deposits and others to securities, for financial instruments form a continuum and categories can be only roughly defined.

The main types of loans and mortgages are listed in Table 3.5. Bank loans form by far the largest market both in terms of amount outstanding and new borrowing; this was clearly the case in 1973, and despite restraints on bank lending, was still very true of 1974. The

Table 3.5.   The main types of loans

Type of loan [a]	Amount outstanding at end 1973		Increase during 1973	
	£b.	%	£b.	%
1. Advanced by government	3·5	4	0·90	4
House purchase loans	1·7	2	0·30	1
Refinanced shipbuilding and export credit	0·9	1	0·25	1
Other government loans	0·9	1	0·35	2
2. Advanced by financial institutions	83·0	96	22·37	96
Bank loans [a][b]	61·4	71	19·49	83
Hire purchase and other instalment credit [c]	1·6	2	0·12	1
House purchase loans [d]	16·9	20	2·26	10
Loans by pension funds to parent organizations	1·0	1	0·34	1
Loans by other financial institutions	2·1	2	0·17	1
3. Total [a]	86·5	100	23·27	100

[a] Figures exclude loans and mortgages received by local authorities apart from normal bank advances (see Table 3.15 below).
[b] Excludes loans for house purchase which are categorized separately.
[c] Figures include a small amount of credit granted by government.
[d] Mainly by building societies, banks and insurance companies.

only other item of any size is loans for house purchase which account for over a fifth of all loans outstanding in 1973 but only a tenth of new lending. New borrowing through bank loans has been increasing in importance over the last decade relative to other types of loans and mortgages. But, since total new lending in the form of loans and mortgages in 1973 was over thirteen times what it was in 1963, the absolute amount of money flowing through the market has increased for virtually every instrument involved.

The figures in Table 3.5 exclude the very substantial loans made within the government group, both to local authorities and national-ized industries. But government lending to other groups has been growing in recent years. All this new lending has gone to the non-financial sectors. The introduction of refinancing for the last stage of shipbuilding and export credits by the Bank of England has assisted both the overseas group and companies; the latter have also been the main beneficiaries of 'other' government loans, while there is now a

substantial flow in the form of house purchase loans made by local
authorities to persons.

The recent expansion in government lending is however, puny
when set beside the growth in loans granted by financial institutions.
Table 3.6 indicates how the amount of different loan instruments
outstanding has expanded. As might be expected from earlier analysis, a major part of the growth in bank loans has come from business
with overseas residents, part of the expanding Eurocurrency operations described in the previous section; overseas loans represented
over half the total of bank loans outstanding in 1973 compared with
just over a fifth ten years earlier. On top of this growth, there has been
a substantial increase in bank lending to companies and persons,
particularly between 1971 and 1973 when the controls on domestic lending were removed. The figures exclude lending to UK
banks through the inter-bank market, but, as Table 3.6 indicates,
in 1973, balances with UK banks, the counterpart of deposits
received from these banks, were thirty times the 1963 level; this

Table 3.6. The growth in loans by financial institutions [a][b]

Type of loan	1963	1971	1972	1973	Growth 1963–73
	Amount outstanding at end period (£b.)				1963 = 1
1. Bank loans [b]	6·50	26·66	41·07	60·25	9·3
of which:					
to UK residents	5·08 [c]	9·94	17·17	24·12	4·7
to overseas residents	1·42 [c]	16·72	23·90	36·13	25·4
2. Hire purchase and other instalment credit	0·74	1·21	1·37 [d]	1·49 [d]	2·0 [d]
3. House purchase loans	4·63	12·08	14·64	16·89	3·6
of which:					
by banks	0·32	0·50	0·84	1·13	3·5
by building societies	3·58	10·41	12·63	14·47	4·0
by insurance companies	0·73	1·17	1·17	1·29	1·8

[a] Main types of loans only.
[b] The figures exclude loans to local authorities and lending in the form of balances held with UK
banks. The amounts involved in the latter are as follows:

Balances with UK banks	1963	1971	1972	1973	Growth 1963–73 (1963 = 1)
Amount outstanding (£b.)	0·64 (est.)	7·78	12·26	19·65	30·7

[c] The split between loans to UK and overseas residents is estimated.
[d] Estimated figures to eliminate effect of reclassification of major institutions.

is a faster growth even than that in lending to overseas residents.

Traditionally, much bank lending has been in the form of over-drafts, that is facilities to borrow by 'overdrawing' on current account up to a stated amount. In theory, such loans were for short periods only; but quite often the short periods have become longer ones and, in the last few years, banks have moved more into lending definite amounts for fixed periods. This has been particularly the case for Euro-Currency loans, and there has also been a tendency for loans to become formally longer-term, for periods of five years or more.

While all the main groups make use of bank loans as a form of borrowing, house purchase loans go entirely to persons; loans to house builders are included in bank lending to companies or persons. Building societies are by far and away the main providers, but insurance companies, and increasingly banks, play a significant subsidiary role; this is in addition to the house loans provided by local authorities, which have already been mentioned. House purchase loans are granted for much longer periods than bank loans, frequently twenty-five years or more; but their average duration is shorter than this, around seven years, owing to early repayment or exchange for a new loan when a person moves house. Most house purchase borrowing is technically in the form of a mortgage, that is a loan specifically secured on the property purchased.

Borrowing in the form of hire purchase and instalment credit is also very largely by persons; the main providers are the specialist finance houses. The total is much smaller than that for either bank or house purchase loans and it has grown much less than both of these. This is partly the result of official restrictions on lending, but the figures have also been influenced by changes in the nature of instalment credit and the consequent reclassification of the financial institutions concerned. Hire purchase credit is technically distinguished from ordinary loans by the fact that the lender retains formal ownership of the item purchased with the 'loan', hiring it out to the borrower until the full amount borrowed is repaid; hence the car or television could, in theory at least, be repossessed and is security for the loan. But, increasingly, the problems and costs of repossession have lessened the value of this security to the lender and the true security has become similar to that for other consumer loans, namely the prospective income of the borrower and his ability to meet the instalments regularly.

Thus, lending in the form of instalment credit has become very similar to a bank loan. An increasing amount of lending for the purchase of consumer durables has been done by means of direct loans and a number of the major finance houses have effectively turned themselves into banks. Hence the figures for instalment

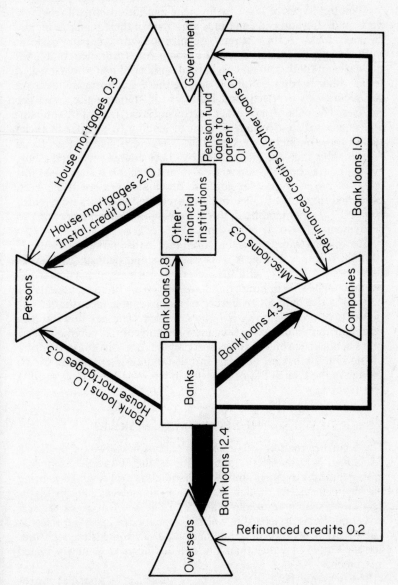

Fig. 3.2 The market for loans in 1973. Arrows indicate the order of magnitude of flows between groups. The size of the main items involved is shown in £b. Some minor flows are omitted.

credit now cover fewer institutions than they did ten years ago.

The other types of loans by financial institutions are all relatively very small. Certain pension funds use a part of their available money to make loans to their parent organization, the company or local authority for whose employees the fund is run. Insurance companies and pension funds also make a limited number of loans not classified under other headings. Notable among these are mortgage loans on the security of property and loans on outstanding life assurance policies. The bulk of such other borrowing is carried out by companies. There is also a certain amount of lending by smaller financial institutions, mainly to persons, that is not identified in the official figures. This includes loans made by check traders, where the borrower buys a check or voucher on an instalment basis and uses this 'piece of paper' to pay for goods at designated outlets. It has been estimated that some £130m. of new checks and vouchers were issued in 1969;[21] the net lending in this form would be much less owing to repayments of existing borrowing.

The various transactions that take place in the market for loans are brought together in Fig. 3.2. As with bills and deposits, the banks dominate the picture, with their overseas business of particular importance. The flow of house purchase loans from building societies to persons is the only other feature of major importance, though the network of smaller flows is quite complex. The net flows shown represent the difference between a more substantial volume of new loans being issued and old ones being repaid. But, this apart, there are in the UK almost no dealings in outstanding loans of any kinds; though in the United States a market in bank loans has developed in recent years.

3.5 SECURITIES—THE SECONDARY MARKET

The securities market, or rather the part of it known as the Stock Exchange, is probably the one section of the financial system that most people are aware of. Indeed, it is sometimes represented as being *the* financial system, though the error of this view should already be very clear; see, for example, Table 3.1. The key feature of the securities market is the extent to which secondary dealings take place; as Table 3.10, p. 80, indicates, purchases and sales of existing securities are far larger in value than the annual increase in newly issued instruments.

The distinguishing characteristic of securities as financial instruments is their negotiability; the contract between borrower and lender is represented by a piece of paper which the lender can easily hand on to another person if he wishes to regain his money. Securities also

Table 3.7.   The main types of securities

Type of securities	Amount outstanding at end 1973		New issues during 1973	
	£b.	%	£b.	%
1. Issued by government [a]				
British government securities [b]	12·0	17	1·55	75
2. Issued by financial institutions	15·2	21	0·28	14
Unit trust units	2·1	3	0·16	8
Other securities	13·1	18	0·12	6
3. Issued by others				
Company and overseas securities	44·9	62	0·23	11
4. Total [a]	72·1	100	2·06	100

[a] Securities issued by local authorities are excluded (see Table 3.15 below).
[b] Holdings by government itself are excluded. Figures for amount outstanding are estimated.

tend to represent borrowing for long or indefinite periods. As discussed in Chapter 1, negotiability, together with a good secondary market, enables those who are uncertain about how long they wish to lend to take on long-term commitments, knowing that they will be able to pass the loan on if necessary. Unlike the situation when a deposit is withdrawn, the sale of a security does not involve extinguishing the corresponding financial instrument; unless of course the security is bought, for this purpose, by the borrower. Equally, however, the lender cannot be sure of regaining the precise value of the original loan he made; he has to take whatever value he can get in the secondary market.

The main types of securities outstanding in the UK in 1973 are shown in Table 3.7. The figures include not only securities quoted and dealt in on the formal Stock Exchange but also the shares and loan stock of smaller unquoted companies, and those of overseas companies and governments to the extent that they are held by people or organizations in the UK. The major category, in terms of outstanding amounts, is the securities issued by companies and the overseas group, which represent nearly two-thirds of the total; securities of financial institutions account for a further fifth of the total, including a small amount of units issued by unit trusts. In both cases, securities quoted on the Stock Exchange form the major part of the total. Issues

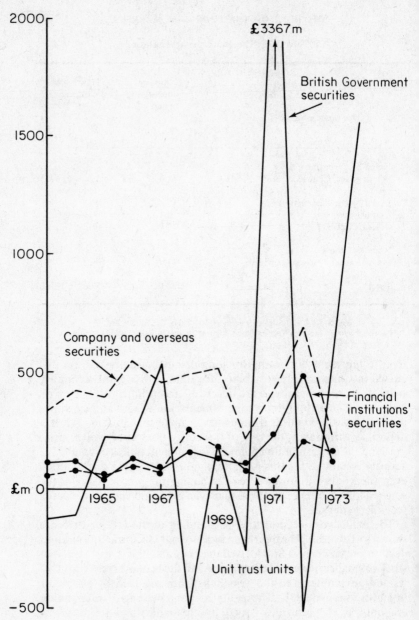

Fig 3.3 New issues of securities, 1963-73.

by the government, excluding those held by it, have a fairly small share of the market in terms of outstandings; though in certain years, like 1971 and 1973, new borrowing in this form has dominated the market. The extent of fluctuation in government borrowing through new securities has already been mentioned and this is illustrated in Fig. 3.3. Compared with these sharp movements, the variations in other kinds of new security issues have been small. But there has been little upward trend in the amount of money raised over the decade, certainly when compared with the substantial increases seen for bills and deposits and loans.

Table 3.8.   The holders of outstanding securities [a]

	British government securities		Company and overseas securities	
	1966	1973	1966	1973
% of total outstanding at market value held by:				
Persons	26	22	50	36
Companies	6	5	8	14
Government [b]	[b]	[b]	2	2
Overseas	13	13	3	3
Banks	22	13	1	2
Other financial institutions	33	47	36	43
All groups	100	100	100	100

[a] All figures, but especially those for 1973, are rough estimates and give a broad indication only of the pattern of holdings.
[b] Government holdings of its own securities are excluded from the total outstanding. At 31 March 1974 such official holdings were 23% of all government securities in issue (at nominal values).

Despite the relatively low level of new borrowing through securities, there have none the less been substantial flows through the securities market in recent years. In the market for government securities the major transactions have been between the government itself and the banks and the other financial institutions. The latter group have been regular buyers, though on a varying scale, but banks have sold government securities in most years. During much of the 1960s persons were selling their existing holdings of government securities, both to the government and the other financial institutions, but, in 1971 and again in 1973–74, they reverted to buying more government securities. In contrast, personal sales of company and overseas securities have been maintained at a high rate, reaching a peak in 1973; these sales, together with new issues by companies, both industrial and financial, have been taken up by rising purchases on the part of most other groups, including companies themselves. Persons have, however, continued to buy some unit trust units, though the scale of purchases has not again reached the high level of 1968.

These transactions have helped to produce some notable changes in the holders of different kinds of securities; their effect has been magnified by simultaneous changes in the market value of outstanding securities. Table 3.8 gives some estimates of the changes in holdings since 1966. Other financial institutions are by far the largest holders of government securities and have increased their share of the total in recent years, at the expense mainly of the banks. Personal holdings of government securities have also declined while, for company and overseas securities, persons are no longer now the major holders. This place has been taken by the other financial institutions, notable among which are the life assurance companies and pension funds. The share of such securities held by companies themselves has also risen sharply.

Changes in market values have had an important influence on the pattern of outstanding securities of different kinds. In fact, as Table 3.9 shows, the bulk of the apparent growth in the value of quoted securities of UK companies between 1963 and 1973 came from increases in the price of ordinary shares rather than through new issues. Furthermore, the new issues of British government and local authority securities were insufficient to offset the declines in price from the 1963 levels. The result has been a rise in the importance of company shares and loan stocks within the total of securities quoted on the Stock Exchange.

This fact is of relevance when considering the turnover in securities that is the total of all purchases and sales. The securities market, at least that in quoted securities, is one of the few areas of the financial system where a measure of turnover is available. Since 1965, when turnover figures were first collected, total stock exchange business by this measure has virtually trebled; the peak level of turnover was actually reached in 1971. In line with movements in market value, turnover in ordinary shares has been rising in importance and that in British government securities has been declining. But Table 3.10 shows that, in both cases, turnover has been rising in relation to the market value of outstanding securities; this has been the general case for all types of security, though there may have been a reversal of the trend in 1974. For company securities the rising ratio of turnover to new issues indicates the increasing importance of the secondary

Table 3.9. The growth in quoted securities [a]

| Type of security | Amount outstanding market value at end year | | | | Increase in amount 1963–73 [a] | | |
| | 1963 [a] | | 1973 [a] | | Total | New issues | Increase in value |
	£b.	%	£b.	%	£b.	£b.	£b.
British government securities	16·45[b]	35	18·82[b]	28	2·37[c]	4·67[c]	[c]
UK local authority securities	0·98	2	1·70	2	0·72	1·32	−0·60
Overseas government and local authority securities	0·87	2	0·40	1	−0·47	−0·26	−0·21
UK company securities [d]	28·41	61	45·79	69	17·38	5·48	11·90
Debentures and loan stock	1·79[e]	4	4·75	7	2·96	3·12	−0·16
Preference shares	1·17	3	0·52	1	−0·65	0·09	−0·74
Ordinary shares	25·45	54	40·52	61	15·07	2·27	12·80
Total of above	46·71	100	66·71	100	20·00	10·49	n/a

1963 figures are for the London Stock Exchange, 1973 ones for the amalgamated Stock Exchange; the increase in amount is thus slightly overstated.
including securities held by the government itself.
issues to non-government bodies only. There was thus a decline in the value of quoted securities greater than 2·30b. (= £2·37b. — £4.67b.).
including securities of financial companies.
figures may include a small amount of foreign company loan stock.

market relative to primary new borrowing in this form. The ratio for ordinary shares fluctuates greatly, but in 1970, and again in 1973 and 1974 total dealings were over 100 times the value of new issues; for debentures and British government securities the ratio in 1973 was just over twenty times.

The flows in the market for securities are illustrated in Fig. 3.4. In contrast to the previous two sections it is the other financial institutions that dominate the picture, though all groups but the overseas one are of significance. The total flows are also much smaller than those in the markets for loans and bills and deposits. It is not possible to determine to what extent personal sales of securities are made direct to borrowing groups (companies and government) or via the institutions; probably the bulk go through the latter route but there must also be some direct flows. A large part of the transactions

Table 3.10. The importance of the secondary market in securities

| | Turnover as ratio of | | | |
| | New issues during year | | Amount outstanding $(mv)^b$ at end year | |
Type of securities	1965	1973	1965	1973
1. British government securities	72·3	22·8	$1·0^b$	$1·9^b$
2. UK local authority securities	1·6	a	0·3	0·7
3. Overseas government and local authority securities	a	a	0·2	0·4
4. UK company securities	8·9	87·5	0·1	0·4
Debentures and preference shares	1·3	21·8	0·1	0·3
Ordinary shares	40·5	124·8	0·1	0·4
5. Total of above	24·2	32·6	0·4	0·5

[a] New issues were negative during the year.
[b] Based on market value of all securities in issue including those held by government.

are carried out through the medium of the formal Stock Exchange; but there are also many private deals in unquoted securities, while the Exchange has recently met direct competition from Ariel, an automated dealing system set up under the aegis of the leading merchant banks.

Whatever the channels, it is clear that transactions in existing securities are of much greater importance than new borrowing through security issues. As a result, the highly developed network that is the new issue market in securities has become increasingly concerned with such secondary transactions.

Two distinct operations are involved here. First there is the refinancing of existing companies that occurs when their shares become quoted on a recognized stock exchange. Although termed 'new issues' in relation to the Stock Exchange, these are essentially secondary transactions since little new money is received by the company. But a significant portion of the existing share capital usually changes hands; the sales form part of the regular selling of company securities by persons. Secondly, much of the expertise developed in the new issue market, particularly among the issuing houses and other merchant banks, is today devoted to assisting companies to acquire outstanding securities through mergers and

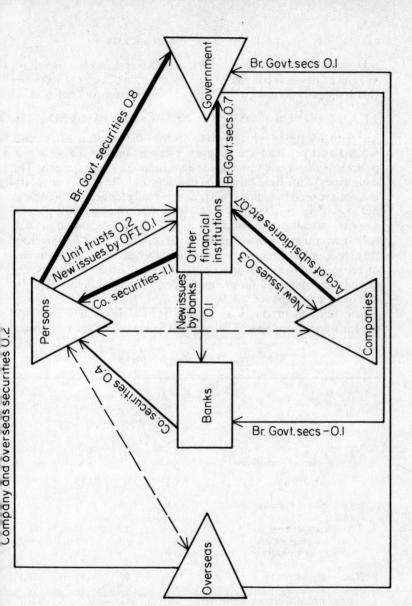

Fig. 3.4 The market for securities in 1973. Arrows indicate the order of magnitude of flows between groups. The size of the main items involved is shown in £b. Dotted lines indicate location of unidentified flows. As a result, some other flows may be overstated. (see text for comment).

takeovers. Finally, the new issue market also undertakes a significant volume of business concerned with international issues of securities that frequently do not involve either UK borrowers or lenders.

3.6 LIFE FUNDS—SOME UNCERTAINTY REMOVED

The term 'life funds' is here used to describe the financial instruments created as a result of the payment of premiums on life assurance policies or the saving towards the acquisition of pension rights. The main types of life funds are listed in Table 3.11. Premiums or contributions are used to build up what is technically termed a fund, that is holdings of assets of various kinds, from which the maturing policies or pensions can in due course be paid. Table 3.12 shows how such funds accumulate, with a substantial part of the increase coming from rent, dividend and interest on assets already held. Each policy-holder or prospective pensioner has rights to a share of the life funds, the amount depending on the premiums or contributions paid either by him or by his employer.

Life funds are in some ways similar types of financial instruments to loans and mortgages. The contract involved between borrower

Table 3.11.   The main types of life funds

| | Amount of funds at end year[a] | | | |
| | 1963 | | 1973 | |
	£b.	%	£b.	%
1. Life assurance funds	7·43	46	18·13	45
2. Self administered pension funds	3·80	24	10·72	27
of which:				
Private sector funds	2·14	13	6·32[b]	16
Local authorities funds	0·73	5	1·71[b c]	4
Other government funds	0·93	6	2·69	7
3. Total funded schemes	11·23	70	28·85	72
4. Value of unfunded pension rights and sinking funds	4·95	30	11·60[b]	28
5. Total life funds	16·18	100	40·45	100

[a] All figures are at book value.
[b] Estimated.
[c] Based on figures for 31 March 1974.

Table 3.12. How life funds are built up[a]

Type of transaction[a]	1963 £b.	1963 %	1973 £b.	1973 %
1. Revenue	2·37	100	6·94	100
of which:				
Employers' contributions	0·77	33	2·15	31
Individual premiums and employees' contributions	0·95	40	2·87	41
Rent, dividends and interest	0·65	27	1·92	28
2. Outgoings	1·29	54	4·12	59
of which:				
Pensions and other benefits paid	1·02	43	3·27	47
Administrative costs, etc.[b]	0·27	11	0·85	12
3. Net increase in funds[a b] (= revenue *less* outgoings)	1·08	46	2·82[c]	41

[a] Figures relate to all life assurance and pension funds in the UK. Revenue and outgoings of unfunded schemes for government employees are also included (see discussion on p. 85).
[b] Includes adjustments made to the book value of funds as a result of actuarial valuations.
[c] Revised figure: see Appendix.

and lender is usually fairly long-term and the instrument has little negotiability. But in other respects they are very different. The accumulation of funds involves dealings between an original lender, usually a person, and a financial intermediary rather than between the latter and a final borrower, and there are of course important special terms that distinguish the life assurance or pension contract.

Although, from the point of view of the financial system, the assurance and pension funds are but another means of channelling money from lender to borrower, the special terms relating to the assurance element of this type of financial instrument are, literally, of vital importance to the lender. For, while life funds are illiquid instruments in the sense that holdings cannot easily be exchanged for money in normal circumstances, there is the security that on certain eventualities, when money is likely to be badly needed, it will be forthcoming. This may be at a certain predetermined time, as with saving for pensions or an endowment policy, or it may be in the case of an emergency as on death. Either way, when the lender commits himself to a long-term contract of this kind he can be sure of certain minimum returns, provided of course the institution involved is a sound one. However, in an inflationary era, he cannot guarantee that the actual sum paid will be adequate to meet his eventual needs.

Individual assurance policies differ greatly in the extent to which they are vehicles for obtaining security or are primarily a means of accumulating wealth to be cashed in at a certain stage. Term life assurance represents the extreme emphasis on security, while pension contracts are almost entirely a vehicle for investing savings. But in virtually all cases there will be some eventual pay-out from a life assurance policy, and it is this that makes the *as*surance contract into a financial instrument representing a form of lending. In contrast, the normal non-life *in*surance contract is not a financial instrument in the sense used here. The payment of an insurance premium on a house or a car will produce a pay-out only in certain restricted circumstances; it is thus in no sense a form of lending but a type of current spending, buying security against certain risks. Hence, while non-life insurance companies are important as financial institutions, the funds they accumulate are the property of the company and its owners; they are not a channel for borrowing and lending in the way that life assurance and pension funds are.

As Table 3.12 indicates, a substantial part of the money flowing into life assurance and pension funds is provided by companies and government organizations as contributions to the pension schemes they run for their employees. But such payments are conventionally seen as being made to the employees as part of their wages and salaries, and the current transactions of both life assurance and pension funds are treated as being undertaken by persons. Hence, in terms of money flows, the lending being accumulated in the form of life assurance policies and pension rights is shown as the net increase in the life funds (the bottom line of Table 3.12); this is a flow between persons and other financial institutions. Part of this flow goes to life assurance companies, both for normal assurance policies and for pensions, and the rest to special pension funds. Table 3.13 shows the

Table 3.13.   The flow of funds into life assurance and pensions [a]

Net lending by persons in the form of £m.	1968	1969	1970	1971	1972	1973
Life assurance funds [a]	791	751	817	964	1,251	1,297
Pension funds [a][b]	717	754	946	1,017	1,123	1,443
All life and pension funds	1,508	1,505	1,763	1,981	2,374	2,740

[a] The split between life assurance and pension funds is estimated.
[b] Pension fund figures include the excess of revenue over expenditure in unfunded pension schemes.

increase in the flows over recent years and the approximate split between the two groups of contributions. The tax advantages associated with both life assurance and pension contributions makes these flows another example of the privileged circuits that exist within the UK financial system.

In addition to the lending flows in the form of acquisition of a share in assurance and pension funds, certain employees accumulate rights to future pensions that are not covered by funded schemes. These unfunded pension schemes, which are mainly for government employees are generally also 'non contributory' as far as the employee is concerned. Current contributions by the employing organization are used to pay pensions in force now, in the same manner as the national old-age pensions are paid out of current taxation. None the less, the pension rights represent a holding of financial assets to the employees concerned. Increases in these assets cannot readily be identified, but Table 3.11 includes some estimates for the outstanding amount of unfunded rights. Funded schemes accounted for over two-thirds of the total in 1973, slightly under half being the funds of life assurance companies and a quarter self-administered pension schemes; the latter have been increasing their share of the total in recent years. In all cases, the funds are shown at the book value of the liabilities they represent rather than at the market value of the assets held (see Section 5.5).

3.7 OTHER INSTRUMENTS—MAINLY OFFICIAL TRANSACTIONS

The residual 'other' category of financial instruments includes a miscellany of items, some important, which are difficult to fit into other classes owing to the lack of detailed data or certain special characteristics. The major item, as Table 3.14 shows, is local authority debt, where published data are inadequate to allow transactions to be separated out into the deposits, loans and securities that are known to be involved. The rest of the items mainly relate to government financing at home and abroad, but certain types of trade credit are also included. The unidentified flows incorporated in this category in the analysis in Chapter 2 are discussed in the next section.

The main types of local authority debt are listed in Table 3.15; they include direct lending by the banks, which was excluded in Table 3.14 since it is covered under bank loans. The bulk of outstanding local authority borrowing is longer-term, with over half in the form of loans and mortgages. But short-term sources are more important in relation to new borrowing. The role of local authorities in the money market has already been mentioned, and, in recent years, their

Table 3.14.   The main types of other instruments

Type of other instrument	Amount outstanding at end 1973		Increase during 1973	
	£b.	%	£b.	%
1. Government financing				
Local authority debt[a]	8·3	57	1·03	39
Government liabilities to the Bank of England Banking Dept	1·8	12	1·03	39
Official gold and foreign exchange reserves and special drawing rights	1·6	11	0·21	8
Official financing including inter-government loans (net)	0·4	3	0·21	8
2. Other items				
Trade credit (net)[b]	2·5	17	0·17	6
3. Total of above	14·6	100	2·64	100

[a] Excludes normal bank advances, classified as bank loans in Table 4.6, and borrowing from government sources.
[b] Figures for government trade credit and that relating to certain overseas transactions only (see discussion on p. 87).

borrowing in the form of deposits has been supplemented by the issue of 'yearling' bonds; these, while securities of over one year in duration and sometimes quoted on the Stock Exchange, are essentially money market instruments. All the main groups provide funds to local authorities from time to time, and, while the other financial institutions have become increasingly important lenders in recent years, the non-financial groups are believed still to be major takers of loans and mortgages. In addition, local authorities obtain a substantial volume of mainly longer-term funds from other parts of the government, notably through the Public Works Loan Board. In 1973 42% of all borrowing was from this source.

The other types of government financing have already been discussed in the course of analysing the sources and uses of government funds. The main flows in recent years are illustrated in Fig. 3.5. The transactions of the Bank of England Banking Department that broadly correspond to the changes in this government liability are considered in the next chapter. As can be seen, the swings in the items have been very substantial from year to year. So also are those in the

Table 3.15.   The main types of local authority borrowing

Type of borrowing	Amount outstanding at 31 March 1974[a]		Increase during fiscal 1973–74[a]	
	£b.	%	£b.	%
1. Short-term borrowing (up to one year)	3·45	27	0·841	53
of which:				
Revenue bills	0·28	2	0·048	3
Bank overdrafts	0·26	2	0·113	7
Other bank loans	0·31	2	−0·079	−5
Loans from OFIs	1·05	8	0·374	24
Borrowing from companies	0·52	4	0·124	8
Borrowing from persons	0·44	4	0·094	6
Other borrowing	0·59	5	0·167	10
2. Longer-term borrowing (one year and over)	9·16	73	0·737	47
of which:				
Negotiable bonds[b]	0·85	7	0·173	11
Other quoted securities[b]	1·73	14	−0·039	−2
Other loans and mortgages	6·56	52	0·603	38
3. Total borrowing from non-government sources[a]	12·61	100	1·578	100

[a] The figures differ from those in Table 3.14 in that they are for a later date and they include all types of bank loans and lending by local authority pension funds to their parent organizations. Borrowing from government sources is still excluded (see p. 40).
[b] Securities are at book value.

various forms of official financing abroad, which are, in Fig. 3.5, separated into some of the different instruments involved, such as reserves, treasury bills and government loans. Comparison with movements in the current account of the balance of payments (the net borrowing or lending of the overseas group—shown in Fig. 2.8) indicates how the need for official financing of this type has arisen.

As mentioned in Chapter 1, transactions in trade credit are one of the worst identified sections of the financial markets. The official figures shown in Table 3.14 cover only credit granted by public corporations (mainly nationalized industries) and certain kinds of credit relating to exports and imports. And, even these transactions are only shown net, so that it is extremely difficult to distinguish the two types of flows involved. Persons appear to be persistent

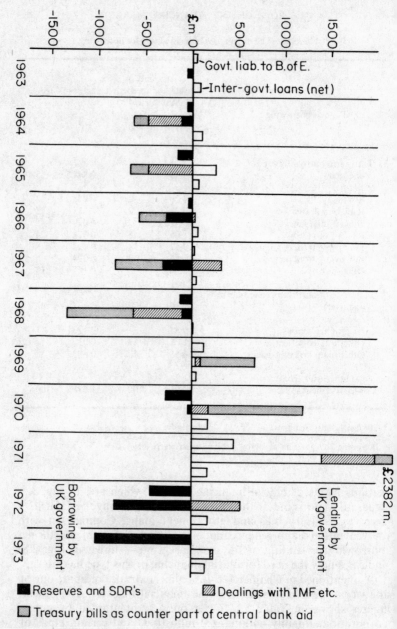

Fig. 3.5 Aspects of government financing.

borrowers in this form, presumably credit from the nationalized electricity, gas, coal and telephone industries. In contrast companies have probably been net providers of trade credit to the nationalized industries in most years and, latterly, they have also been lending in this form to the overseas group.

Some idea of the true importance of the direct borrowing and lending between groups that takes place in the form of trade credit and similar loans can be gained by looking at the total of such credit that is outstanding. Table 3.16 gives estimates of the situation in 1966. Companies are seen to be both the main source and the major recipients of trade credit, but a significant amount is both granted and received by persons (unincorporated businesses) and public corporations. The totals involved are quite large. In place of a net figure of just over £2b., the difference between the credit granted by companies and that received, the gross amount of trade credit outstanding is shown at some £8b. in 1966. In addition, there were thought to be other forms of miscellaneous credit, like payments due in the form of wages and salaries, taxes, rates and insurance premiums and claims, totalling a similar amount.

Together, these types of credit represent a volume of lending well above the total of bank loans outstanding at that date and nearly half the value of company and overseas securities. The rate of expansion in new lending in the form of trade and other credit has probably been well below the exceptional growth in new bank loans and deposits

Table 3.16.   Trade credit and other loans in 1966 [a]

		Trade credit		Other misc. credit [b]
£b.	Granted	Received	Granted	Received
Persons	0·5	1·5	4·2	2·1
Industrial and commercial companies	6·9	4·3	0·5	3·4
Government	0·7	1·3	3·5	1·5
Overseas	0·1	0·6	0·2	—
Banks	—	—	—	—
Other financial institutions	—	—	0·4	1·0
All groups [a]	8·2	7·7	8·8	8·0

[a] These figures are taken from reference 50 (The Financial Interdependence of the Economy 1957–66). As explained there, the total amounts of credit granted and received do not balance, as they in theory should, owing to the inadequacy of available data.

[b] Wages and salaries, taxes, rates and insurance payments due, etc.

since 1966. But, even a fairly conservative estimate of a doubling of the total to some £30b. by 1973 makes this a significant segment of the financial system, of comparable size to life assurance and pension funds and nearly double the volume of house purchase loans that are outstanding. (Compare the figure of £30b. with those items identified in Tables 3.1 and 3.5.)

3.8 UNIDENTIFIED FLOWS

It will be clear from the above that the granting of new trade credit by both companies and other groups is one of the major flows in the financial system that the official statisticians have so far been unable to identify. Trade credit is, however, not the only problem area. Fig. 3.6 shows the financial flows that are left as unidentified in the flow of funds table. These represent the amount required to balance the estimate of net lending and borrowing by each group derived from saving and capital spending figures with the net result of the identified borrowing and lending transactions. For, while in theory the two should be the same, in practice this is usually not the case.

The unidentified flows are themselves probably the net result of a number of transactions in different instruments. The main pattern of the flows is the persistent net borrowing by persons and net lending by companies that was mentioned in Chapter 2. In addition there are some unidentified transactions by the overseas group (the so-called 'balancing item' in the balance of payments figures) and more limited discrepancies for the other groups. While flows of trade credit and similar lending almost certainly account for a considerable part of the unidentified element, it is unlikely that this represents the whole of the story. Some transactions in securities, particularly personal sector sales to companies, may also be involved. But the official statisticians believe that part of the explanation lies in inadequacies in the estimates of the savings and capital spending flows rather than in unidentified borrowing and lending.[42, 45] In particular, savings by persons are thought to be underestimated and the figure for companies may be too high, while there is in any event normally a discrepancy between the estimates of total saving and total investment which should in theory be equal.

To put the unidentified flows into perspective, Fig. 3.7 illustrates the transactions that took place in 1973 in the various financial markets discussed in the last three sections. Of the identified movements, the flows of lending from persons to life assurance and pension funds and from banks to the government via the Bank of England are the most significant. But the unidentified items are also of considerable importance.

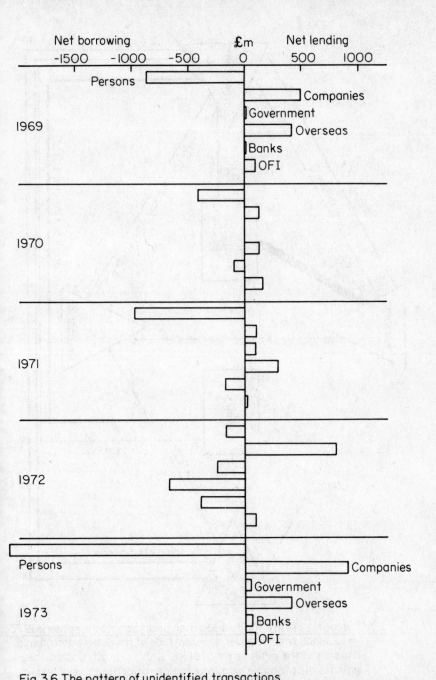

Net borrowing   £m   Net lending

-1500   -1000   -500   0   500   1000

Persons

1969

Companies
Government
Overseas
Banks
OFI

1970

1971

1972

Persons

1973

Companies
Government
Overseas
Banks
OFI

Fig. 3.6 The pattern of unidentified transactions.
  The figures represent the balacing item required to reconcile identified
financial transactions with the group's net financial surplus or deficit.
See text for comment on their composition.

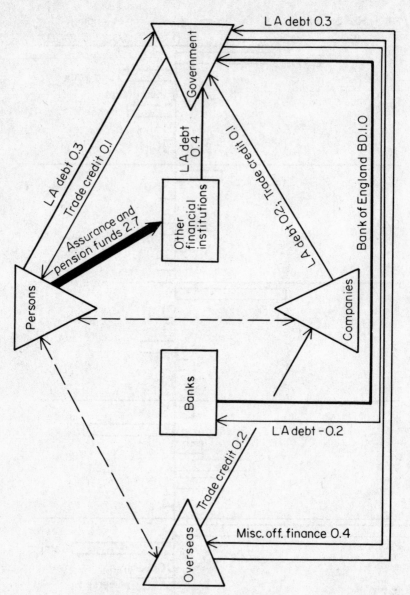

Fig. 3.7 The market in life funds and other financial instruments in 1973. Arrows indicate the order of magnitude of flows between groups. The size of the main items involved is shown in £b. Dotted lines indicate the probable location of unidentified flows (see text for comment).

3.9 HOW THE MARKETS COMPARE

A complete picture of the flow of funds through the financial markets, bringing together the various circuits discussed here under the separate markets, cannot be given yet. For it is necessary first to study in

Table 3.17. The largest markets [a]

Type of financial instrument [a]	Amount outstanding at end 1973		Increase during 1973	
	£b.	%	£b.	%
1. Bank deposits	71·7	22	20·85	38
2. Bank loans	61·4	19	19·49	36
3. Company and overseas securities [b][h]	44·9	14	0·23	—
4. House purchase loans	18·6	6	2·56	5
5. Life assurance funds	18·1	6	1·30	2
6. Deposits with building societies	16·4	5	2·07	4
7. Securities issued by financial institutions [h]	13·1	4	0·12	—
8. British government securities [h]	12·0	4	1·55	3
9. Unfunded pension rights	11·6 [c]	4 [c]	n/a	n/a
10. Self administered pension funds	10·4	3	1·44 [j]	3
11. Local authority debt [d]	8·3	3	1·03	2
12. National savings	7·6	2	0·14	—
13. Notes and coin	4·3	1	0·54	1
14. Deposits with savings banks [e]	2·5	1	0·17	—
Trade credit (net) [f]	2·5	1	0·17	—
16. Commercial bills	2·3	1	0·24	—
17. Unit trust units	2·1	1	0·16	—
Loans by other financial institutions [g]	2·1	1	0·17	—
19. Hire purchase instalment credit	1·6	—	0·12	—
20. Treasury bills	1·3	—	−0·33	−1
Total all instruments [f][i]	320·6	100	54·30	100

[a] See text for comment on arbitrary elements in classification.
[b] Excluding securities issued by financial institutions.
[c] Rough estimate only.
[d] Excluding bank loans.
[e] Investment accounts.
[f] For consistency with earlier analysis (e.g. Table 3.1), trade credit is included only on the limited net basis shown in official figures. If, however, the estimate of £30b. + for outstanding trade and other credit, made on p. 90, is used, this market represents 9% of all instruments outstanding, ranking fourth in size, after bank deposits, bank loans and company and overseas securities.
[g] Excluding house purchase loans and hire purchase and other instalment credit.
[h] At market value: all others are at book value.
[i] Includes some other smaller groups of instrument.
[j] Includes revenue less expenditure in unfunded pension schemes.

more detail the crucial role that the financial institutions, both banks and others, play in integrating the business of the various markets; this is the subject of the next two chapters. But the role of the markets is compared in another way in Table 3.17, which lists the individual types of financial instrument discussed in this chapter in order of their size by total amounts outstanding at end 1973; the increase in new borrowing in each form during that year is also shown.

These figures summarize the historic importance of particular markets and show how far this importance is being maintained. Inevitably there is an element of arbitrariness in the listing since it depends on the degree of detail with which individual types of financial instrument are distinguished. But, even allowing for this, it is very clear that it is the markets in bank deposits and bank loans that form the most important part of the mechanism for channelling borrowing and lending flows through the UK financial system. As has been discussed a considerable part of these flows represents financing of the overseas group; if this element is excluded from the loan and deposit figures, bank business becomes of a roughly similar size to the outstanding value of company and overseas securities, or of all assurance and pension funds taken together. But, in terms of new borrowing and lending flows in 1973, bank deposits and bank loans formed by far the most important vehicles for domestic fund flows; this was still true in the more restrained conditions of 1974. It will be seen, in due course, that this is reflected in the relative importance of the financial institutions concerned.

The other feature of the financial markets evident from the analysis in this chapter is the limited role played by secondary dealings. Only in the securities market are these of any real substance. The bulk of the activity taking place in financial markets is concerned directly with facilitating new fund flows, handling the creation of new financial instruments rather than dealing in ones already outstanding. Secondary markets have developed only where the holders of the financial instruments concerned have felt the need for additional flexibility; the growth of the secondary market in CDs is a particularly interesting example of how this process occurs.

4.   What the financial institutions do: (a) the banks

4.1 THE THIRD STAGE: BRINGING ON THE PRINCIPALS

To some people, the analysis of the financial system that has been presented so far must seem rather like *Hamlet* without the Prince. For it is the financial institutions that are the most visible part of the system in everyday terms. Yet, while we have here seen them as one of the groups operating in the financial markets and have noted their dominance in connection with many types of financial instruments, little has been said about the individual institutions and the way they operate. This omission will now be remedied.

First of all, as a summary of the picture given to date, Table 4.1 shows how important the financial institutions, taken together, were in the market for the main types of financial instrument in 1973. The figures distinguish between the institutions' role as borrowers and that as lenders, in terms of both outstanding holdings and new flows during the year. Overall the institutions hold 40% of the outstanding financial instruments as assets and 42% as liabilities; that is, they are involved in one way or another with over 80% of outstanding financial instruments. For new flows the shares are even higher, 49% and 50% respectively.

These figures need careful interpretation. They do not mean that institutions are involved in almost all current financial transactions. Rather, because of the layering process mentioned earlier, more than one institution may be involved in any given set of flows from initial lender to final borrower; in another set of flows there may be no intermediary at all. For example, the initial deposit of money in a bank may be lent on through several other banks, creating several other deposits before it is finally turned into a loan to a person or a company. In contrast, the granting of new trade credit involves a direct transaction between companies or between a company and a person. In addition, the outstanding instruments and new flows do not allow properly for the known but statistically unidentified borrowing and lending transactions that also take place; as discussed earlier, many of these involve direct dealings between non-financial groups. Hence the figures in Table 4.1 probably overstate the total share of financial institutions.

None the less, it is clear that financial institutions do play a very

Table 4.1.   The importance of financial institutions[a]

| Type of financial instrument | What institutions held at end 1973 as | | | |
| | Assets | | Liabilities | |
	£b.	% of all outstanding	£b.	% of all outstanding
Bills and deposits[b]	6·7	6	91·2	85
Loans	82·7	96	2·8	3
Securities	33·5	46	15·2	21
Life funds	—	—	29·0	71[c]
Other instruments	6·3	43	0·8	5
Total of above	128·0	40	136·9	42

| Type of financial instrument | How institutions' holdings increased during 1973 | | | |
| | Assets | | Liabilities | |
	£b.	% of all increases	£b.	% of all increases
Bills and deposits[b]	1·50	6	23·29	99
Loans	22·37	96	0·75	3
Securities[c]	1·56	76	0·28	14
Life funds	—	—	2·74	100[d]
Other instruments	1·26	48	0·06	2
Total of above	26·69	49	27·01	50

[a] The figures show how institutions' holdings of different instruments either as assets or liabilities relate to the total of all instruments in the various categories.
[b] Inter-bank transactions are excluded. See discussion on p. 95 for interpretation of the percentages.
[c] Figures are for cash transactions only, not changes in market values.
[d] Outstandings include but increases exclude the value of unfunded pension rights.

important part in the financial system. The interesting feature of Table 4.1 is the way in which their share of the different markets varies, in particular the fact that they are seldom dominant as both borrowers and lenders in the same market. They play a major role as borrowers in the form of bills and deposits and life funds but hold few deposits and no life funds. Similarly they dominate the loan market as lenders but do little borrowing in this way. Only in the securities market are they involved on both sides of the fence, and even here their role as lenders is far more important than that as borrowers.

In this way, the financial institutions act as links between the different parts of the financial system, channelling money out of deposits into loans, out of life funds into securities and so on. This reflects their essential role as financial intermediaries. By putting themselves between the borrower and lender and creating new kinds of financial instrument more attractive to both parties than the alternative instruments for direct lending, they ease the flow of funds through the financial system.

One of the key aspects of this role is that the institutions are acting as *principals*. That is, they take the original lender's money on to their own book, as their own liability, accepting a contract to repay the money with interest in a certain period, or under certain conditions. From the depositor's or saver's point of view, that is the end of the matter. What the financial institution does with the money is up to the institution, provided that it fulfils the contract made. Similarly, when the institution lends out money to a borrower, the loan or security is the institution's own asset. The borrower is concerned only with his particular contract with the institution; where the institution gets its money from, and under what conditions, is its own problem.

The true character of this role as principal is perhaps most clearly seen when it is contrasted with the other ways in which financial institutions act to assist the flow of funds between potential lenders and borrowers. For example, they can act as *agents* for borrowers or lenders, finding the necessary partner to the financial contract that the person or organization wishes to make. This is a traditional broking function, where the broker helps to put a deal together but is not financially involved himself, and institutions like *stock* brokers or *insurance* brokers specialize in this type of activity in their respective markets. Financial institutions may also act as *advisers* or *consultants*, suggesting to the borrower or lender possible sources of or uses for the funds in question, perhaps with recommendations about the best of these for the purpose in hand. The advice may even include the provision of contacts with possible partners and it is frequently linked in practice with subsequent work carried out on an agency basis. But the two roles are clearly distinct from each other, as well as being very different from activity as a principal.

Most financial institutions carry out a variety of functions as agents and consultants. This is often not reflected in the figures they publish, but it is mentioned below where relevant. However, while this business is important, it is the role of the institutions as principals that is critical to the operating of the financial system. It is the way in which they perform this function, the particular types of borrowing and lending that they bring together, that distinguishes the different varieties of institutions. This is also the key to success or failure in the management of financial institutions.

As principals the institutions borrow money in one form in order to lend it on in another; they thus enter into two contracts, and their ability to fulfil the one (to those who lend to them) depends on the other (on the part of their borrowers) being in its turn fulfilled. One might think that this would lead the institutions to lend in a safer way than they borrow. But banks that provide a secure outlet for short-term funds lend on in the form of loans that are both longer-term and more risky. The same is true of building societies, while assurance companies and pension funds invest their secure funds in what can be very insecure securities. In virtually every case, the financial institutions take one kind of lending and turn it into another of a more risky kind, thus obtaining the extra return that provides them with their revenue. They also offer either borrower or lender, or both, a more attractive deal than a direct transaction between the two would normally produce.

Behind this apparent sleight of hand lies a law of statistics called the law of large numbers. Because the institutions handle large numbers of individual contracts, the outcome of their business is inherently much more predictable than the characteristics of the individual borrowing and lending contracts would suggest. Whereas it may be impossible to tell *a priori* whether an individual deposit will or will not be withdrawn in a period, or whether a particular borrower will default, the proportion of a large number of deposits or loans that will suffer such fates can be predicted fairly accurately in reasonably stable conditions. So can the proportion of assured people who will die or fall ill within a given period. In consequence, banks or assurance companies or any other institution dealing with large numbers of individuals can, in principle at least, tell how much money they need to keep by for such contingencies and how much of their short-term borrowing can be lent on in longer-term or more risky forms.

Even so, it is clear that, while the individual depositer may not usually worry about how his money is used, the analyst of the financial system must. For the relationship between the term or risk character of the institution's borrowings and lendings is of vital importance. Hence, in what follows much attention will be paid to the structure of assets and liabilities held by the different financial institutions. It is also important to take into account not only the nature but the size of individual borrowing and lending contracts; for the law of large numbers will obviously not work where numbers are

Table 4.2.   Banking business in 1973

Amount outstanding end 1973	Deposit banks	Overseas banks	Merchant banks	All banks
		% of deposits		
1. Borrowing[a]				
Deposits[a]	100	100	100	100
	(£25,137m.)	(£54,994m.)	(£16,682m.)	(£96,813m.)
of which:				
in sterling	91	16	57	43
in other currencies	9	84	43	57
from				
UK banks	10	26	34	22
Other UK residents	73	6	28	28
Overseas residents	8	58	25	39
Negotiable CDs	9	10	13	11
2. Lending[a]	106	102	108	104
of which:				
Notes and coin, etc.	5	—	—	1
Balances with UK banks	13	27	25	23
Money at call	6	1	4	3
Sterling bills	4	1	1	2
Special deposits	4	—	2	2
Negotiable sterling CDs	3	2	7	3
British government securities[b]	6	1	—	2
Loans to UK local authorities	1	2	5	2
Advances	62	66	58	63
to UK residents	53	11	31	25
to overseas residents	8	55	27	38
Other assets	2	2	6	3
3. Acceptances	—	2	5	2

[a] Deposits represent the banks' main, but not their only, source of borrowing. The relationship of total lending to deposits indicates how far other sources of funds are important to the various groups. These sources include long-term capital in the form of securities.
[b] At book value.

few. Thus institutions dealing in the money market in large sums need to pay closer attention to the way in which the contracts represented by their outstanding borrowing and lending are matched in time and riskiness. This question is considered further in connection with the different groups of banks.

4.2 THE CHANGING STRUCTURE OF THE BANKING SYSTEM

As mentioned in Chapter 1, the distinction conventionally made between the banks and the 'other' financial institutions is in ways an arbitrary one. It derives from a period when the borrowing and lending activities of various groups of institutions were more clearly differentiated than they are today. But it is evident from the analysis in the previous chapter that the emphasis of banking business still differs from that of other institutions. The banks are primarily involved with the shorter-term forms of borrowing and lending, in the markets in deposits and loans, other than those for house purchase. In contrast the other financial institutions are more active in granting house purchase loans and in the securities markets.

The main types of institution normally included in the banking group are listed in Table 4.3. Table 4.2 (p. 99) gives a fuller picture of the outstanding business of the three main groups in 1973; here their dealings with other banks are included. Taking all banks together, over half their deposits were in currencies other than sterling and over a third were from overseas residents; this excludes any certificates of deposit held abroad. Nearly a quarter more of all bank borrowing through deposits came from other banks; so other UK residents, that is mainly persons and companies, provided only 28% of the total. The major use for this borrowing was in loans (advances), of which over half were to overseas residents. The only major outlet for bank lending other than advances was balances held with other banks, which were (as must be the case) of the same order of magnitude as deposits from them. Items such as money at call, mainly with discount houses, and various forms of government borrowing like treasury bills and securities were in 1973 of very little significance in the total.

These figures show how important the new Euro-currency and inter-bank markets have become in the total activities of the banks. But their significance varies greatly for the different groups of banks. Each of the groups is discussed in detail below, but Table 4.2 summarizes the essential differences between them. The overseas banks in London are by far the most heavily involved in dealings with overseas residents, while the deposit banks are very much less so; the last

Table 4.3.   The main kinds of banks

| Type of bank [a] | Deposits at end year [a] | | | |
| | 1963 | | 1973 | |
	£b.	%	£b.	%
1. Deposit banks	8·09	62	25·14	25
London clearing	7·17	55	21·63	22
Scottish	0·76	6	1·99	2
Northern Ireland	0·16	1	0·80)	
Other	c	—	0·71)	1
2. Discount houses [b]	1·23	9	2·57	3
3. Overseas banks in London	2·85	22	55·00	55
British overseas	1·36	11	12·70	13
American	0·67	5	26·29	26
Foreign	0·40	3	8·75	9
Other overseas	0·42	3	7·26	7
4. 'Merchant' banks	0·88	7	16·68	17
Accepting houses	0·84	6	5·37	5
Other UK banks [d]	0·04	1	11·31	12
5. Total of above [a]	13·05	100	99·39	100

[a] Figures include inter-bank transactions but exclude activities of Bank of England Banking Department, the National (formerly Post Office) Giro and the so-called secondary banks (see text for comments on these three groups).
[b] Figures are for borrowed funds.
[c] Not available; probably very small.
[d] This group included many more organizations in 1973 than in 1963. But many of the newcomers either did not exist or were very small in 1963.

group includes all the well known 'street corner' banks like Lloyds and Midland but not their merchant banking type subsidiaries. The latter, together with the other independent merchant banks, occupy an in-between position; they have a substantial overseas business, but it is not the dominant factor as for the overseas banks. They are, however, the group most heavily involved in inter-bank dealings, with over one-third of their deposits and a quarter of their lending in this form; the discrepancy reflects in part the way in which the parent deposit banks have used their subsidiaries as a channel for the new money market activities. They are also the group of banks most interested in the CD market.

The varying involvement of the banking groups in the new and rapidly growing money markets has affected their ranking in terms of the size of business carried out. As Table 4.3 indicates, deposit banks were the major group in 1963, with nearly two-thirds of total deposits. In 1973, though their outstanding borrowings had trebled, they had only a quarter of the total business; these figures exclude the activities of their merchant banking subsidiaries.

Their pre-eminent position has been taken by the overseas banks in London, whose share of outstanding business rose from under a quarter in 1963 to over a half by 1973; deposits with these banks rose nearly twentyfold in this period, while the expansion of the American banks was even faster. Another group whose business expanded almost as fast is the merchant banks, who are now a significant force in the banking field. But the split given in the table indicates that this is due entirely to the growth for the 'other UK banks' which include the merchant banking subsidiaries of the deposit banks; the share of deposits held by the long-established merchant banks, which are classified as accepting houses, declined over the period.

Apart from the publicly owned giro system, of which more later, the one institution normally included within the banking group but not shown in Table 4.3 is the Banking Department of the Bank of England. The importance of the Banking Department does not arise from the size of its dealings; as Table 4.4 shows, these are relatively small compared with other groups, roughly the same size as those of a largish merchant bank. Its significance comes from its dual role as banker both to the government and to the banking system as a whole. In the latter role, it acts as lender of last resort to the system, providing by virtue of its government backing an ultimate source of funds to the system should other borrowing and lending get seriously out of balance. Traditionally, this function was carried out by lending to the discount houses (see Section 4.6). Latterly, in the support operations for secondary banks discussed on p. 117, it has operated more directly. The Bank also acts as a sort of moral guardian to the banking system, indeed sometimes to the financial system as a whole. And it is the major channel through which government monetary policy is put into effect.

The ways in which the government exercises control over the financial system are considered in Chapter 8. They consist in part of direct controls, like limits on the growth in lending or movements in interest rates under their own jurisdiction. In addition, a variety of measures can be taken which involve the Bank of England in dealings with the financial system. It is the latter that have the main effect on the flows that take place between the Bank and the government and are summarized in the net liability of the government to the Banking Department.

As part of these transactions, the Banking Department will buy and sell both treasury bills and government securities in what are known as open market operations. The action is distinct from new government borrowing in these forms which is handled by the Issue Department of the Bank of England. More important, in terms of the flows through the Banking Department in recent years, have been the special deposits that the banks have from time to time been required

Table 4.4.   The Bank of England Banking Department

Amount outstanding end year	1963		1973	
	£m.	%	£m.	%
1. Borrowing[b]	290	100	1,968	100
Deposits	216	75	1,657	84
of which, from:				
Public sector	12	4	23	1
Special deposits	—	—	1,439	73
Other bankers' deposits	204	71	195	10
Reserves and other accounts[a]	73	25	311	16
2. Lending	308	106	1,983	101
of which:				
Notes and coin	54	18	13	1
Government securities[a]	204	71	1,675	85
Advances and other accounts[a]	28	9	32	2
Premises, equipment, etc.[a]	22	8	263	13

[a] Definitions of these items changed somewhat between 1963 and 1973. See *Notes and Definitions of Financial Statistics* for details.
[b] Excludes long-term capital.

to make with the Bank of England. As Table 4.4 shows, these deposits have been lent on by the Banking Department to the government and they have latterly been a much more important source of funds to the Bank than other bankers' deposits; the latter represent the portions of their liquid reserves that the banks customarily hold with the Bank of England. The fluctuations in the net liability of the government to the Banking Department have in recent years been closely tied to changes in the level of special deposits; Fig. 4.1 illustrates the relative movements in the two items.

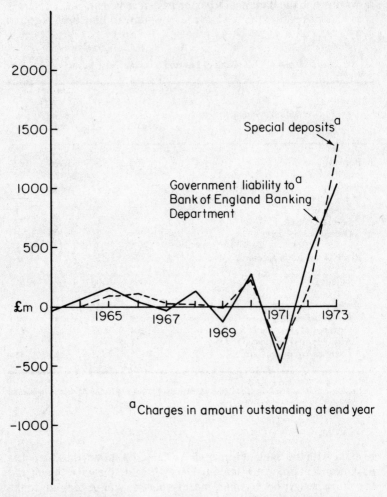

Fig 4.1 Special deposits and the government's liability to the Bank of England (Banking Department)

4.3 HOW DEPOSIT BANKING HAS ALTERED

When most people think of the banking system it is the deposit banks that come to mind. Many of these banks, also called commercial or joint stock banks, are household names and they are best known for their network of branch offices, one in virtually every town in the UK. Their business originated with the bullion merchants, who offered people a safekeeping service for their spare money, then mainly in the form of gold coins and similar valuables. Gradually it became easier for people to make payment by handing over their titles to the gold held by the merchant rather than going to the bother of withdrawing the gold and physically transferring it. Thus the use first of bank notes and subsequently of the current account deposit as money and a means of payment was born.

It is their role as providers of the main payments mechanism used today that primarily distinguishes the deposit banks from the other banking groups. They are the only banks to take deposits that are withdrawable without notice on any scale, and the system that transfers these deposits from holder to holder in the course of payment forms a major part of their business. This can be seen from the figures of bank clearings, the process by which cheques, drawn on one bank and credited to an account at another, are presented for payment. In 1973 the total value of such clearings was £1,457b. compared with a figure for the outstanding deposits of deposit banks of £25b. and gross domestic product for the year of £62b. The only other organization at present offering a comparable type of payments system is the National Giro, a publicly owned organization set up in 1968 to provide a cheap money service based on the Post Office. But the scale of its activities is very much smaller; at end 1973, its outstanding deposits were only £93m. The Trustee Savings Banks also offer limited chequing facilities on their current accounts, and there are plans for this service to be extended (see Section 5.4).

In addition to their role in handling payments, the deposit banks perform a major function in channelling funds between borrowers and lenders. The original merchants found that, as business built up, a large amount of the gold they were safekeeping remained continuously in their vaults. At any one time, few of their deposits were actually being withdrawn, and these amounts were often matched by the new deposits being made. As a result it seemed reasonably safe, as well as remunerative, to lend out some of the idle money, provided enough was always kept in reserve to meet unusually large withdrawals. Only in the event of a real run of withdrawals, with everyone wanting their money at the same time, would the 'bank' be caught out.

Although such runs on the bank have from time to time occurred, the deposit banks were able to develop a very substantial lending business alongside their safekeeping and payments services. Loans were made to businesses and to private individuals, and money was also lent to the government through the purchase of securities and bills. Traditionally, the intention was that all loans should be short-term only and essentially self-liquidating, for example to tide over seasonal fluctuations in business. In addition, in order to meet contingencies the banks kept a substantial portion of their deposits, normally around 30%, in a highly liquid form, with a smaller proportion, around 10%, actually in 'cash', in this case mostly the deposits with the Bank of England mentioned in the last section.

This traditional type of business was still the norm for deposit banking during much of the postwar period. It was sustained by the agreement, reached between the major banks over fifty years ago, not to compete for deposits through the interest rates paid and to set their lending rates in relation to a common base. The result, as seen in the previous chapter, has been a substantial growth in competition from other banks and the development of the various parallel deposit and money markets. Initially, the deposit banks reacted to this by setting up their own subsidiaries to operate in the new markets, but ultimately the growth led to the abandoning of the cartel agreement between the banks in 1971. Since then, there have been some radical changes in the business of the parent deposit banks themselves.

Most notable, perhaps, is the growth in importance of interest-bearing deposits as compared with the traditional current account deposits. For most of the 1950s, the latter represented two-thirds or more of the total deposits with deposit banks, and by end 1970 were still well over half the total. At end 1972 current accounts were less than 45% of the total, and the share has fallen further since then.

Some of the other changes that have taken place are illustrated in Fig. 4.2; once again the figures exclude the merchant banking subsidiaries of the deposit banks. The process of change in the forms of lending undertaken by the deposit banks in fact began well before 1963. In 1957 advances formed only 25% of deposits compared with 55% in 1963 and 63% in 1973. Investments, mainly in government securities, were 40% of deposits in 1957; by 1963 they had fallen to 19% and there was a further sharp fall to the present 9%. The proportion of liquid assets declined less drastically between 1963 and 1973, from 37% to 31%, but the types of assets changed markedly; a substantial part of the holdings of traditional liquid assets like notes and coin, money with the discount market and bills, was replaced by deposits with other banks (shown in other money at call, etc.).

Possibly of even greater significance, but not so evident in the

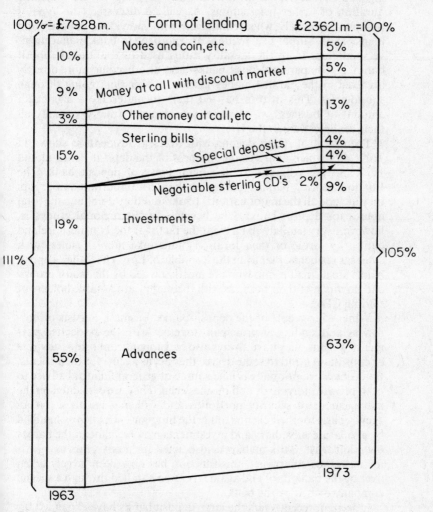

100%= £7928m.   Form of lending   £23621m. =100%

10%	Notes and coin, etc.	5%
9%	Money at call with discount market	5%
3%	Other money at call, etc	13%
15%	Sterling bills	4%
	Special deposits	4%
	Negotiable sterling CD's 2%	9%
19%	Investments	
55%	Advances	63%

111%   105%

1963   1973

Fig. 4.2 Changes in deposit banking. Figures are percentages
of deposits outstanding at year end

figures, is the extent to which the banks have moved towards borrowing and lending on a fixed-term basis in place of the indefinite
duration of earlier transactions. As will be discussed, this type of
business, especially when conducted with individual deposits and
loans of substantial size, requires an approach to bank management
very different from the liquidity ratios used in traditional deposit
banking. The parent deposit banks have also become more directly
involved in the parallel money markets rather than going through
subsidiaries. This in turn has led them to undertake a significant
amount of business with overseas residents; formerly virtually all
their dealings were in the UK.

The extent of recent dealing with overseas residents is shown in
Table 4.5, which analyses the business of the deposit banks at end
1973 and gives figures for the main types of deposit bank. The
London clearing banks form by far the most important sub-group;
they include all the major national banks and they dominate the total
figures for deposit banks. The business of the regional groups is,
however, very similar, apart from the fact that the Northern Ireland
banks, by virtue of their location, undertake more business with
overseas residents, mainly in the Republic of Eire. The 'other' deposit
banks are a small group who are mostly owned by the major groups
and do much of their business with them; they are notable holders of
sterling CDs.

While a large part of the deposit banks' business consists of borrowing and lending as principals, together with the associated payments systems, they have always also had a significant role as advisers
or consultants, and to some degree they act as agents for their clients.
Banks have traditionally been a source of general financial advice to
both private individuals and businessmen. They are consulted on the
management of security portfolios and will manage these on an
agency basis for their clients; today the function is frequently handled
by a separate subsidiary and investments may be made in the bank's
own unit trust. Bank managers also acted for many years as agents
for insurance companies; this function has now been largely taken
over by the bank itself and again it is often handled through a special
company owned by the bank.

Indeed, in recent years the large deposit banks have expanded far
beyond their basic banking business to include a wide range of
activities covering virtually all areas of the financial system. The main
types of business that banking groups have so far not entered are
insurance underwriting and first mortgage lending on houses; as will
be seen, the latter is the prerogative of the building societies, but the
banks are now active in secondary lending for house improvements.
The activities other than deposit banking have mostly been carried

Table 4.5.   The business of the deposit banks today

Amount outstanding end 1973	London clearing banks	Scottish banks	Northern Ireland banks	Other deposit banks	All deposit banks
	% of deposits				
1. Borrowing [a]					
Deposits [a]	100	100	100	100	100
	(£21,632m.)	(£1,989m.)	(£803m.)	(£713m.)	(£25,137m.)
in sterling	91	92	86	99	91
in other currencies	9	8	14	1	9
from UK banks	9	6	22	33	10
Other UK residents	73	82	51	63	73
Overseas residents	8	3	27	—	8
Negotiable CDs	10	9	—	4	9
2. Lending [a]	103	117	95	108	106
of which:					
Notes and coin, etc.	4	13	3	1	5
Balances with UK banks	13	6	19	15	13
Money at call	5	8	5	6	6
Sterling bills	4	3	1	1	4
Special deposits	4	4	—	3	4
Negotiable sterling CDs	2	3	5	32	3
British govt securities [b]	6	7	6	10	6
Loans to UK local authorities	1	2	2	2	1
Advances	63	68	49	32	62
to UK residents	54	66	30	32	53
to overseas residents	9	2	19	—	8
Other assets	1	3	5	6	2
3. Acceptances	—	2	—	—	—

[a] Deposits represent the banks' main, but not their only, source of borrowing. The relationship of total lending to deposits indicates how far other sources of funds are important to the various groups. These include long-term capital in the form of securities; for Scottish banks notes issued are also important. Figures for Northern Ireland banks show that there are some unidentified forms of lending.
[b] At book value.

out, like the merchant banking interests, through separate subsidiary companies, and so are not reflected in the parent company figures analysed above. But the annual report of a typical group gives the following list of activities at end 1973; 'Providing services in banking, instalment finance, leasing, insurance, portfolio management, foreign travel, shipping and forwarding and acting as trustees and executors'.

4.4 THE EXPLOSION OF OVERSEAS BANKING IN LONDON

Four main types of bank have been grouped together under the heading of overseas banks. These are the British overseas banks, the American banks, the foreign banks and the other overseas banks. Of the four, the British overseas banks stand out by virtue of the fact that they are a group of British-owned banks that traditionally operated overseas, particularly in the countries of the old British Empire in Africa, India and the Far East. In contrast, the other three groups are all foreign-owned banks operating in London; the so-called foreign banks are mainly of European origin, while the 'other overseas' group comprises mostly the Japanese and other Eastern banks with offices in London.

Despite their different origins, all the groups of overseas banks in London are today heavily involved in the parallel money markets and the Euro-currency business. The British overseas banks were among the first British banks to become involved in this business, stimulated by the threat that nationalist movements presented to their activities in certain traditional areas. Some foreign banks have long had offices in London, designed to handle the international business of their domestic clients, and the expanding operations of the American banks were initially provoked by their wish to regain the dollar business lost to their home offices as a result of regulation Q. Subsequently the great growth in the Euro-currency business attracted both more American and many other foreign banks to London. The expansion in both numbers and business of these foreign banks has been enormous. The latter was illustrated in Table 4.3. As regards the former, there were at end 1973 some 226 foreign banks with direct representation in London and a further 50 with stakes in consortia banks; this compares with 77 with direct representation in 1960, when there were virtually no consortia in existence.

The pattern of business of the four overseas groups is now very similar. As Table 4.6 indicates, they all receive over half their deposits from overseas and around half are lent back to foreign residents; the other overseas group has an even greater emphasis on overseas lending. Business in the inter-bank market is substantial, over a quarter of deposits for the group as a whole, and both the British overseas and American banks have significant dealings in certificates of deposits.

The emphasis on foreign dealings apart, the main difference between the overseas banks and the deposit banks that shows up in their figures is the different structure of their lending other than through advances (Table 4.2). Virtually all the overseas banks' other holdings

Table 4.6.   The business of the overseas banks today

Amount outstanding end 1973	British overseas banks	American banks	Foreign banks	Other overseas banks	All overseas banks in London
			% of deposits		
1. Borrowing [a]					
Deposits [a]	100 (£12,697m.)	100 (£26,285m.)	100 (£8,750m.)	100 (£7,262m.)	100 (£54,994m.)
of which:					
in sterling	26	15	13	9	16
in other currencies	74	85	87	91	84
from UK banks	24	26	22	32	26
Other UK residents	10	6	5	2	6
Overseas residents	53	56	64	63	58
Negotiable CDs	13	12	9	3	10
2. Lending [a]	106	101	100	100	102
of which:					
Notes and coin etc.	—	—	—	—	—
Balances with UK banks	31	27	34	16	27
Money at call	1	1	1	1	1
Sterling bills	1	—	—	—	1
Special deposits	1	1	—	—	—
Negotiable sterling CDs	4	2	1	1	2
British govt securities [b]	2	—	—	—	1
Loans to UK local authorities	4	1	1	1	2
Advances	58	68	60	78	66
to UK residents	14	10	8	8	11
to overseas residents	44	58	52	70	55
Other assets	4	1	3	3	2
3. Acceptances	2	—	1	6	2

[a] Deposits represent the banks' main, but not their only, source of borrowing. The relationship of total lending to deposits indicates how far other sources of funds are important to the various groups. These include long-term capital in the form of securities.
[b] At book value.

are in the form of deposits with UK banks, while the deposit banks still hold a significant amount of such liquid assets as notes and coin, money at call and bills of various kinds, as well as retaining some British government securities. This reflects the fundamental distinction between the type of banking that is involved. Although, as mentioned earlier, the deposit banks are moving away from their traditional open-ended borrowing and lending commitments, they still hold a considerable part of their assets in the form of a reserve that can readily be realized should circumstances require it: deposits at the Bank of England can be withdrawn; money with the discount houses can be called; bills and short-term government securities can be sold.

In contrast, the banks operating in the wholesale money markets like the overseas group rely on a different strategy to meet contingencies. Since their borrowing and lending tends to be in large lumps, the concept of keeping a reserve to meet contingencies is no longer so relevant; to be of use, the reserve would have to be so large that the benefit would be vitiated by the loss of profitability owing to the lower yield on liquid assets. Instead, a close watch is kept on the balance between the amounts borrowed and lent for different lengths of time, in different currencies and over the extent of risk involved in each case. The matching process is assisted by the fact that the conditions of borrowing and lending are normally fixed; indeed, this type of banking would be virtually impossible to operate without a considerable degree of certainty about, at least, the length of life of deposits and loans and the interest payments involved.

The only published information that illustrates how this type of banking business operates in practice relates solely to the banks' activity in the Euro-currency markets. This shows (Table 4.7) that the length of life of the banks' outstanding borrowing and lending in foreign currencies is broadly matched, though as would be expected the average term of lending is slightly longer than for borrowing.

Table 4.7.   The maturity structure of bank business in foreign currencies[a] at end March 1974

Life of instruments involved	Liabilities[b]		Assets[c]		Net Position[d]
	£b.	%	£b.	%	£b.
Less than 8 days	13·39	22	11·37	18	−2·02
8 days to less than 3 months	29·47	47	26·28	42	−3·19
3 months to less than 1 year	15·86	25	15·33	25	−0·53
1 year and over	3·48	6	9·32	15	+5·84
All periods	62·20	100	62·30	100	+0·10

[a] The figures are for all UK banks.
[b] Deposits.
[c] Loans, balances with other banks and CDs.
[d] Assets less liabilities.

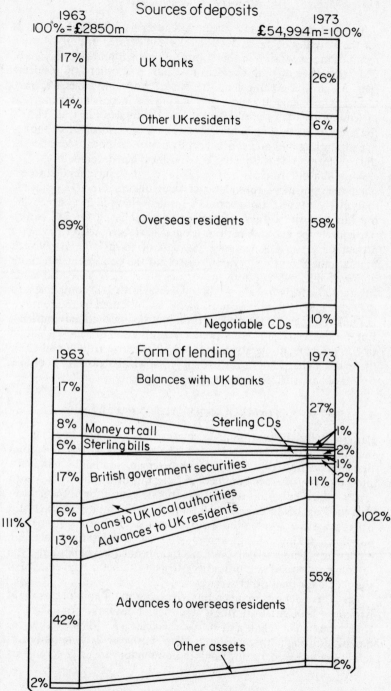

Figures are percentages of deposits outstanding at year end.

Fig. 4.3. Changes in overseas banking, 1963-73

The growing importance of the UK inter-bank market as a basis for the activities of the overseas banks is illustrated in Fig. 4.3. As a result of the expansion in this source of deposits and also the use of CDs, the share of both overseas residents and other UK residents (persons and companies) in the banks' borrowing has declined. Overseas residents are, however, taking an increasing proportion of lending by the overseas banks, and the figures illustrate clearly the great reduction in holdings of reserve type assets, like money at call, sterling bills and short-term British government securities, as the new form of wholesale banking business has developed.

Although the overseas banks, taken together, have tended to expand their business abroad faster than that in the UK domestic market, their transactions with UK residents have in fact been growing rapidly. And certain of the longer established foreign banks, particularly the major American groups, have been actively trying to attract domestic UK business. Several of them have established branch offices outside London, or set up the equivalent but more approachable 'money shops' in various areas. They have also made substantial efforts to enlarge their dealings with UK companies. In the aggregate figures, these movements are obscured by the continuing influx of new banks concentrating in the international markets. But, for the American banks alone, the proportion of deposits lent on to UK residents doubled, from 5% to 10%, between 1969 and 1973; there was a sharp fall in the earlier years, which saw the initial and very rapid expansion of their international dealings.

4.5 THE MERCHANT BANKS ARE NOW BANKS

Paradoxically, the traditional business of the merchant banks in the banking field was relatively limited. The accepting houses, the group that includes most of the long established merchant banks, handled a substantial business in commercial bills, but their main role was to 'accept' these bills, that is to act as ultimate guarantor of the debt so that the bills could be sold (discounted) in the money market at a better price than would otherwise be the case. Their direct business as principals, taking deposits and making loans, and thus channelling money from lender to borrower through the medium of banking type instruments, was small, primarily carried out for the convenience of the clients for their other services.

Apart from commercial credits, the other main area of merchant banking was originally business in the new issue market for securities, where the banks acted, and still act, as agents for those wishing to borrow through this channel. The business was initially internationally based, raising funds in London for foreign governments

and organizations; but exchange restrictions and the changed economic environment of the interwar years led to a decline in foreign
dealings. In place of this activity, the merchant banks developed the
domestic equivalent, raising money for UK companies, and, in the
years following the Second World War, the domestic new issue
business has been extended into the general field of corporate finance,
providing financial advice of all kinds to companies as well as acting
as their agents in takeover and merger deals. Latterly, foreign issue
business has revived and, at the same time, a further agency business
has developed in the form of the management of substantial investment portfolios, particularly those of company pension funds. In
addition, a number of banks have set up their own unit trusts, thus
taking on a principal's role in this area.

But the most notable change in the business of the established
merchant banks has been the extent to which these institutions have
become banks in a very real sense. The expansion of their activities as
principals in the banking field dates from the late 1950s, when many
of the accepting houses were involved in the early stages of both the
Euro-currency and the new domestic money markets. Between 1958
and 1963 the total deposits of the accepting houses quadrupled, a rate
of expansion exceeded only by the American banks, and there has
been a sixfold increase in the last decade. This represents a growth
rate less than that of the main overseas groups, but there have been
virtually no new entrants to the ranks of the accepting houses in the
period, compared with the vast growth in the number of the overseas
banks. In addition, in recent years the accepting houses have been
active in developing new types of short- to medium-term lending to
industry, notably in the areas of leasing and factoring.

The banking activities of the established merchant banks are summarized in Table 4.8 under the heading of 'accepting houses'. While
they are heavily involved in both Euro-currency and inter-bank
markets, they still do a substantial amount of their business with UK
residents; over a third of their deposits and nearly a quarter of their
advances at end 1973 represented dealings with UK persons and
companies, very largely the latter. But, despite the substantial growth
in their banking business, the accepting houses are still only small in
relation to the other banking groups; in total they had but 5% of the
deposits outstanding at end 1973, notably less than any of the overseas banking groups which operate in the same markets.

More important today, in terms of the volume of their banking
business, are the 'other UK banks'. This group, with 12% of total
deposits, includes three types of bank: the merchant banking subsidiaries of the deposit banks, a number of the recently established
organizations carrying out merchant bank activities, and certain of

Table 4.8.   The business of the merchant banks today

Amount outstanding end 1973	Accepting houses	'Other UK banks'	All 'merchant' banks
		% of deposits	
1. Borrowing [a]			
Deposits [a]	100	100	100
	(£5,372m.)	(£11,310m.)	(£16,682m.)
of which:			
in sterling	46	62	57
in other currencies	54	38	43
from UK banks	22	39	34
Other UK residents	34	26	28
Overseas residents	34	21	25
Negotiable CDs	10	14	13
2. Lending [a]	109	108	108
of which:			
Notes and coin, etc.	—	—	—
Balances with UK banks	22	27	25
Money at call	3	4	4
Sterling bills	1	1	1
Special deposits	1	2	2
Negotiable sterling CDs	11	5	7
British government securities [b]	—	1	—
Loans to UK local authorities	6	5	5
Advances	54	59	58
to UK residents	23	34	31
to overseas residents	31	25	27
Other assets	11	4	6
3. Acceptances	16	—	5

[a] Deposits represent the banks' main, but not their only, source of borrowing. The relationship of total lending to deposits indicates how far other sources of funds are important to the various groups. These include long-term capital in the form of securities.
[b] At book value.

the hire purchase finance houses that have been reclassified as banks.

Much of the phenomenal growth shown in Table 4.3 has come, as with the overseas banks, from new entrants into this category of business; in particular, the deposit bank subsidiaries were mostly established in the early 1960s, and their business has expanded very rapidly since then. The importance of this last group shows up in the analysis of borrowing and lending through the much greater emphasis on inter-bank transactions than for accepting houses; the 'other UK banks' are also more involved in lending to UK residents.

The growth of other merchant banks with their difference in emphasis from the accepting houses is reflected in the changing make-up of the borrowing and lending of the merchant banks shown in Fig. 4.4. The increasing importance of inter-bank and CD dealings for the group as a whole is evident, and there has been a reduction in the significance of overseas as well as other UK residents as a source of deposits. Advances of all kinds have however grown more prominent in total lending, and, as with the overseas banks, there has been a sharp decline in holdings of reserve type assets; loans to UK local authorities have also grown much less rapidly than other forms of lending.

While the other merchant banking group includes a number of the new independent merchant banks, it does not cover what have been generally described as the fringe or secondary banks; that is the set of banking type organizations established in the late 1960s, which grew very rapidly in the early 1970s and then mostly collapsed in the difficult market conditions of 1973–74. None of the well-known names in this group, like Cedar Holdings or London and County Securities, are included, though Dalton Barton came in through its merger with Keyser Ullmann which is classified as an 'other' UK bank.

These secondary banking operations are not documented in the official statistics and their importance has varied greatly. At their peak in 1973, total deposits were estimated to be around £1000m. or 7% of the total for all banks, but the figure must have declined sharply since then. This borrowing came both from financial institutions and persons and companies, and much of it was very short-term; it was channelled largely into longer-term loans and direct purchases of securities or physical assets such as land and buildings. The problems that arose when security and property values dropped and borrowings were not renewed illustrate clearly why banks tend normally either to hold considerable liquid reserves to meet contingencies or to match borrowing and lending fairly closely, or to do both to some degree; they show that financial institutions cannot perform their

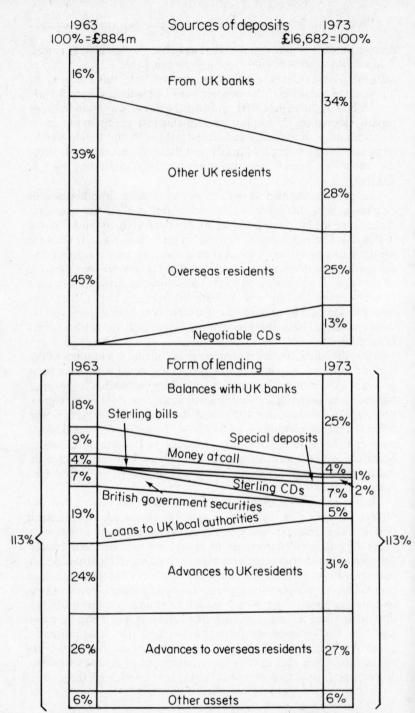

Figures are percentages of deposits outstanding at year end.
Fig. 4.4. Changes in merchant banking, 1963-73.

channelling function successfully if there is too great a degree of disparity between the average term and risk characteristics of their borrowing and lending.

4.6 THE UNKNOWN MONEY MARKET OPERATORS

The least known members of the banking group are those that specialize almost entirely in money market operations. Two types of institution are involved here: the discount houses that act as principals in this area, and the various money market brokers who operate as agents. To some degree these two functions are becoming linked together within one institutional group.

Figures for the discount houses were included in Table 4.3 and it is clear that they have been declining in importance in recent years; their share of total deposits in 1973 was one-third what it was in 1963. This reflects the degree to which their operations have been tied to the traditional money market discussed in the previous chapter. The analysis for 1963 in Table 4.9 illustrates the essentials of this type of activity. Two-thirds of their borrowing came from the deposit banks, and this was lent on to the government and companies in the form of treasury and commercial bills and short-dated government securities. Historically, the emphasis on commercial bills was much greater, the business of the discount houses being originally to provide short-term funds for commerce and industry by discounting the bills of exchange relating to domestic and international trade, often after these bills had been 'accepted' by the accepting houses. As in 1963, they used to borrow their funds mainly from the banking system, but this money has increasingly been employed to finance the government not industry, the discount houses becoming the main intermediaries between the banks and the government.

As the new money markets developed, the traditional business of the discount houses, being tied to the deposit banks, declined in importance within the banking system. Gradually, like the deposit banks, the discount houses have gone out into the new markets to compete for themselves. Their main development has been in the market for sterling certificates of deposits, where a number of houses have become very active as secondary dealers in outstanding certificates. This is a role for which they were well equipped as a result of their similar activities in the market for government securities, and the effect on the assets held by the discount houses can be seen in Table 4.9; by end 1973 over one-third of their outstanding lending was in the form of sterling CDs with a further 4% in US dollar certificates.

Table 4.9.   The business of the discount houses

Amount outstanding end year	1963		1973	
	£m.	%	£m.	%
1. Borrowing[a]	1,232	100	2,567	100
of which, from:				
Bank of England	4	—	—	—
Deposit banks	802	65	1,420	55
Other UK banks	265	22	953	37
Other UK residents	⎰ 162	⎱ 13	135	5
Overseas residents			60	2
2. Lending	1,305	106	2,621	102
of which:				
Treasury bills	529	43	321	12
Other public sector bills	⎰ 249	⎱ 20	94	4
Other bills			590	23
British government securities[b]	442	36	48	2
Local authority securities	17	1	379	15
Negotiable sterling CDs	—	—	922	36
US dollar CDs	—	—	113	4
Balances with UK banks and other assets	67	5	155	6

[a] Total of borrowed funds, but excludes longer-term capital and reserves.
[b] At nominal values.

As well as acting as principals in the sterling CD market, the discount houses have as a group also performed a broking role, finding buyers for outstanding certificates that the holders wish to sell. To date, the Bank of England has required individual houses to choose whether they act as principals or agents in the market for non-sterling certificates; they may not do both. The houses that operate as agents have in a number of cases linked up with the firms of independent money market brokers, which have been established as the various new money markets developed. These brokers initially concentrated on business in the markets for local authority and finance house deposits, sometimes combined with foreign exchange broking, that is handling the switches of funds between different currencies, acting as agents for other parties like the banks and industrial companies. But the broking business has now grown to include a function in the inter-bank market as well as handling transactions in certificates of deposit. Thus the independent brokers and the discount house groups now play an important role in both the primary and the secondary money markets.

4.7 THE SHAPE OF THE BANKING SYSTEM

The overall picture of the banking system is one of an extremely complex network of transactions, both between the banking groups themselves and between them and the other groups in the economy. This situation is summarized in Fig. 4.5 in terms of the outstanding borrowing and lending by the banks at end 1973. Each of the main banking groups is shown separately, though in some cases flows to and from merchant and overseas banks have to be combined owing to lack of data. In a similar way, it is not possible to identify the other parties to transactions in the inter-bank or CD markets; these markets are indicated by circles in the diagram.

The differing roles of the banking groups show up clearly. Deposit banks deal primarily with the domestic sectors, acting as a channel for money flowing from persons to companies and the government. Relatively, their dealings with other banks are small. In contrast, the business of the overseas banks in London is dominated by the overseas group; such banks are the major force in inter-bank dealings, though merchant banks are also active in this area. It is notable that inter-bank activity is as important, in terms of size of outstanding assets and liabilities, as many of the direct flows between banks and the non-financial groups. The specialized role played by discount houses is evident, while the figure also shows how limited are the dealings between the banks and the other financial institutions.

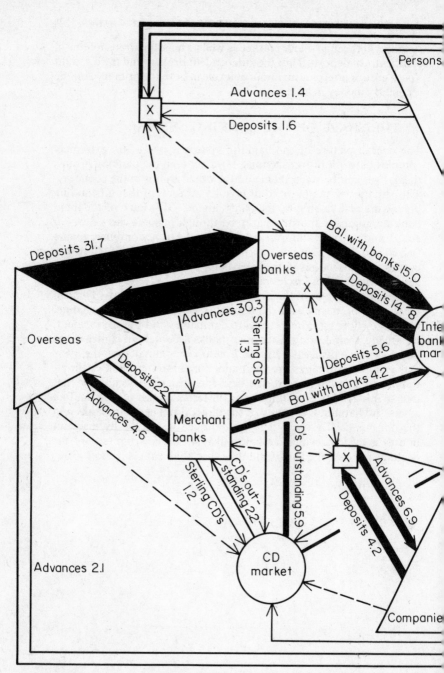

Persons

Advances 1.4

Deposits 1.6

Deposits 31.7

Overseas
banks

X

Bal. with banks 15.0

Deposits 14.8

Overseas

Advances 30.3

Sterling CD's 1.3

Deposits 5.6

Inter
bank
mar

Deposits 2.2

Advances 4.6

Bal with banks 4.2

Merchant
banks

CD's out-
standing 2.2

Sterling CD's 1.2

CD's outstanding 5.9

X

Advances 6.9

Deposits 4.2

Advances 2.1

CD
market

Companie

Arrows indicate the order of magnitude of the <u>outstanding assets and liabilitie</u>
are in £b. Details of the other parties to transactions in the inter-bank and CD
merchant banks are available. Dotted lines indicate unidentified flows.

Fig. 4.5. The banking system in 1973

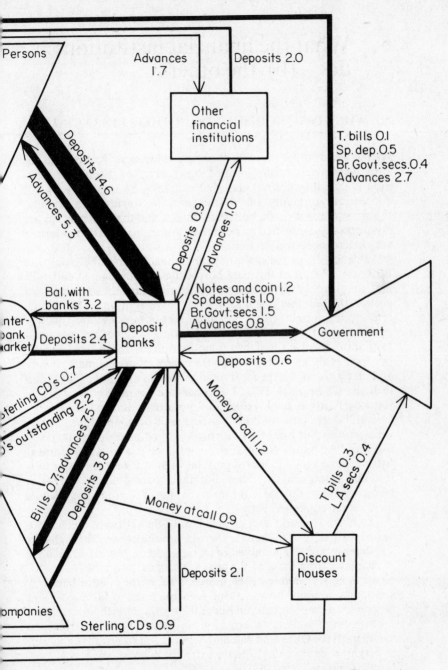

Persons

Advances 1.7

Deposits 2.0

Other financial institutions

T. bills O.1
Sp. dep. O.5
Br. Govt. secs. O.4
Advances 2.7

Deposits 14.6

Advances 5.3

Deposits O.9

Advances 1.O

Bal. with banks 3.2

Notes and coin 1.2
Sp deposits 1.O
Br. Govt. secs 1.5
Advances O.8

Inter-bank market

Deposits 2.4

Deposit banks

Government

Deposits O.6

Sterling CD's O.7

Money at call 1.2

's outstanding 2.2

Bills O.7; advances 7.5

Deposits 3.8

T. bills O.3
LA secs O.4

Money at call O.9

Discount houses

Deposits 2.1

ompanies

Sterling CDs O.9

the various banking groups in relation to the other main groups. Figures given
arkets are not available. In some cases only combined figures for overseas and
ome minor flows have been omitted.

5. What the financial institutions do: (b) the others

5.1 WHAT DISTINGUISHES THE 'OTHER' FINANCIAL INSTITUTIONS

As the word 'other' implies, the main thing that the financial institutions conventionally grouped together as the OFIs have in common is that they are not classified as banks. That is, they do not concentrate primarily on shorter-term borrowing and lending, though some of them do both these things, and their borrowings are not normally considered to be money. Apart from this, they form a very heterogeneous collection.

Table 5.1 shows the institutions that make up the OFI group and their size in terms of the main borrowings outstanding at end 1973 and ten years earlier. Here the institutions are divided into two groups, the near banks and the investment institutions. As the name implies, the former group are those whose business most closely resembles that of the banks. The building societies are the main institutions involved, and they alone account for over a quarter of the borrowings by all OFIs; in 1963 they were relatively much smaller and they have shown the most rapid growth of any in the OFI group over the ten years to 1973. Life assurance companies, whose outstanding funds at book value have more than doubled since 1963, were still larger than the building societies in absolute terms in 1973, with one-third of total OFI borrowings. And pension funds, taken together, accounted for nearly one-fifth of the total. Investment trusts are the only other group of any significance in terms of outstanding assets and liabilities; but their growth up to 1973 was primarily due to the rise in the market value of their holdings, which have a large equity element.

The borrowing and lending activities of the OFIs are much more varied than those of the banks. There is some borrowing through bills and deposits and a fair number of loans are made; but the latter differ in character from those of the banks, and these two types of instruments in no way dominate the transactions, as they do for banks. A substantial amount of borrowing is in the form of life funds, and securities are important as an outlet for lending. Furthermore, there are significant two-way transactions in most types of instruments; members of the OFIs hold bills and deposits and receive loans, as well as making security issues, and the extent of this two-way activity has been growing in recent years.

Table 5.1. The 'other' financial institutions

Type of institution	Main borrowings[a] at end year			
	1963		1973	
	£b.	%	£b.	%
1. Near banks	5·31	27	17·69	32
Finance houses[b]	0·55	3	0·78	2
Building societies[c]	4·01	20	14·37	26
Trustee Savings Banks[d]	0·75	4	1·99	4
National Savings Bank[d]	—	—	0·55	1
2. Investment institutions	14·42	73	36·93	68
Life assurance companies[e]	7·43	38	18·13	33
Pension funds[e]	3·80[h]	19	10·72[h]	20
Investment trusts[f]	2·82	14	5·72	10
Unit trusts[g]	0·37	2	2·06	4
Property unit trusts[h][i]	—	—	0·30	1
3. Total of above	19·73	100	54·62	100

[a] Form of borrowing is as indicated in subsequent notes.
[b] Deposits, bills and other borrowings.
[c] Shares and deposits.
[d] Investment account deposits.
[e] Funds at book value.
[f] Total investments at market value.
[g] Outstanding units at market value.
[h] Estimated values.
[i] Outstanding units at book value.

5.2 THE DECLINE OF HIRE PURCHASE

The group of institutions listed above as finance houses are more correctly described by their full name of hire purchase houses. This draws attention to the fact that, historically, these institutions specialized in the particular form of instalment credit known as hire purchase. The nature of the transactions involved was discussed in Chapter 3. The bulk of this lending is made direct to persons to finance the purchase of consumer durables. But, in addition, the finance houses have always provided loans to companies in the retail and motorcar business, either directly or by buying from them the hire purchase agreements they have outstanding with their customers.

Table 5.2.   The business of finance houses

Amount outstanding end year	1963[c]		1973[c]	
	£m.	%	£m.	%
1. Borrowing[a]	775	93	1,077	79
of which:				
Deposits	390	47	477	35
Bills discounted	62	7	150	11
Other loans	101	12	155	11
Unearned finance charges	71	9	122	9
Capital and reserves	151	18	173	13
2. Lending[a]	836	100	1,357	100
of which:				
Hire purchase debt	659	79	884	65
Other advances	77	9	126	9
Leased assets	40[b]	5	254	19
To other financial institutions	9	1	2	—
Securities other than trade investments	19	2	33	2
Trade investments	32	4	58	4

[a] Because data are available on borrowing from certain sources only, figures are shown as percentage of total identified lending.
[b] Rough estimate only.
[c] The two sets of absolute figures are not fully comparable owing to the reclassification of certain institutions.

As mentioned earlier, the nature of instalment credit business has changed over the last decade and the original finance houses have become more involved with other types of lending. The latter include not only direct personal loans to people wishing to buy consumer durables, but also new types of instalment credit for companies, such as the provision of plant and equipment that can be leased from the finance house. Unlike hire purchase credit, the leasing of assets does not count as a formal loan for statistical purposes, since there is no option for the lessee to acquire the assets at the end of the period. Instead, the plant and equipment is treated as the property of the finance house and the leasing payments are operating costs to the business using the assets. But the effect is the same as providing a loan, and the growth in this type of business is illustrated in Table 5.2.

The published figures for finance houses unfortunately do not show fully the changes in the nature of the business of this group of institutions, owing to the reclassification of the major organizations to the banking group (see p. 72). This reflects not only the growing emphasis on direct personal lending by the groups, but also the extension of their range of business to include a variety of merchant bank type activities including agency and consultancy work for companies in the corporate finance field. They have also entered the field of property finance, which led them to share some of the problems of

Table 5.3.   The balance sheet of a major finance house

	Amounts outstanding at 30 September 1973
	%
Liabilities	
Deposit, current and other accounts	73
Loans and acceptances from other banks	11
Creditors	4
Tax, investment grants, etc.	3
Minority interests	—
Loan capital	3
Share capital and reserves	6
Total	100
Assets	
Balances with other banks and short-term deposits	20
Customers and other accounts	58
of which:	
Instalment debts that include interest and charges	42
Less unearned interest or charges	8
	34
Instalment debts on which interest is charged as it falls due	5
Other loans and sundry debtors	19
Investments	2
Equipment in hands of lessees	15
Land for development and work in progress	3
Stock and work in progress	1
Property and equipment	1
Total	100

the secondary banks in 1973 and 1974. A clearer picture of the current nature of finance house business is shown by an analysis of the accounts of a major group which is given in Table 5.3.

In addition to the finance houses, there is a variety of much smaller financial institutions active in different ways in the field of consumer credit. They were examined in considerable detail by the Crowther Committee on Consumer Credit.[21] The most notable of them are the check traders, mentioned in Section 3.4. Outstanding loans of this group were estimated to amount to some £90m. in 1969; they are financed partly by retailer credit and partly by sources similar to the smaller finance houses.

5.3 HOW BUILDING SOCIETIES BORROW SHORT AND LEND LONG

The building societies constitute one of the better known groups of financial institutions. They have also, to date, been one of the most specialized groups within the financial system. Like the deposit banks, they have extensive branch networks, and deposits with the societies provide a major alternative outlet for the private individual's spare cash. But, unlike banks, they deal almost exclusively with persons, and their lending is concentrated by statute in one area, the provision of long-term loans on first mortgage for the purpose of house purchase or improvement.

Most of the special characteristics of the building societies arise from their historical development. Originally private savings groups designed to enable people to club together to buy houses by pooling their savings, the societies have retained both their non-profit-making status and their sense of being a social service. The potential tax advantages given to their depositors have already been mentioned; in addition, because of the wish to encourage wider home ownership, borrowers can obtain substantial tax reliefs on their loans.

Paradoxically, while the building societies thus form a separate and privileged circuit of borrowing and lending within the financial system, they are one of the institutions whose actions and dealings are most closely watched in the political arena. Unlike most other interest rates, the mortgage rate, set by the Building Societies Association though not mandatory, has long been a matter of keen political interest. Furthermore, though building societies are isolated in that they do not normally deal directly with sectors other than persons, they are in no sense immune from the effect of what is going on elsewhere in the financial system. In order to attract adequate funds for lending, they must offer competitive interest rates, which in turn

Table 5.4. The business of the building societies

Amount outstanding end year	1963		1973	
	£m.	%	£m.	%
1. Borrowing	4,359	100	17,709	100
of which:				
Shares and deposits	4,005	92	16,471	93
Reserves	201	5	672	4
Accrued interest, etc.	153	3	566	3
2. Lending [a]	4,359	100	17,709	100
of which:				
Mortgages	3,578	82	14,624	83
British government securities	294	7	1,201	7
Local authority debt (long-term)	248	6	598	3
Misc.: short-term assets	186	4	1,059	6
Other assets	53	1	227	1

[a] At book values.

affects the mortgage rate they charge. And the political wish to keep this last rate low has led to government intervention in other sectors of the financial market; for example, as mentioned earlier, the imposition in September 1973 of the $9\frac{1}{2}\%$ limit on interest payment for small deposits with banks, with the aim of protecting building society borrowing and lending.

The other peculiarity about building societies concerns the relative terms of their borrowing and lending. Table 5.4 shows that their business bears a broad similarity to that of the deposit banks. The bulk of their borrowing is in the form of deposits, shares being effectively deposits withdrawable after a short period of notice. And loans, here called mortgages, are the main form of lending. But, in contrast to the banks, the societies' holdings of liquid assets are small, little over 10% of the total, while virtually all lending is long-term in character and so is in no way matched with the length of life of borrowings.

It may be wondered how the building societies manage to use such short-term borrowing for long-term lending and survive. This is, after all, basically what the so-called secondary banks tried to do and failed dismally at. Yet there have been very few building society failures this century; though there have been many amalgamations in recent years.

Three factors contribute to the building societies' ability to borrow short and lend long simultaneously. First, while the loans they make are apparently very long-term, the average duration is much less (see Section 3.4), and the security for them is excellent. This last fact derives partly from the cautious lending policies of the societies. Also, since loans are granted mainly to people living in the house concerned, default on mortgage payments will be avoided at virtually all costs, since loss of the house means a major family dislocation. Furthermore, should the building society ultimately have to call in its loan, it is relatively easy to realize the asset involved, certainly when compared, for example, with the problems of repossession under hire purchase agreements. And in an inflationary era, the value of the underlying security has usually been well in excess of the outstanding loan.

Secondly, because building societies are long established, depositors have come to accept their business practices and to consider deposits with the societies as very secure holdings, as indeed they have been for many years. Close official supervision of the societies' activities has also contributed to this situation, for the industry had its problems in the nineteenth century. And, while most deposits and shares may be withdrawn at very short notice, the average period of holding is much longer. Thirdly, in their day-to-day business, building societies have a much greater degree of flexibility than might seem to be the case, owing to the continuing flow of money being received in the form of interest and loan repayments.

Building societies are one of the few groups for whom it is possible to analyse the turnover in borrowing and lending, the total receipts and payments, as well as the net changes over a period. In 1973, repayments of loans amounted to £1·5b. compared with new advances of £3·5b. In the same year, £6·1b. of shares and deposits were received and £4·5b. worth were withdrawn; in addition, £0·7b. of interest due was retained and credited to outstanding accounts. The importance of repayments on existing mortgages as a source of funds, as well as that of withdrawals of deposits as a use, is very evident. Established building societies are thus in a position to undertake a substantial volume of new lending, even if new deposits barely exceed withdrawals. And, if new advances are cut right back, the flow of money from repayments provides the societies with a substantial cushion of liquid funds with which to meet any net withdrawals.

However, the turnover in building society deposits has been rising rather more rapidly than that in advances in the last few years. This represents a potential weakening of the situation, since it would be difficult for the societies to increase turnover in advances much further, owing to the long-term nature of these loans. The change is connected with the problems that the societies have had in securing an acceptable flow of new house purchase loans without raising deposit and therefore mortgage rates too high. As a result, building societies have recently been examining possible ways of obtaining some longer-term funds, to give them a better match to the term of their lending. They have also, in the last few years, moved closer to providing a banking type service for making payments, and they generally appear to be anxious to enlarge the range of their activities beyond their traditional specialized role.

5.4 NATIONAL SAVINGS AND INVESTING

As discussed in Chapter 3 the various national savings media represent another of the privileged circuits designed to encourage private saving. They are privileged in the sense that the government-owned or -controlled institutions involved offer tax advantages to those who deposit money with them; though it could be said that, in terms of the interest rates paid to depositors, the latter are under- rather than over-privileged. The main institutions concerned are the National Savings Bank (formerly the Post Office Savings Bank) and the network of Trustee Savings Banks; the latter are long-established savings institutions run independently, but under close government supervision. Since the money deposited with these banks is lent on to the government, a large part of their activities is closely linked with official financing; their current account borrowing is thus treated as being that of the government itself, as part of national savings. But the investment accounts operated by both National and Trustee Savings Banks offer more competitive interest rates and their activities are more closely integrated with those of other financial institutions. They are thus conventionally included in this group.

Table 5.1 showed that the investment account activities of these two groups are relatively small compared with those of other financial institutions, though they are comparable to unit trusts in terms of outstanding borrowings and larger than the remaining finance houses. Deposits with Trustee Savings Banks increased two and a half times over the decade to 1973, slightly faster than the funds of life assurance companies but notably slower than building society deposits. Table 5.5 indicates how the two savings bank groups allocate their funds between different forms of government borrowing. The National Savings Bank puts greatest weight on British government securities, but, even so, over a third of its borrowing in 1973 was channelled through to local authorities. For the Trustee Savings Banks, the proportion of lending going to local authorities was well over 50%; a large part of this was in the form of mortgage loans,

Table 5.5.   The savings banks' investment accounts

Amount outstanding at end 1973	Trustee Savings Banks		National Savings Bank [b]	
	£m.	%	£m.	%
1. Borrowing				
Deposits on investment accounts	1,990	115	548	119
2. Lending				
Total investments [a]	1,733	100	460	100
of which:				
Cash	27	2	—	—
Local authority debt (short-term)	57	3	3	—
Local authority debt (long-term)	1,156	56	162	35
British government securities	439	25	281	61
Overseas government securities	2	—	—	—
Agricultural corporation securities	52	3	14	3

[a] At market value.
[b] Formerly the Post Office Savings Bank.

though the share of securities in the total has been increasing.

A feature of Table 5.5 is the fact that, at end 1973, the amount of deposits outstanding for both savings banks substantially exceeded the market value of their total investments. The deposits are not normally for a fixed term and are withdrawable at one month's notice, and it is doubtful whether a privately owned institution with short-term borrowings could for any period maintain such a discrepancy between the value of its outstanding assets and liabilities. However, since the government effectively stands behind the savings banks, depositors do not worry about any temporary book deficit. And so long as new deposits exceed withdrawals, there is no need for the savings banks to realize the holdings at their depressed market values; they can wait until the securities mature at their higher nominal values.

Latterly, the Trustee Savings Banks, like the building societies, have been trying to move beyond their traditional range of activities and to provide more general banking and financial services. They administer a unit trust and provide limited current account chequing facilities. Following the report of the Page Committee on the whole National Savings movement,[24] there are plans for a major reorganization of the Trustee Savings Banks. This will lead to their becoming fully independent of the government, with powers to carry out a complete range of banking activities, including lending.

5.5 ASSURANCE AND INSURANCE

The life assurance companies and pension funds are the two main groups of investment institutions. The dual nature of their borrowing contracts, providing both an outlet for regular saving plus the assurance that money will be available in certain circumstances, has already been discussed. Because of the wish to encourage people both to save and to provide against certain contingencies, premiums for life assurance policies and contributions to pension funds have long attracted favourable tax treatment; so also have the institutions involved. Life assurance companies also resemble building societies and savings banks in another way. Many of them have a long history and a tradition based on their origins as mutual help organizations. A large number of them are still non-profit-making bodies, owned by their policy-holders, while the separately administered pension funds are run by boards of trustees on behalf of their members.

The process by which assurance and pension funds accumulate was considered in Section 3.6. All borrowing is treated as coming from persons, though part of the revenue is actually received from companies and government in the form of employers' contributions to pension schemes. From the point of view of the channelling function performed by this group of institutions, the essential feature of their borrowing is that it is very long-term in nature. A 'fund' of assets is gradually accumulated to meet the payments specified in the contract. There will of course eventually be an outflow of money on each policy. But, provided sufficient new business is being taken on, premiums and contributions being received will largely cover current claims and payments; any balance can usually be met out of the interest and dividends received on the invested fund (see Table 3.12). Hence an assurance company or pension fund will normally not only retain its existing assets effectively in perpetuity, but should regularly be adding to them. Only if it issues policies whose terms and conditions lead to an unusual volume of claims or surrenders, or if there is some exceptional catastrophe, would the institution's expenditure be likely to exceed receipts, thus making it necessary to dispose of any part of the outstanding holdings.

As a result, assurance companies and pension funds can in principle afford to lend their money out on a very long-term basis. What is essential, however, is that the income that they receive on their investments should exceed the rate of interest allowed for when the premiums on the policies issued were set. For this reason, the institutions have tended to go some way towards matching the term of their lending to their borrowing, thus securing the income they need for future solvency. But in recent years an increasing proportion of life assurance business has been written on a with-profits basis, where the policy holder has a share in any extra return that the assurance company can make over and above that contracted for. In this situation the assurance company has an incentive to obtain as high return as possible, while still maintaining adequate security of income, an aim that can conflict with that of matching assets and liabilities. Similarly, most pension funds nowadays have liabilities that are not fixed in money terms but rise with wage and salary levels, and a matching approach to lending is not feasible in this circumstance.

Unlike similar institutions overseas, UK assurance companies and pension funds are not subject to any official controls on their investments. How they resolve the choice between security and extra return depends on them, subject only to the constraint that the actual (market) value of their assets must exceed the present value of all their contractual liabilities; this last is what the book value of their 'funds' represents.

The way in which the various groups have chosen to distribute their investments is shown in Table 5.6. In all cases the bulk of holdings in 1973 were in the form of marketable securities. Life assurance companies lay the most importance on British government securities, with nearly a quarter of their 1973 investments in this form (at nominal values); they are also substantial investors in both company debentures and loans and non-quoted loans and mortgages. But even allowing for valuation differences, they place much less weight on ordinary shares than do the pension funds. Both the company and the 'other' government pension funds held over half their 1973 investments in this form and they also both had substantial direct holdings of property and land; so did the assurance companies. In contrast, local authority pension schemes lend a significant proportion of their funds back to their parent authorities; at end 1973 they also held an exceptional amount of their investments in short-term assets of various kinds.

Because new premiums normally exceed current claims, the life assurance companies and pension funds effectively undertake a large amount of new borrowing each year; the money so raised has then to be invested. The distribution of this new investment is an important factor within the area of the financial markets in which the institutions operate, and Fig. 5.1 illustrates how it has changed over the last decade. There are marked fluctuations in the emphasis on different types of investment from year to year. This is especially true of British

Table 5.6.   How assurance funds and pension funds invest

Amount outstanding at end 1973[a]	Life assurance funds	Self-administered pension funds of:		
		Private companies	Local[a] authorities	Other government bodies
		% of all investments		
Total investments[b]	100 (£18,125m.)[b]	100 (£6,199m.)	100 (£1,587m.)	100 (£2,719m.)
of which:				
Short-term assets	2	7	12	4
British government securities	23	11	18	6
Local authority securities	2	1	1	1
Overseas government securities	1	—	—	—
Company securities	40	64	43	61
Debentures and loans	14	11	6	7
Preference shares	1	—	—	—
Ordinary shares	25	53	37	54
Unit trust units	1[c]	3[c]	10	1[c]
Loans and mortgages[d]	15	1	14	9
Property, land, etc.	15	12	1	18
Agents' balances	2	—	—	—
Other assets	—	1	1	—

Figures for local authority pension funds are as at 31 March 1974.
Figures for pension funds are at market value, for life assurance companies at book value (with British government and local authority securities at nominal value).
Mostly property unit trusts.
Includes loans to local authorities.

government securities. The proportion of new money going into property has been rising fairly steadily, but allocations to ordinary shares have been through a number of cycles; they declined relatively in the middle 1960s, recovered towards the end of the decade but dropped back sharply in 1973 and 1974. Purchases of company debentures and loans also showed a marked fall in both absolute and relative terms in 1973–74, and in the three years 1972–74 a large proportion of new money was being retained by both groups in short-

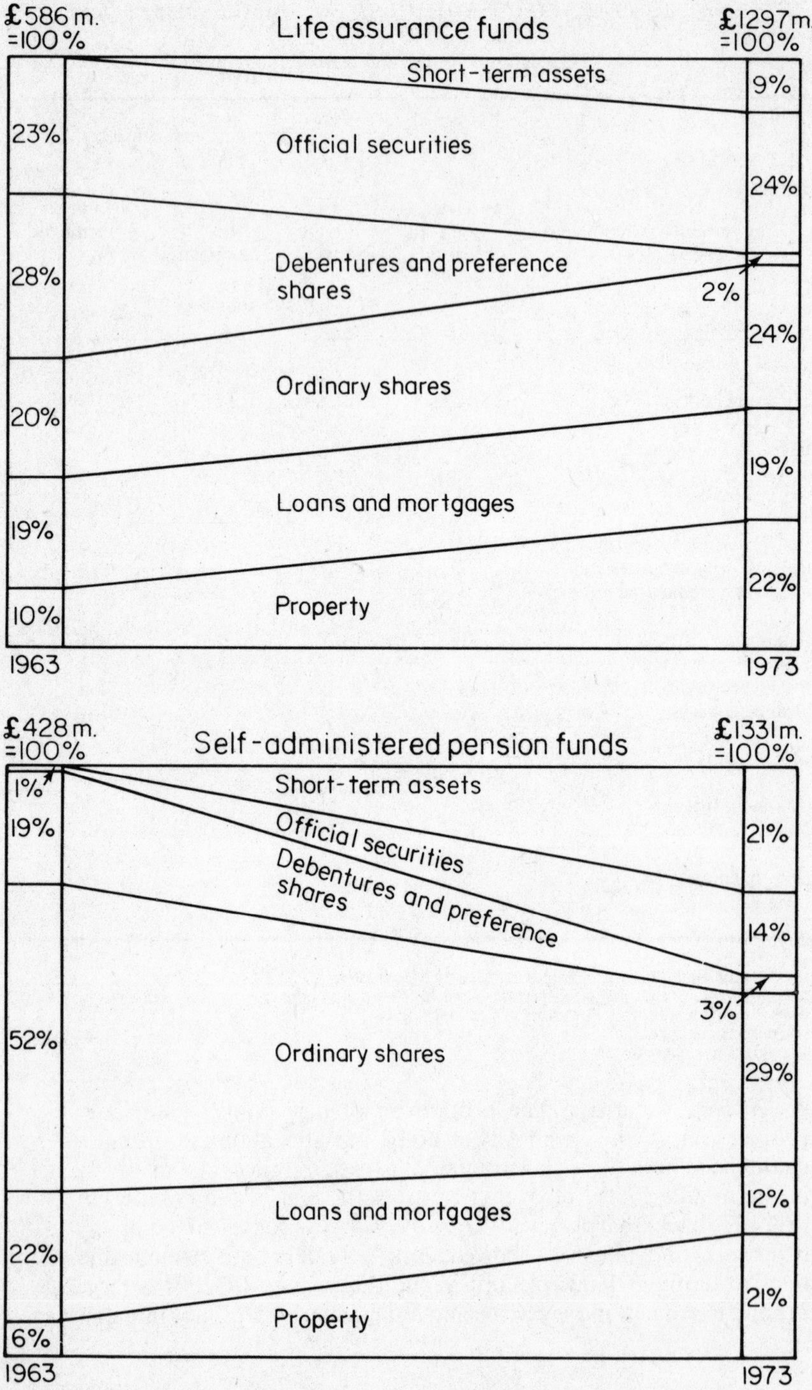

Life assurance funds

£586 m. = 100%

£1297m. = 100%

	1963	1973
Short-term assets		9%
Official securities	23%	24%
Debentures and preference shares	28%	2% / 24%
Ordinary shares	20%	
Loans and mortgages	19%	19%
Property	10%	22%

Self-administered pension funds

£428 m. = 100%

£1331m. = 100%

	1963	1973
Short-term assets	1%	21%
Official securities	19%	14%
Debentures and preference shares		3%
Ordinary shares	52%	29%
Loans and mortgages	22%	12%
Property	6%	21%

Fig. 5.1 The changing pattern of new investments

term holdings. The institutions were thus a much less important source of funds to the securities market than they had formerly been.

The nature of non-life insurance was discussed briefly in Chapter 3. In particular, the reason why non-life funds are not treated as a formal channel for borrowing and lending was examined. But while non-life funds are in practice the property of the insurance business and its owners, whether shareholders, partners or policy-holders, they represent a significant element in the financial market. At end 1973 the amount of non-life funds outstanding was some £2·9b., larger than unit trusts though well below the figures for the life assurance companies and pension funds; over the previous decade they had more than trebled in size.

The investment constraints on non-life funds are not the same as those of life assurance and pension funds, reflecting the different nature of the contracts that produce the funds. For non-life insurance, the contract taken on by the insurance company in exchange for the premium payment is essentially short-term; it involves a payment out should an event, like a fire or an accident, occur within a short period, generally a year. In principle, therefore, the 'fund' held to meet this liability must be short-term too. In practice, provided new business is continually being taken on, many claims can be met out of the new premiums being received, and the company will retain a continuing fund of investments. It will also normally hold a further reserve fund designed to meet special contingencies.

The large-scale nature of some of the risks insured and the possibility of having to make large payments in the event of a natural disaster mean that non-life insurance funds have to retain a degree of liquidity. But they also have an incentive to earn as high a return as possible so as to build up their reserves and to provide profits for their owners. The actual balance adopted by the main funds at end 1973 is shown in Table 5.7. While the proportion of short-term assets was in fact no higher than for certain pension funds, the holdings of British government securities provide a form of second line reserves; most of the latter are short-dated stocks, in contrast to the longer-term maturities that predominate in the portfolios of life assurance and pension funds. However, the concern to improve investment return, and in particular to insulate reserves against the ravages of inflation, has led the non-life companies to invest a growing proportion of their funds in equity-type holdings, both ordinary shares and property; in 1973 these were as important to them as they were to life assurance companies.

Probably the major difference between the investments of non-life and life funds lies in the significance of the item agents' balances. This accounted for nearly one-fifth of non-life investments in 1973

Table 5.7.   The investments of non-life insurance funds

Amount outstanding end year	1963		1973	
	£m.	%	£m.	%
Total investments [a]	972	100	2,933	100
of which:				
Short-term assets	65	7	364	12
British government securities	202	21	351	12
Local authority securities	41	4	40	1
Overseas government securities	39	4	40	1
Company securities	203	35	1,134	38
Debentures and loans	71	7	139	4
Preference shares	38	8	128	4
Ordinary shares	194	20	867	30
Unit trust units	—	—	1	—
Loans and mortgages	54	6	145	5
Property, land, etc.	66	7	296	10
Agents' balances	185	19	561	19
Other assets	17	2	—	—

[a] At book value, with British government and local authority securities at nominal value.

compared with 2% for life funds. The money represents the sums that the companies are due to be paid by their agents, mainly the premiums that have been collected on their behalf. Agents of many kinds play a major role in selling and administering both life and non-life policies, and the difference in the importance of balances is due primarily to the much greater size of life than non-life funds in relation to the premium income handled. While many agents are individuals work- ing on their own account, there are also some substantial firms of insurance brokers involved. The latter are particularly significant in the pension business handled by the life assurance companies and also deal with a lot of the non-life insurance of industrial companies. There are, in addition, some networks of broking offices, dealing mainly with motor and certain other personal insurances.

Insurance brokers act as both agents and consultants. They also purport to operate simultaneously on behalf of both the buyer and the seller of insurance and assurance. That is, on the one hand they provide advice to the individual or company wishing to take out a policy and will handle his premium payment and any subsequent claims; on the other hand they normally receive their income from the insurance companies whose policies they sell, being paid a commission related to the amount of business they introduce to the company. Where the commission rates on different types of policies or on those offered by different companies vary, the broker has obviously an incentive to sell his client the policy most profitable in terms of commission, a policy that may not necessarily be the one most suited to the client's need. This potential conflict of interest illustrates some of the problems of agency operation. It has led to criticism of the present structure of insurance broking and a call for more direct fee payments to brokers by those seeking their advice; the latter, after all, effectively pay the existing commissions through higher premiums on their policies.

5.6 SPREADING INVESTMENT RISK

The remaining institutions in the OFI group operate almost exclusively in the securities market. In addition to the two groups identified in Table 5.1, the investment and unit trusts, these institutions include stockbrokers and stockjobbers as well as certain special investment agencies.

In statistical terms, most stockbrokers and jobbers are not treated as financial institutions; as unincorporated businesses they are included with the personal sector though some of the major firms are now limited companies. They perform a major role in the market for quoted securities. The extent of the dealings that they handle can be gauged from the turnover figures for the Stock Exchange discussed in Section 3.5. Stockbrokers are primarily agents in this market; they act on behalf of people or organizations who wish to buy or sell securities, finding the corresponding buyer or seller to complete the deal. For this service they are paid a commission based on the size of the transaction carried out.

The sort of conflict that occurs in insurance does not normally arise in stockbroking, since, according to Stock Exchange rules, the broker is required to find the other party to the deal from among the stockjobbers. The latter act as principals in the market, buying and selling stock on their own account. The amount of stock that they retain is limited by the volume of funds they have available, which is in turn constrained by the extent of their owned capital. Thus, while the volume of transactions that jobbers handle is very substantial and they play a major part in facilitating the exchange of security holdings for money or other holdings, they are not themselves major channels for new borrowing and lending. Indeed, the limits imposed by the amount of capital available to them has tended in recent years to lessen their ability to handle large-scale deals in securities. This has not only forced many amalgamations among the stockjobbers; it has also led the brokers to look beyond the jobbers for the other party to the deal their clients wish to make. Having found a partner, this arranged deal is then usually 'put through' the jobber's book on a nominal basis.

In addition to their activities as agents, stockbrokers have an extensive role as advisers. The provision of research services has in fact become one of their main ways of attracting clients, especially the major investing institutions, since the commission rates that they charge are based on a fixed scale. They have also developed further agency roles in connection with the flotation of new issues on the Stock Exchange and in the form of investment management services for clients. This merchant banking type activity has led some of them, in turn, to set up unit trusts which they run for their clients. In this role, as unit trust managers, the brokers are in fact acting like principals, taking money in exchange for units and investing it in securities. But the activity is carried out through a separate company, not as an integral part of the broking firm; and the real principal is the trustee of the unit trust.

Both investment and unit trusts act as principals in the securities markets. They borrow money in this form and invest it in other kinds of securities. As Table 5.8 shows, the bulk of their money is in fact held in ordinary shares, an important part especially for investment trusts being in shares of overseas companies. In 1973 the only other major holding was that of short-term assets which, as in the case of life assurance and pension funds, was unusually high.

The investment and unit trusts do not make their money from the differential in interest rates that occurs when borrowing shorter and lending longer as most other institutions do. Instead the service they provide is the reduction of risk through diversification of holdings; that is, by giving the investor a small share in a large number of holdings, in place of a larger amount in only a few holdings, the risk of losing all on one investment is reduced. Furthermore, in theory at least, the saver gains by delegating the management of his funds to professionals; by using their expertise they should be able to obtain a higher return for a given level of risk than he could on his own. For both these functions the trusts charge an annual management fee; in addition unit trust managers make some money by having a small differential between the prices at which they stand ready to buy and to sell units.

The ability to buy and sell units at virtually any time at a price

Table 5.8.   What investment and unit trusts hold

Amount outstanding at end 1973	Investment trusts	Unit trusts
	% of all investments	
Total investments [a]	100 (£5,723m.)	100 (£1,887m.)
of which:		
Short-term assets	8	18
British government securities	1	—
Local authority securities	—	—
Overseas government securities	—	—
Company securities	89	82
Debentures and loans	3	2
Preference shares	2	2
Ordinary shares	84	78
of which:		
quoted UK companies	46 ⎫	62
unquoted UK companies	3 ⎬	
overseas companies	35 ⎭	16
Other investments	2	—

[a] At market value.

closely geared to the underlying value of the investments held is what mainly distinguishes unit trusts from investment trusts. It is not necessary to find someone else who wishes to sell or buy existing units; new units can always be bought from the trust and existing ones can be sold back to them. In this sense unit trusts are said to be open-ended. In contrast, investment trusts are closed-ended. They operate as companies with a share capital and other borrowings, most of which are normally quoted on the stock exchange. New shares are issued only at irregular intervals and anyone wishing to acquire a holding must buy the shares in the trust company from an existing holder. There is no automatic mechanism relating the market price of the trust's borrowing to the value of the assets that it holds, and, for a variety of reasons, investment trust shares tend to stand at a discount on their asset value.

This, plus their closed-ended nature, makes investment trusts rather unsuited as a medium for small savers to put their money into a diversified securities portfolio, and in practice a substantial part of their outstanding shares tend to be held by other investment institutions, notably insurance companies and pension funds. Unit trust units however are held almost entirely by persons. The trusts were developed as a vehicle to channel the money of small savers into company securities and so to provide finance for industry. Their behaviour is supervised more closely than that of investment trusts and there was quite substantial growth in new personal lending in this form during the 1960s. In addition to straight purchases of units on an *ad hoc* basis, many trusts run contractual savings schemes for the regular investment of small amounts. And, latterly, such investment has often been linked with life assurance schemes, thus enabling savers to take advantage of the tax benefits offered by the latter while holding an investment more closely geared to movements in security prices.

The unit trust system has been used by other groups of financial institution as a way of both spreading the risk associated with certain types of investment and obtaining professional management in specialized fields at reduced cost. Some of the pension funds run by smaller local authorities have participated in a trust called the Local Authorities Mutual Investment Trust, which is in fact a unit trust managing a portfolio of Stock Exchange investments. Various other pension funds have used this vehicle for their property holdings, participating in newly established property unit trusts; these specialized trusts enable the smaller funds to take a stake in a field where individual lumps of investment are large even in relation to an institution's funds, and where the type of management expertise needed differs from that required to handle a portfolio of securities. At end 1973, property unit trusts held over £300m. of investments at book value; this compares with a total for the direct holdings of property by the main investment institutions of more than £4,000m. (see Table 5.9, p. 146).

With the exception of the property unit trusts, most investment and unit trusts use their money to buy quoted securities. Their holdings of the securities of companies that are not quoted on a stock exchange either at home or abroad are very small. There are, however, a number of investment institutions that specialize in this type of finance. Most of them are broadly of the investment trust type, that is they borrow the money that they invest in unquoted companies in the form of securities (both ordinary shares and loan stocks). Their holdings are usually in a similar form though a few, like the Agricultural Mortgage Corporation, provide mortgage loans to unincorporated businesses.

Some of the major organizations who specialize in investment in unquoted companies have backing from the banks, who hold part of their outstanding borrowings; these include ICFC (Industrial and Commercial Finance Corporation—now part of Finance for Industry), EDIT (Estates Duties Investment Trust) and the Charterhouse Industrial Development Corporation. There are also a number of smaller companies, some privately owned and others financed by different institutional groups. The total volume of funds invested by these specialized institutions is believed to have been of the order of £200m. in 1972 with annual new lending of £50m.[34] The amounts are not large compared either with institutional investment in quoted companies or with the total borrowings by unquoted companies; but they are important in that this is the main channel, other than bank loans, by which money flows through the formal financial system to the unquoted company group.

5.7 THE OFIs COMPARED

To pull together this analysis of the other financial institutions, Fig. 5.2 illustrates the outstanding dealings that the various groups had with each other and with the other main groups in the economy at end 1973. Apart from confirming the importance of the building societies and life assurance companies, the feature of the system is the limited extent to which the OFIs have dealings with each other. In contrast to the banks (see Fig. 4.5), virtually all their outstanding transactions are with the non-financial groups, and in many cases each type of institution specializes in dealing with only one or two other groups, building societies with persons, savings banks with persons and government and so on.

Table 5.9 provides a more detailed comparison of the relative importance of the different types of investing institutions in 1973. In addition to showing the size of their holdings of various investments, it also contrasts their new lending in the different forms and the extent of their activity (turnover) within each market. While life assurance companies are the main investing institutions in the markets for British government securities and company debentures and loans, pension funds are of greater significance in the case of ordinary shares. Investment trusts are also important in the last market, while the weight of unit trust turnover in ordinary shares far exceeds their relative share of total institutional holdings. But for all institutional investors, new purchases of ordinary shares were unusually low in 1973, and they fell further in 1974. In the property market, pension funds were of almost as great importance as the life assurance companies in terms of new lending in 1973 and again in 1974, though their outstanding holdings are much smaller.

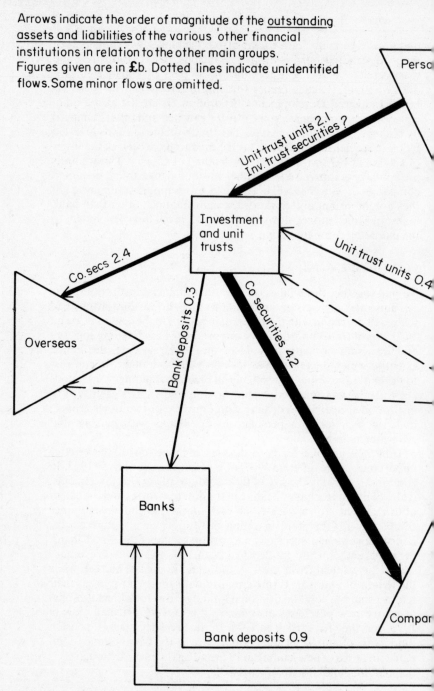

Arrows indicate the order of magnitude of the <u>outstanding assets and liabilities</u> of the various 'other' financial institutions in relation to the other main groups.
Figures given are in £b. Dotted lines indicate unidentified flows. Some minor flows are omitted.

Perso

Unit trust units 2.1
Inv. trust securities ?

Investment and unit trusts

Co. secs 2.4

Unit trust units 0.4

Overseas

Bank deposits 0.3

Co securities 4.2

Banks

Bank deposits 0.9

Compar

Fig. 5.2. The position of the 'other' financial institutions in 1973.

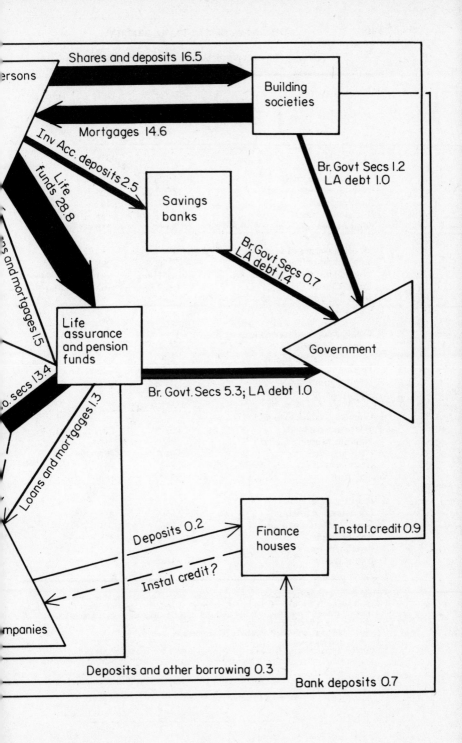

Table 5.9.   A comparison between the investing institutions

	Size of[a] holdings end 1973 £m.	New investment in 1973 £m.	Turnover[e] in 1973 £m.
1. All investments			
Life assurance funds	18,125	1,297	
Non-life insurance funds	2,933	253	
Pension funds	10,507	1,199	n/a
Investment trusts	5,723	−35	
Unit trusts[b]	2,189	218	
2. British government securities			
Life assurance funds	4,156	296	5,383
Non-life insurance funds	351	23	744
Pension funds	1,122	182	2,219
Investment trusts	66	14	241
Unit trusts	8	8	46
3. Company debentures and loan stocks			
Life assurance funds	2,594	30	426
Non-life insurance funds	139	33	84
Pension funds	997	31	343
Investment trusts	174	−16	n/a
Unit trusts	35	−5	41
4. Company ordinary shares[c]			
Life assurance funds	4,597	277	1,540
Non-life insurance funds	867	80	387
Pension funds	5,317	380	2,217
Investment trusts	4,802	−93	2,531
Unit trusts	1,477	84	1,551
5. Property, land, etc.			
Life assurance funds	2,636	285	
Non-life insurance funds	296	21	
Pension funds	1,243	258	n/a
Investment trusts	—	—	
Unit trusts[d]	244	57	

[a] Holdings are at market values except for life assurance and non-life insurance funds, where figures are for book values (with British government and local authority securities at nominal values). Figures for pension funds include local authority schemes as at 31 March 1974.
[b] Including property unit trusts.
[c] Includes holdings in overseas as well as UK companies.
[d] Property unit trusts.
[e] Turnover = purchases plus sales.

Table 5.10. The largest institutions

Type of institution [b]	Outstanding borrowings [a] at end 1973		Growth in outstanding borrowings 1963–73
	£b.	%	1963 = 1
1. American banks	26·3	17	39.2
2. London clearing banks [g]	21·6	14	3·0
3. Life assurance companies	18·1	12	2·4
4. Building societies	14·4	9	3·6
5. British overseas banks	12·7	8	9·3
6. Other UK banks [g]	11·3	7	282·2 [c]
7. Pension funds	10·7	7	2·8
8. Foreign banks	8·8	6	21·8
9. Other overseas banks	7·3	5	17·3
10. Investment trusts [d]	5·7	4	2·0
11. Accepting houses	5·4	4	6·4
12. Discount houses	2·6	2	2·1
13. Unit trusts [d]	2·1	1	5·6
14. Scottish banks	2·0	1	2·6
Trustee Savings Banks	2·0	1	2·7
16. Northern Ireland banks	0·8	1	5·0
Finance houses	0·8	1	1·4 [e]
18. Other deposit banks	0·7	—	[f]
19. National Savings Bank	0·6	—	[f]
20. Property unit trusts	0·3	—	[f]
Total all institutions [a]	154·2	100	4·7

[a] Main types of borrowing only. For banks, figures are for deposits, for discount houses, borrowed funds; thus outstanding long-term capital is omitted. Figures differ from those used in Table 4.1 for this reason and because inter-bank transactions are included here. Bank of England Banking Department and National Giro are omitted. For details for other institutions see notes to Table 5.1.
[b] See text for arbitrary elements in the classification.
[c] Many new institutions have been added to this group but many of the newcomers were small or did not exist in 1963.
[d] Borrowings are at market value: all other institutions are at book value.
[e] Growth has been affected by reclassification of some major finance houses as banks.
[f] Group was small or non-existent in 1963.
[g] Merchant banking subsidiaries of London clearing banks are included in other UK banks.

5.8 BREAKING DOWN THE BARRIERS

Two important facts emerge from the discussions, in this and the previous chapter, of the role played by the various types of financial institution. The first is how greatly the institutions differ, not only in their functions but also in their size and the extent to which they have expanded in recent years. Table 5.10 lists the main groups in order of their outstanding borrowings at end 1973 and also shows their growth over the decade from 1963. As with the similar table for types of financial instrument (Table 3.17), the order is affected by the degree to which groups are subdivided; but the effect of bringing several similar groups together, for example all overseas banks, can readily be seen.

The clear message is that in 1973 the UK financial system was dominated by banking institutions. This was suggested by the importance of bank deposits and loans in Table 3.17 and is fully confirmed here. It remained the case in 1974, despite some curtailment of both domestic and international banking business. Even the large OFI groups like building societies and assurance companies are notably smaller than the American or London clearing banks. Furthermore, the banking groups have shown by far the most rapid growth in recent years. Between 1963 and 1973, only discount houses had a growth rate slower than certain of the 'other' financial institutions.

The other key feature of UK financial institutions is the extent to which the traditional demarcation lines between the types and functions of the institutions have now broken down. The major financial companies not only spread across activities as principals, agents and consultants within a particular area, but also incorporate the business of a number of different institutions within the group. As mentioned, this is particularly the case in the large banking groups, which have both crossed boundaries within banking and moved into other fields like insurance broking and unit trust management. Now other institutions appear to be developing a counter-reaction. For example building societies and Trustee Savings Banks are wanting to develop banking type services, while one insurance company operates its own bank. One key question concerning the future of the financial system is how far this trend will, or should, be carried.

6. The complete picture

6.1 REASSEMBLING THE PIECES

It is now time to pull the various strands of analysis together and to see what the complete UK financial system looks like. To revert to an earlier analogy of the system as a complex piece of electric circuitry, we have thus far looked at each of the batches of coloured wire separately and have seen what function they perform and how they each fit together with the other components of the system. The final step in the analysis is to put all the pieces back in their places and examine how the individual circuits and components combine to make up the instrument that is the UK financial system.

One aim of this chapter is to identify the key characteristics of the UK financial system. Among the questions to be considered are: what are the major flows taking place within the UK financial system today; how have these changed in recent years; which are the main groups involved in financial transactions; how far do the main flows take place through the medium of the financial institutions?

To some extent each of these questions has already been answered. For example Tables 3.17 and 5.10 together give a broad indication of the significance of different parts of and participants in the financial system. But to show the system as a whole, we need to return to the full flow of funds presentation discussed in Chapter 1. A simplified form of this, using the five main groups of financial instruments, was given in Table 2.9; this will now be enlarged to show the pattern of financial transactions in more detail.

6.2 THE PATTERN OF FUND FLOWS

The main flows of funds through the UK financial system during 1973 are shown in Table 6.1. This gives the net borrowing and lending undertaken by each of the main groups through the different types of financial instrument. It also shows the focus of the flows that are taking place, by marking the main borrowing (or for loans lending) group involved. In Fig. 6.1 this is translated into a pattern of aggregate flows between the main groups, a form that helps to indicate the major circuits within the system rather more clearly than does the detail of Table 6.1.

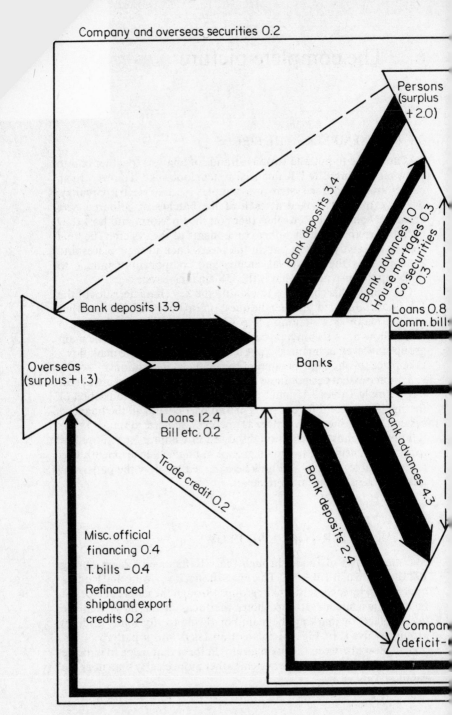

Fig. 6.1. The financial system in 1973.

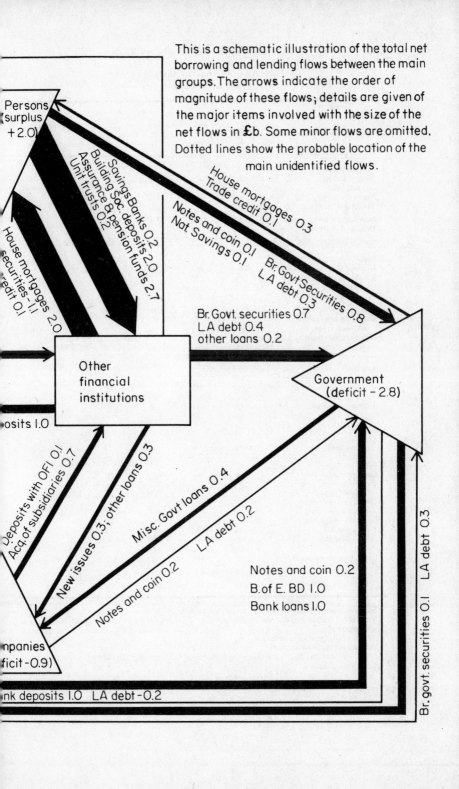

This is a schematic illustration of the total net borrowing and lending flows between the main groups. The arrows indicate the order of magnitude of these flows; details are given of the major items involved with the size of the net flows in £b. Some minor flows are omitted. Dotted lines show the probable location of the main unidentified flows.

Persons (surplus +2.0)

House mortgages 0.3
Trade credit 0.1

Savings Banks 0.2
Building Soc. deposits 2.0
Assurance & pension funds 2.7
Unit trusts 0.2

Notes and coin 0.1
Nat. Savings 0.1
Br. Govt. Securities 0.8
L A debt 0.3

House mortgages -1.1
securities 0.1
credit 0.1

Br. Govt. securities 0.7
L A debt 0.4
other loans 0.2

Other financial institutions

Government (deficit -2.8)

...osits 1.0

Deposits with OFI 0.1
Acq. of subsidiaries 0.7

New issues 0.3; other loans 0.3

Misc. Govt loans 0.4

L A debt 0.2

Notes and coin 0.2

Notes and coin 0.2

Notes and coin 0.2
B. of E. BD 1.0
Bank loans 1.0

Br. govt. securities 0.1
L A debt 0.3

...npanies
ficit -0.9)

...nk deposits 1.0   LA debt -0.2

Table 6.1. The flow of funds in 1973[a]
Net lending (+) or borrowing (−) by[a]

Type of financial instrument (£m.)	Persons	Industrial and commercial companies	Government	Overseas	Financial companies Banks	OFIs
1. Bills and deposits						
Notes and coin	129	176	−544*	—	239	—
Treasury bills[b]	−7	7	328*	−352	29	−5
National savings	138	—	−138*	—	—	—
Tax reserve certificates	−90	−67	206*	—	−41	−8
Deposits with banks	3,390	2,375	100	13,942	−20,851*	1,044
Deposits with OFIs	2,216	75	—	54	—	−2,345*
Commercial bills	—	7	17	−170	240	−94
2. Loans						
House purchase loans by govt	−301	—	301*	—	—	—
Refinanced shipbuilding and export credits	—	−54	250*	−196	—	—
Other government loans	—	−355	352*	—	3	—
Bank loans	−1,047	−4,309	−953	−12,425	19,491*	−757
Hire purchase and other instalment credit	−123	−6	13	—	—	116*
House purchase loans by financial institutions	−2,256	—	—	—	290*	1,966*
Other loans by OFIs	−40	−326	−138	—	—	504*
3. Securities						
British government securities	817	—	−1,552*	82	−35	688
Company and overseas securities	−1,450	482	8	175	295	490
New issues	—	−262*	—	30*	−62*	−61*
Other transactions	−1,450	744	8	145	357	551
Unit trust units	156	—	—	—	—	−156*
4. Life funds						
Life assurance and pension funds	2,740	—	—	—	—	−2,740*
5. Other						
Local authority debt	329	164	−1,033*	308	−160	392
Government liability to Bank of England	—	—	−1,027*	—	1,027	—
Official gold and foreign exchange reserves	—	—	210*	−210	—	—
Other official financing (net)	—	—	190*	−190	—	—
Trade credit (net)	−98	−186	59	225	—	—
Other assets[c]	−39	−97	243	−140	—	33
Unidentified transactions[d]	−2,995	1,465	151	473	508	
6. Total of above[d]						
= net surplus or deficit	1,469	−649	−2,957	1,576	163	

[a] Borrowing and lending within the groups are excluded.
Asterisks * indicate the main borrowing (or for loans lending) groups involved for each instrument.
[b] Includes Northern Ireland bills.
[c] Includes accruals adjustment.
[d] These lines do not add to zero owing to discrepancy between estimates of total saving and total capital spending.

Before looking more closely at the flows, a reminder of what they do, and do not, represent is probably useful. The figures are those for net borrowing and lending only. They show the direction of flows through any one circuit, but not the total transactions being carried out; the latter figures can be much larger, as was seen in the data for building societies' borrowing and lending and for turnover in the securities market. The transactions shown are those involving borrowing and lending between the groups, companies from banks, persons from OFIs and so on. Thus the flows between members of the same group, between individual banks, companies or persons are omitted.

The significance of these intra-group flows for the banks and the other financial institutions was considered above and they were presented schematically in Fig. 4.5 and 5.2. In principle, they could be incorporated in Fig. 6.1, but only at the cost of a much more complicated presentation. Instead, the blocks representing these two groups may be thought of as representing the boundaries of another set of flows between such groups of institutions; only the flows within the banking group are of real importance. A similar approach can be adopted to the triangles for the major non-financial groups; but in the area of persons and companies there is the further problem that there is little firm information about the extent of the transactions involved. The volume of flows like private lending between persons (and by) persons to unincorporated business, or trade credit between companies cannot at present be estimated, though it is believed to be quite substantial. There are also some complex flows within the government group, relating to the financing of local authorities and nationalized industries.

Even when attention is fixed on flows between the groups, there are still some problems of identification. The lack of data on flows of trade credit and other loans between persons and companies has been mentioned several times earlier, and in Fig. 6.1 these are indicated in an illustrative manner only. In addition, it is not possible to tell exactly through which channels persons and companies carry out their transactions in securities, in particular how far company acquisitions involve direct purchases of securities held by persons or represent sales by the investing institutions, who are at the same time buying other securities from persons. In Fig. 6.1 most of these security transactions are shown as going via the OFIs, rather than directly between companies and persons or between the overseas group and persons; but there is undoubtedly some money flowing through the latter circuits as well.

None the less, while Table 6.1 and Fig. 6.1 do not show all the flows within the UK financial system, they do indicate clearly the way in which the system operates to channel money from borrower to lender. Three characteristics stand out as features of the system in 1973.

First, in virtually all cases, there were two-way flows between the groups. Companies lent to the banks as well as borrowing from them. Persons deposited money with other financial institutions as well as getting loans from them. There was some tendency for money to flow from persons both to companies (via the banks) and to the government (via banks and OFIs). But a large amount of borrowing and lending between members of any one group was carried out not directly but through the medium of another group; banks, OFIs and even the government channelled back to persons or companies a substantial part of the funds that other people or companies lent to them.

The second feature is that virtually all the major flows were going through one of the two groups of financial institutions. Even allowing for the unidentified direct transactions between persons and companies, it is the circuits between persons and OFIs, and between banks and both the overseas group and companies, that dominate Fig. 6.1. Finally, in terms of the funds flowing through them, the banks clearly form the main element within the UK financial system. Their two-way transactions with the overseas group were the single largest circuit in 1973, and in domestic business their dealings with companies and the government overshadowed those of the OFIs. Only in relation to personal transactions are the latter of major importance.

6.3 HOW THE PATTERNS HAVE CHANGED

The picture presented above is that of a single year. Naturally the pattern of flows will change from year to year as the financial circumstances of the non-financial groups, who initiate the borrowing and lending, alter. As Fig. 2.8, p. 54, showed, the net surplus or deficit of these groups can vary greatly from year to year, but the normal picture has been for persons to be net lenders and the government net borrowers, with the overseas group and companies fluctuating round a balanced position. In this respect 1973 was a fairly typical year, exceptional only in the extent of the government deficit. In 1974, both the latter and the net borrowing by companies increased further, with a corresponding rise in the surpluses of both persons and the overseas group. This change, and the accompanying monetary restraint, served to reduce the significance of the two-way flow between the banking system and both persons and companies, new personal borrowing being sharply cut back while company deposits were run down. But in other respects, there was little change in the general pattern of fund flows as compared with 1973.

The way in which money flows through the financial system also changes for more fundamental reasons, reflecting underlying changes in the structure of the system. A number of major developments have been noted in the earlier analysis, in particular the substantial growth in money markets of all kinds. It remains to show the way these have affected the overall flow of funds picture, and how far the features identified in the preceding section are of long standing or represent quite recent developments.

For this purpose Fig. 6.1 above may be compared with equivalent analyses of fund flows both ten years ago (Fig. 6.2), and in 1957 (Fig. 6.3). The latter year is one of the earliest for which a reasonably detailed fund flow picture can be constructed for the UK; it also represents a point when the financial system had fully recovered from wartime and immediate postwar distortions but when the growth in new money markets had not yet begun. The three pictures are comparable in that they each show the relative order of magnitude of the aggregate flows between groups in the year in question and they are constructed on the same principles; but the scales used for flows differ, especially as between 1963 and 1973, owing to the enormous growth in the money values involved.

The comparison shows some major changes in the pattern of flows between 1963 and 1973 and even more between 1957 and 1973. In both the earlier years, it is the circuit between persons and other financial institutions that stands out as most important. Banking transactions, especially those overseas, were of far less importance than they are today though their growth had already begun by 1963. Over the period as a whole, the emphasis in flows has shifted from right to left in the diagrams, away from government and OFIs towards banks and the overseas group and, to a lesser extent, companies.

Thus, one of the key features identified earlier as a characteristic of the UK financial system today, the importance of the banking system as a channel for fund flows, is evidently a relatively recent development. In earlier years the banks were important in the payment mechanisms but much less so as a medium for new borrowing and lending transactions. The other two characteristics appear to be of longer standing. Even in 1957, a very large part of the borrowing and lending flows went via the financial institutions rather than direct between non-financial groups, though direct flows between persons and government loomed larger than in 1973. And most flows were two-way ones, transactions between members of the same group being then, as now, frequently carried out through an outside intermediary.

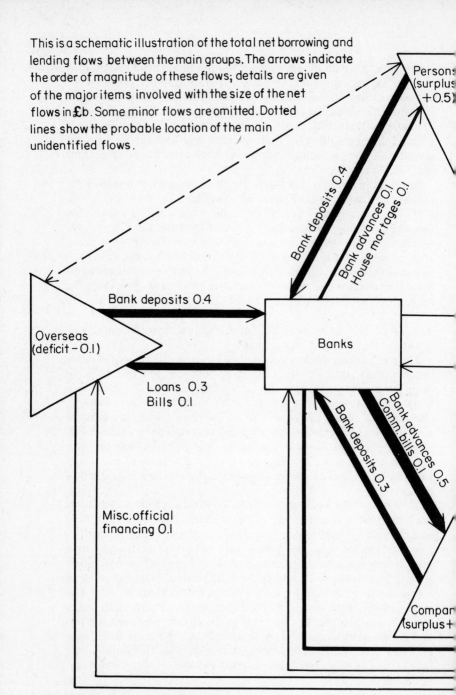

This is a schematic illustration of the total net borrowing and lending flows between the main groups. The arrows indicate the order of magnitude of these flows; details are given of the major items involved with the size of the net flows in £b. Some minor flows are omitted. Dotted lines show the probable location of the main unidentified flows.

Persons
(surplus +0.5)

Bank deposits 0.4

Bank advances 0.1
House mortages 0.1

Overseas
(deficit – 0.1)

Bank deposits 0.4

Banks

Loans 0.3
Bills 0.1

Bank advances 0.5
Comm. bills 0.1

Bank deposits 0.3

Misc. official financing 0.1

Compar
(surplus +

Fig. 6.2. The financial system in 1963

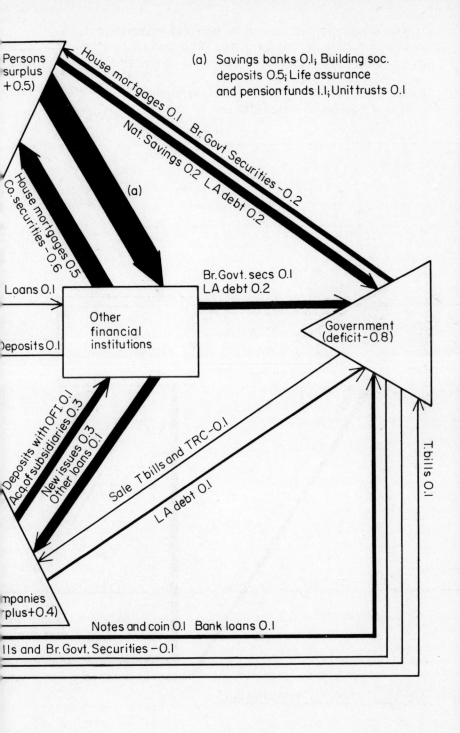

Persons
surplus
(+0.5)

(a) Savings banks 0.1; Building soc.
deposits 0.5; Life assurance
and pension funds 1.1; Unit trusts 0.1

House mortgages 0.1 Br. Govt Securities -0.2

Nat. Savings 0.2 L A debt 0.2

(a)

House mortgages 0.5
Co. securities -0.6

Loans 0.1

Deposits 0.1

Other
financial
institutions

Br. Govt. secs 0.1
LA debt 0.2

Government
(deficit -0.8)

Deposits with OFI 0.1
Acq. of subsidiaries 0.3

New issues 0.3
Other loans 0.1

Sale T bills and TRC -0.1

L A debt 0.1

T.bills 0.1

Companies
(surplus +0.4)

Notes and coin 0.1   Bank loans 0.1

T.bills and Br. Govt. Securities -0.1

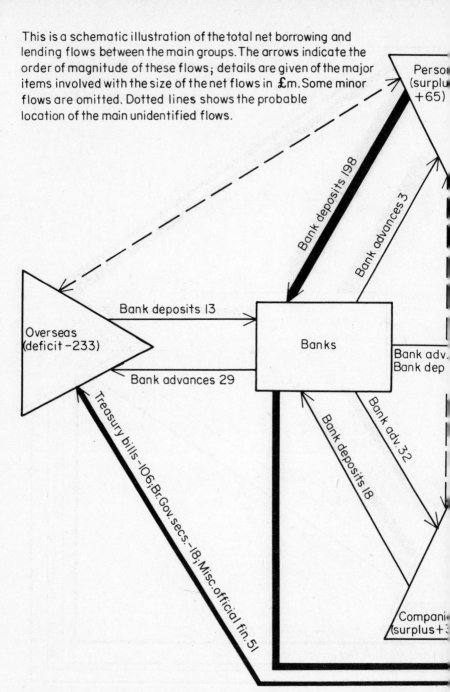

This is a schematic illustration of the total net borrowing and lending flows between the main groups. The arrows indicate the order of magnitude of these flows; details are given of the major items involved with the size of the net flows in £m. Some minor flows are omitted. Dotted lines shows the probable location of the main unidentified flows.

Persor (surplu +65)

Bank deposits 198

Bank advances 3

Bank deposits 13

Banks

Overseas (deficit −233)

Bank advances 29

Bank adv. Bank dep

Bank adv. 32

Bank deposits 18

Treasury bills −106; Br. Gov. secs. −18; Misc. official fin. 51

Compani (surplus +3

Fig. 6.3. The financial system in 1957

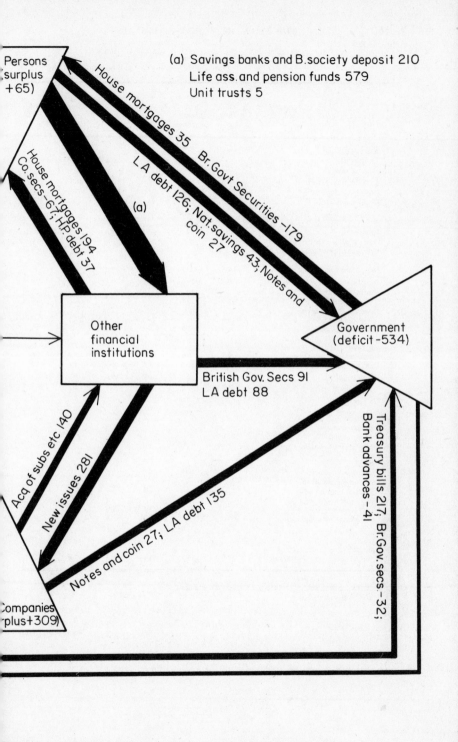

(a) Savings banks and B.society deposit 210
    Life ass. and pension funds 579
    Unit trusts 5

Persons
(surplus
+65)

House mortgages 35   Br. Govt Securities -179

House mortgages 194
Co. secs -6; H.P. debt 37

L A debt 126; Nat.savings 43; Notes and
coin 27

(a)

Other
financial
institutions

Government
(deficit -534)

British Gov. Secs 91
LA debt 88

Acq of subs etc 140

New issues 281

Notes and coin 27; LA debt 135

Treasury bills 217;
Bank advances - 41

Br.Gov.secs -32;

Companies
(surplus+309)

Table 6.2.   Who owed money to whom in 1973 [a]

Outstanding lending (+) and borrowing (−) by [a]

Type of financial instrument (£b.)	Persons	Industrial and commercial companies	Govern-ment	Overseas	Financial companies	
					Banks	OFIs
1. Bills and deposits						
Treasury bills	—	—	−1·3	0·4	0·9	—
National savings	7·6	—	−7·6	—	—	—
Tax reserve certificates	0·1	0·1	−0·2	—	—	—
Deposits with banks [b]	18·6	10·6	−3·6	42·6	−70·5	2·3
Deposits with OFIs	18·8	0·6	—	—	—	−19·4
Commercial bills	—	−1·7	—	−0·5	2·3	−0·1
2. Loans						
House purchase loans by govt	−1·7	—	1·7	—	—	—
Refinanced shipbuilding and export credits	—	−0·2	0·9	−0·7	—	—
Other government loans	−0·2	−0·7	0·9	—	—	—
Bank loans	−5·5	−14·0	−3·0	−36·1	61·4	−2·8
Hire purchase and other instalment credit	−1·6	0·1	0·2	—	—	1·3
House purchase loans by financial institutions	−16·9	—	—	—	1·1	15·8
Other loans by OFIs	−0·3	−1·9	−0·9	—	—	3·1
3. Securities						
British government securities	2·7	0·6	−12·0	1·5	1·6	5·6
Company and overseas securities	21·1	−31·4	1·3	−4·2	−1·8	15·0
of which: issues	—	−39·3	—	−5·6	−3·0	−10·1
holdings	21·1	7·9	1·3	1·4	1·2	25·1
Unit trust units	2·1	—	—	—	—	−2·1
4. Life funds						
Life assurance and pension funds	29·0	—	—	—	—	−29·0
Unfunded pension rights etc.	11·6	—	−11·6	—	—	—
5. Other						
Local authority debt	2·5	0·7	−8·3	0·6	1·2	3·3
Government liability to Bank of England	—	—	−1·8	—	1·8	—
Official gold and foreign exchange reserves	—	—	1·6	−1·6	—	—
Other official financing (net)	—	—	0·4	−0·4	—	—
Trade and other credit (net)	1·0	−1·7	1·4	0·1	—	−0·8
6. Total of above = net lending (+) or borrowing (−)	88·9	−38·9	−41·9	1·7	−2·0	−7·8

[a] Borrowing and lending within the groups are excluded.
[b] Includes notes and coin.

6.4 THE RESULT: WHO OWES MONEY TO WHOM

Each year's flow of funds leads to an accumulation of holdings of financial instruments as assets and liabilities by the various groups. While these holdings are also affected by changes in the market value of certain types of instrument, their distribution acts as a kind of summary of past flows through the financial system. When compared with the current pattern of flows it can help to illuminate the long-run changes that have taken place in the structure of the financial system. In addition, the analysis of outstanding borrowing and lending is itself of interest, for the insight it gives into who owns the wealth in the country.

Outstanding holdings of different types of financial instrument at end 1973 are shown in Table 6.2, and Fig. 6.4 summarizes the aggregated indebtedness between groups in a way similar to the flow of funds presentation in Fig. 6.1. Once again, the figures relate to dealings between groups only; within each oblong or triangle there are further amounts of outstanding borrowing and lending, inter-bank deposits and loans, trade credit and the like. Some of the transactions not identified in the flow of funds data can now be more clearly presented; this applies particularly to personal holdings of securities, though a precise split between UK company securities and those issued by overseas organizations is not possible. The main problem still relates to the flow of trade credit between companies and persons; in Table 6.2 the holdings are given on a net basis, while in Fig. 6.4 only an indication of gross indebtedness can be given. Altogether, the figures must be seen as broad orders of magnitude only.

None the less, they serve to provide an interesting comparison with the pattern of new borrowing and lending in 1973. Most of the outstanding dealings between groups are again two-way and those through financial institutions are of major importance. But some of the direct indebtedness between non-financial groups is substantial, for example personal holdings of both company and government securities. There is also much more imbalance between the outstanding borrowing and lending between sectors than in the new flows; persons have lent far more to both the financial groups and the government than they have borrowed from them; and likewise for OFIs and companies. Only in the case of transactions between banks and overseas and, to a lesser extent, between banks and companies are outstanding borrowing and lending of roughly similar size. And, while dealings between banks and overseas are clearly of considerable importance, they do not dominate the picture of holdings in 1973, as they did that of new flows.

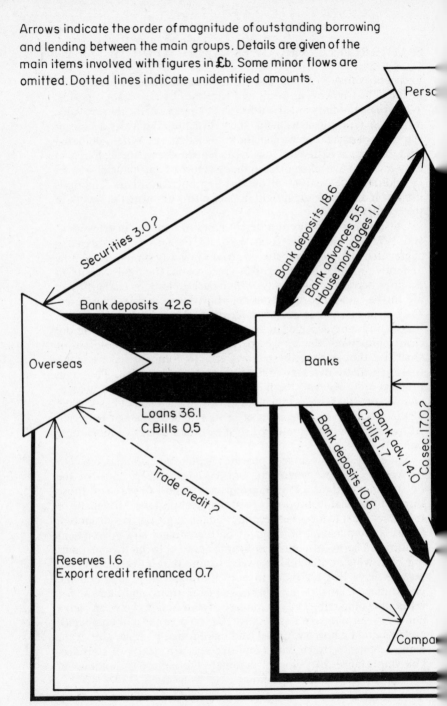

Arrows indicate the order of magnitude of outstanding borrowing and lending between the main groups. Details are given of the main items involved with figures in £b. Some minor flows are omitted. Dotted lines indicate unidentified amounts.

Persc

Securities 3.0?

Bank deposits 18.6

Bank advances 5.5
House mortgages 1.1

Bank deposits 42.6

Overseas

Banks

Loans 36.1
C.Bills 0.5

Co sec.17.0?

Bank adv. 14.0
C.bills 1.7

Bank deposits 10.6

Trade credit ?

Reserves 1.6
Export credit refinanced 0.7

Compa

Fig. 6.4. The pattern of holdings in 1973

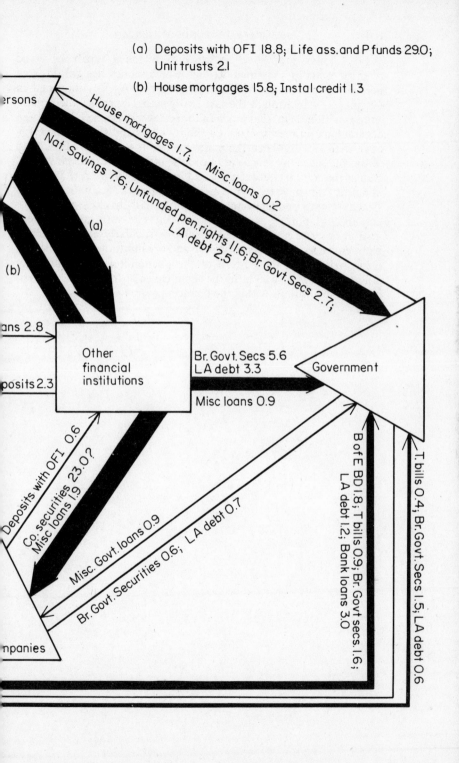

(a) Deposits with OFI 18.8; Life ass. and P funds 29.0;
Unit trusts 2.1

(b) House mortgages 15.8; Instal credit 1.3

Persons

House mortgages 1.7; Misc. loans 0.2

Nat. Savings 7.6; Unfunded pen. rights 11.6; Br. Govt. Secs 2.7;
LA debt 2.5

(a)

(b)

...ans 2.8

...posits 2.3

Other
financial
institutions

Br. Govt. Secs 5.6
LA debt 3.3

Misc loans 0.9

Government

Deposits with OFI 0.6

Co: securities 23.0 ?
Misc loans 1.9

Misc. Govt. loans 0.9

Br. Govt. Securities 0.6; LA debt 0.7

B of E BD 1.8; T bills 0.9; Br. Govt secs. 1.6;
LA debt 1.2; Bank loans 3.0

T. bills 0.4; Br. Govt. Secs 1.5; LA debt 0.6

...mpanies

Fig. 6.4 illustrates the way in which the financial system has served over the years as a channel through which money has passed from persons to companies and the government. As was indicated in Chapter 2, it is through the last two groups, or rather the organizations within them, that much of the real wealth in the UK has been accumulated in recent years. Of the two financial groups, the OFIs have until recently been the main channel for these domestic fund flows, and securities represent one of the prime instruments involved. But, as the contrast between Figs 6.1 and 6.3 made clear, the changes in recent years have tended to alter the emphasis within the financial system, giving greater weight to shorter-term banking-type transactions and putting more stress on the two-way flows between institutions and non-financial groups, particularly on the dealings between banks and overseas people and organizations. This is slowly being reflected in the pattern of the outstanding indebtedness of different groups as well as in the significance of the various types of financial institutions within the financial system.

7. Some overseas alternatives

7.1 THE BASIS FOR COMPARISONS

The analysis of the UK financial system and how it relates to the rest of UK activity immediately raises further questions. For example, why is the UK system as it is? And how does it differ from the financial setups that exist elsewhere?

The question of why financial structures have developed in the way they have is considered in the next chapter. In this chapter the financial structures in a number of other countries are studied with a view to isolating some of the special features of the UK system. Attention is concentrated on countries of broadly the same level of development as the UK, that is the major countries of North America and Western Europe plus Japan. Specifically, in addition to Japan, the financial systems looked at are those of the United States, Canada, France, West Germany and the Netherlands. Space and data limitations mean that the analysis of the foreign systems is much less detailed than that for the UK. Rather than describing each set of markets separately, the various other countries are compared with the UK from a number of standpoints.

All the countries examined, as well as the UK, are members of the Organization for Economic Co-operation and Development (OECD), which provides a major service by collating various types of financial data for member countries and putting these on to a broadly comparable basis. *OECD Financial Statistics* has been the main source of data for the subsequent analysis. The emphasis is primarily on current flows of funds in the form of new borrowing and lending, rather than on the analysis of the financial instruments that are outstanding as a result of past transactions. For, as in the UK, most countries do not provide comprehensive data on the holdings of assets and liabilities.

It was indicated in Chapter 1 that the OECD approach to the analysis of fund flows differs from that used in earlier chapters, all transactions in liabilities being classified as sources of funds and all dealings in assets as uses, regardless of the direction of the transaction. In Table 1.4, the effect of this approach was compared with that used in Chapters 2 to 6. There are a number of others ways in which OECD definitions differ from those employed in analysing the UK. Notable among these are the classification of certain types of financial instruments, the constituents of each of the main groups (especially the location of unincorporated businesses), and the extent of consolidation of intra-group transactions. The main differences are set out in the Appendix and they are mentioned in subsequent comments where significant for the interpretation of the figures.

Because of these differences the OECD figures cannot be used to identify small variations between the financial systems, even though the OECD presentation of UK data is used as a basis of comparison. However, the data are adequate at least to indicate whether there are any major variations in the financial structure and habits of the countries selected. Unfortunately the degree of detail available does not enable a schematic picture of each system, along the lines of Fig. 6.1 above, to be presented. But a fairly detailed study of borrowing and lending transactions is possible. In what follows, for simplicity the figures presented will be mainly those for 1972, the latest year for which OECD data on all countries was available at the time of writing.

7.2 HOW THE GENERAL FINANCIAL CHARACTERISTICS DIFFER

The first step, in examining the alternative financial systems that exist in other countries is to see how important these systems are within the economies concerned. This can be done at the most general level by contrasting financial magnitudes with comparable economic quantities, for example the total outstanding financial instruments with the value of all physical assets, or new borrowing and lending with gross domestic product.

In view of the absence of data on physical assets, the first of these alternatives is not possible here, but Table 7.1 shows how new borrowing in 1972 compared with gross domestic product. The countries fall into three groups. The United States, Canada and Germany all had broadly comparable ratios; France and the Netherlands were at a slightly higher level, while the figures for the UK and especially Japan were notably higher, new borrowing in Japan being nearly as large as the total addition to national wealth during the year. With the exception of Germany and the Netherlands, new borrowing in all countries has risen a good deal faster than GDP in recent years. But the expansion for the UK has been particularly marked. In 1970 the UK ratio was at a more average level of one-third, but the figure for Japan in both 1970 and 1971 was still exceptionally high, around 65%.

Table 7.1. How important is the financial system?

1972		Total new borrowing (= new lending)	Gross domestic product	New borrowing as % of GDP	Saving (= investment)	Saving as % of GDP	Total sources (= uses) of funds (borrowing and saving)	Borrowing as % of all sources
USA	$b.	375·3	1178·5	32	297·1	25	672·4	56
Canada	$b.	38·1	104·0	37	23·4	22	61·5	62
Japan	Y000 b.	83·5	90·7	92	35·2	39	118·7	67
France	Fr b.	462·3	1001·9	46	270·0	27	732·3	63
Germany	DM b.	293·5	829·4	35	246·7	30	540·2	54
Netherlands	Fl b.	67·9	147·1	46	45·4	31	113·3	60
UK	£ b.	39·8	61·2	65	12·5	20	52·3	76

These figures suggest that the financial system, or more specifically current financial transactions, is of particular importance in the UK and Japan today. The next question is how far this reflects differences between the underlying economies, notably variations in the importance of saving and investment transactions which current borrowing and lending facilitate. Table 7.1 shows that there is some relationship between the two measures. Both Japan and the Netherlands have relatively high ratios of borrowing and lending and saving and investment to GDP, while the figures for Canada and the United States are low. But this is by no means always the case. Germany, with fairly low borrowing to GDP, has a fairly high savings figure, while the UK is very much in the opposite position.

The relationship between borrowing and saving, or lending and investing, is summarized in the final column of Table 7.1. This gives the share that borrowing (or lending) represents of the total sources (or uses) of funds for capital transactions. It is clear that, when allowance is made for differences in the significance of savings and investment, in 1972 the financial system was notably more important in the UK than in other countries; this is despite the fact that UK borrowing figures do not include a full allowance for trade credit. To a large extent, the high Japanese borrowing to GDP ratio reflects the exceptional importance of saving and investment in the economy, whereas this is in no way true of the UK. In terms of sources and uses of funds, the financial system as a whole appears to be least important in Germany and the United States.

In order to look more closely at what lies behind these apparent differences, it is helpful to examine the position of the various groups active in the financial system. As background to this, Table 7.2 indicates the significance of the six main groups in total saving and investment in the various countries; financial companies are here divided into banks and other financial institutions (the exact split is shown in the Appendix table). The figures relate to saving and investment, after allowing for capital transfers, like tax payments and grants, between groups. In the case of Germany, in this and subsequent tables, data on persons include all housing transactions, some of which are in fact carried out by companies and government.

In all countries, persons, companies and government are the main groups both saving and investing in physical assets. Their importance differs quite considerably between countries. In the United States persons, which here excludes unincorporated businesses, are the major group. In Canada, and to a lesser extent Germany, it is companies that are most important (despite the fact that, in both these countries, unincorporated businesses are included with persons). The feature of the UK figures is the exceptionally large role of

Table 7.2.   Who saves and who invests [a]

| | % of 1972 total accounted for by | | | | | |
	Persons	Companies	Government	Overseas	Banks	OFIs
1. Saving [b]						
USA	64	34	—4 [d]	3	1	2
Canada	35	44	14	4	2	1
Japan	42	38	20	—	— [f]	— [f]
France [c]	n/a	n/a	n/a	n/a	n/a	n/a
Germany	39 [e]	39	18	—	3	1
Netherlands	73		23	1	—	3
UK	34	27	33	—	2	4
2. Investment [b]						
USA	53	45	— [d]	—	1	1
Canada	19	61	18	1	—	1
Japan	25	44	25	6	— [f]	— [f]
France [c]	n/a	n/a	n/a	n/a	n/a	n/a
Germany	26 [e]	53	19	—	1	1
Netherlands	70		22	8	—	—
UK	25	23	46	—	—	6

[a]   The precise coverage of the groups differs from country to country (see Appendix).
[b]   Including capital transfers but excluding discrepancies (balancing item required to reconcile
     saving and investment figures with identified financial transactions).
[c]   An adequate breakdown of the French figures is not available.
[d]   All spending by US government is classified as being current expenditure.
[e]   Figures include all transactions relating to housing, part of which is in fact carried out by other
     groups (companies and government). The role of persons is thus slightly overstated.
[f]   Saving and investment by Japanese financial institutions is assumed to be nil.

government in both saving and investing and the low figures for
companies, especially for their share of total investment. In addition,
the other financial institutions in the UK play an unusually large role
in investment and, to a lesser extent, savings.

Comparison of each group's share in saving and investment gives
an indication of how far they are net borrowers or lenders through
the financial system. In 1972, persons in all countries had a higher
share of saving than investment, showing that they were net lenders.
This is generally the case in most years, and the reverse is normally
true of companies who invest more than they save. The UK was,
however, a notable exception to this in 1972 when identified savings
by companies exceeded their physical investment. Table 7.2 suggests

that the position of both government and the overseas group varies a lot from country to country; in the United States, all government spending is treated as being on current account; hence the negative saving and nil investment.

The general pattern of net borrowing and lending can be seen in another way in Table 7.3, which shows the contribution of each group to the net flows through the financial system. The figures relate to the

Table 7.3.   How the financial behaviour of the main groups differs [a]

| Net borrowing [b] or lending | % of total in 1970–72 accounted for by | | | | | |
	Persons	Companies	Government	Overseas	Banks	OFIs
USA	80	—59	—41	13	3	4
Canada	91	—90	—2	—8	8	1
Japan	100	—62	—18	—20	—[c]	—[c]
France	85	—73	—19	—8	7	8
Germany	85 [d]	—99	4	—	11	—1
Netherlands [e]	(55)	(—68)	(—32)	(2)	(10)	(34)
UK	81	—34	—24	—25	19	—17

[a] The precise coverage of the groups differs from country to country; see Appendix.
[b] The figures are for identified borrowing and lending transactions only. They show each group's share in the total of net borrowing/lending flows through the financial system.
[c] Assumed to be nil, probably small.
[d] Includes all the financial transactions, almost entirely borrowing, relating to housing; part of this should probably be under Companies and Government.
[e] Recent OECD figures do not show the split between borrowing and lending by persons and companies in the Netherlands. Figures shown in brackets are for 1968.

period 1970–72 as a whole, in order to smooth out some of the fluctuations that take place from year to year in the net transactions by government and the overseas group. The table confirms the fact that persons have been the major net lenders in all countries in recent years; in Japan, and to a large degree in Canada also, they were indeed the only net lenders in this period. Everywhere but in the UK, companies have accounted for well over half the net borrowing, with only a limited amount going to government and the overseas group; the latter represents the counterpart of balance of payment surpluses. In this particular period, UK companies were net borrowers, though on a much smaller scale than elsewhere; as was seen in Fig. 2.8, they were net lenders for much of the 1960s. In addition, a substantial volume of UK funds flowed through to both government and the overseas group in 1970–72; the analysis above showed that the UK

Table 7.4.   The importance to different groups of borrowing and lending

1972	Persons	Companies	Government	Overseas	Banks	OFIs	All groups
1. Borrowing as % of all sources of funds.							
USA	26	44	164[d]	48	95	95	56
Canada	43	42	63	73	96	96	62
Japan	45	66	63	100	100[a]	100[a]	67
France[c]	n/a	n/a	n/a	n/a	n/a	n/a	63
Germany	31[b]	40	28	97	94	93	54
Netherlands	40		41	97	98	90	60
UK	55	54	45	100	97	92	76
2. Lending as % of all uses of funds.							
USA	43	26	100[d]	100	97	98	56
Canada	69	21	53	91	99	97	62
Japan	68	61	52	39	100[a]	100[a]	67
France[c]	n/a	n/a	n/a	n/a	n/a	n/a	63
Germany	54[b]	20	26	95	98	92	54
Netherlands	43		44	71	100	99	60
UK	67	61	23	100	100	90	76

[a] Savings and investment by Japanese financial institutions is assumed to be nil.
[b] Includes all transactions relating to housing, some of which are actually carried out by other groups.
[c] An adequate breakdown of the French figures is not available.
[d] All spending by US government is classified as being on current account.

government has normally been a substantial net borrower, but the position of the overseas group has fluctuated from year to year, a situation common to most countries.

In addition to the unusual position of industrial companies in the UK in this period, the net borrowing and lending position of the two groups of financial companies is also of interest. The net flows for these groups appear to be far more important in the UK than elsewhere. It is particularly noticeable that other financial institutions have been quite important as net borrowers, reflecting the extent to which their funds have been used to acquire physical assets like property rather than financial instruments; such action is often not permitted under the regulations governing financial institutions abroad.

While the pattern of net borrowing and lending is important, in that it shows the main direction of fund flows through the financial system, it does not, of course, show the full role played by the different groups in the system. For this details on total borrowing and lending transactions are required. Table 7.2, p. 169, indicated the significance of borrowing and lending in the economy as a whole; Table 7.4 shows how the position of the various groups differs, relating borrowing by each of them to their total sources of funds and lending to their total uses; the other part of sources and uses of funds are saving from current transactions and investment in physical assets.

As might be expected, borrowing and lending form the major sources and uses of funds for the two financial groups in all countries, though the significance of both saving and physical investing to other financial institutions in the UK is again evident. Borrowing or lending, and sometimes both, are also of prime importance for the overseas group; for those countries in balance of payment deficit in 1972, the United States and Canada, the deficit provided an important source of funds to the overseas group, while the reverse was true for surplus countries like Japan and the Netherlands. In the case of persons and companies, borrowing and lending are notably more important in the UK and Japan than for most other countries. This is especially true of lending by companies; as will be seen, in Japan the figures include a substantial volume of trade credit, but in the UK this is not the case. In contrast, financial transactions by the UK government are relatively unimportant compared with its saving and investment, and the same is also true for Germany.

Table 7.5 summarizes the role that, as a result of their varying involvement in borrowing and lending, the main groups play in the total of such transactions. Once again, there are quite marked differences between countries. It is notable that the high ratio of borrowing and lending to total sources and use of funds in the UK is *not* attributable to an exceptionally high share of financial institutions in the total. The combined figures for banks and OFIs in France are higher than in the UK, and they have grown more rapidly in recent years. Nor is the importance of the banks significantly higher in the UK than elsewhere; they are clearly particularly important in Germany where the OFI group is small. In contrast, OFIs are more than usually important in the United States and France, but their share has been declining in most of the countries in recent years, while that of banks has been rising.

The most notable distinction in the UK figures is the major role played by the overseas group in the total of borrowing and lending. Only in the Netherlands is this group anywhere near as important.

The role of UK companies in total borrowing is very small compared with, for example, Japan, Germany or the United States, and their lending is also small despite its size in relation to their physical investment (Table 7.4); this reflects the low level of investment. The UK government is also of relatively little importance as either borrower or lender, especially the latter; this contrasts with the role played by authorities in Canada and Japan, though the lack of consolidation for these two countries may be affecting the figures here.

7.3 THE CHANNELS FOR BORROWING AND LENDING

It is clear that the broad structure of the financial system varies from country to country. The significance of borrowing and lending transactions is different, both in total and in respect to the other capital transactions of the main group. As a result the groups play varying roles within the financial system. The next stage of the comparison is to see how far the position of the formal financial system, that is the structure of organized markets and institutions, differs.

The main financial institutions that exist in the different countries are listed in the Appendix table, which shows how they are classified under the two main groups. In general terms, the nature of the services offered by the financial institutions that exist in the different countries is remarkably similar. In all cases there are deposit banks, savings banks, and insurance companies; there are also normally institutions offering house mortgages as well as a variety of other specialist, often government-sponsored, organizations. There is always some kind of organized money market and a formal market in longer-term securities. But, behind this broad uniformity, there are some quite wide differences in the make-up and behaviour of the institutions and in the conditions and regulations governing apparently similar financial transactions. And the significance of different markets and institutions as channels for borrowing and lending varies.

Table 7.5, p. 174, shows the role played by the two main groups of institutions in the total of borrowing and lending in 1972. Together, the financial companies were most important in France and Germany and least in the United States and the Netherlands. Except in the United States, the banks have generally been the more important of the two groups in terms of new borrowing and lending; as mentioned, this is especially the case in Germany, but, in both the UK and Canada, the significance of the banks was in 1972 over twice that of the other financial institutions.

Table 7.5. Who borrows and who lends

1972	% of total transactions accounted for by:					
	Persons	Companies	Government	Overseas	Banks	OFIs

1. Total borrowing

	Persons	Companies	Government	Overseas	Banks	OFIs
USA	18	21	9	2	21	29
Canada	16	18	16	6	31	13
Japan	9	33	16	4	21	17
France	13	14	8	10	33	22
Germany	15 [a]	22	6	7	43	7
Netherlands	33		11	18	23	15
UK	13	10	9	19	32	16

2. Total lending

	Persons	Companies	Government	Overseas	Banks	OFIs
USA	31	9	3	5	21	30
Canada	24	10	13	8	32	13
Japan	23	25	12	2	21	17
France	20	8	7	10	32	23
Germany	25 [a]	11	5	6	45	7
Netherlands	35		11	13	24	17
UK	16	9	4	21	33	16

[a] Includes all transactions relating to housing, some of which are actually carried out by other groups.

Unfortunately it is not possible to see for all countries how the individual financial institutions compare in terms of outstanding borrowings. Some figures are available for the United States, Japan and the Netherlands and these are contrasted with UK data in Table 7.6; the Japanese figures include government financial institutions, which are grouped with government in the rest of the analysis. Figures for shares of new business in 1972 are also given in Table 7.6 for all the selected countries other than Germany.

The commercial banks are by a considerable margin the most important group of institutions in all the countries examined. But this is particularly true in the UK, especially in terms of new business in recent years. Only in the Netherlands does any other single group, in this case the pension funds, approach the banks in size. In Japan and

Table 7.6. The size of the institutions

(1) Outstanding business

Type of financial institution [a]	end 1972	USA	Japan	Netherlands	UK
		Each group's share % of total outstanding borrowings in			
1. Banks		40	47	54	48
Central bank		5	5	7	48
Commercial banks		35	42	30	
Other monetary institutions		—	—	17 [b]	—
2. Other financial institutions		60	53	46	
Savings banks		20 [c]	6 [d]	9	12
Housing finance institutions			—	n/a [e]	14
Life assurance companies		12	5	12	13
General insurance companies		2		n/a [e]	2
Pension funds		13	—	25	11
Other private financial institutions [f]		10	26	n/a [e]	18
Government financial institutions		3	16	n/a [e]	— [g]
3. Total of above		100	100	100	100
Amount (b.)		$1,755	Y.175,439	Fl.196	£105

(2) New business

1972	USA	Canada	Japan	France	Netherlands	UK
	Each group's share % of new borrowings in					
1. Banks	42	46	48	60	58	84
Central bank	1	6	3	14	8	84
Commercial banks	41	40	45	46	30	
Other monetary institutions	—	— [h]	—		20 [b]	—
2. Other financial institutions	58	54	52	40	42	16
Savings banks	27 [c]	9 [h]	7 [d]	11	8	—
Housing finance institutions		11 [i]	—	n/a [j]	n/a [e]	6
Life assurance companies	8	8	4	4	9	3
General insurance companies	2	2			n/a [e]	1
Pension funds	7	9	—	—	25	3
Other private financial institutions [f]	11	6	27	25 [j]	n/a [e]	3
Government financial institutions	3	9	14		n/a [e]	— [g]
3. Total of above	100	100	100	100	100	100
Amount (b.)	$184.6	$16.6	Y.35,775	Fr.253.4	Fl.27.3	£37.4

[a] Inevitably, the institutions classified to the same broad group differ somewhat from country to country.
[b] Includes co-operative agricultural credit banks.
[c] Includes credit unions who provide some instalment loans.
[d] Includes trust departments of trust banks; banking departments are classified as commercial banks.
[e] 1972 figures for these groups are not available but at end 1973 they accounted for the following percentage of the enlarged total of outstanding borrowing:

Housing finance institutions	3%
General insurance companies	2%
Other private financial institutions	4%
Government financial institutions	10%

[f] Includes investment and unit trusts and consumer credit companies.
[g] Figures exclude current account activities of National and Trustee Savings Banks. Their investment accounts are included under savings banks.
[h] Quebec Savings Banks and credit unions are here classified as savings banks. In the earlier analysis they were grouped under other monetary institutions, i.e. as banks, according to OECD's convention.
[i] Includes trust companies.
[j] The Mortgage Loan Bank is included with other financial institutions.

France the bulk of the remaining business is carried out by various specialist, mainly deposit-taking, institutions, a good number of which are government-owned or -controlled. Neither insurance companies nor pension funds play a major part in either of these two countries. Both these institutions are of importance in the United States and Canada as well as in the Netherlands, and, in terms of outstanding business, in the UK; private savings and housing finance institutions also have a significant role in these countries.

An alternative approach to looking at the channels for borrowing and lending, and one that avoids some of the problems of classifying institutions to different groups, is to look at the main character of the

Table 7.7. The share of different types of financial instrument

1972	USA	Canada[a]	Japan[a]	France	Germany	Nether-lands	UK
% of total new borrowing during year in the form of:							
1. Bills and deposits	34	33	32	46	30	32	56
Cash and transferable deposits	6	32	10	20	7	15	50
Other deposits	24		21	28	24	20	7
Money market paper, etc.	4	1	1	—2	—1	—3	—1
2. Loans	34	25	34	41	35	40	36
Short-term loans	15	12	34	20	9[b]	1	23
Long-term loans	18	13		21	26	39[c]	13
3. Securities	14	18	10	9	13	7	2
Bonds	11	17	7	5	10	4	—
Shares	3	1	3	4	3	3	2
4. Life funds: equity on life assurance and pension funds	7	8	3	1	4	12	6
5. Other	11	16	21	3	18	9	—
Gold and foreign exchange	—	—	1	—	5	—	—
Trade credit	4	10	12	2	—	2	—
Other instruments	7	6	8[d]	1	13[e]	7	—
6. Total all instruments	100	100	100	100	100	100	100
Amount (b.)	$375.3	$37.4	¥78,883	Fr.462.3	DM.293.5	Fl.66.3	£38.4

[a] Figures for these countries include transactions within groups. Hence, for example, figures for trade credit are on a gross rather than a mainly net basis. Comparisons are correspondingly distorted (see text and Table 7.8).
[b] Bank loans up to one-year term only.
[c] Includes debt certificates which are really part mortgages, part securities.
[d] Includes most instruments arising from transactions with overseas residents.
[e] Includes some dealings within group.

Table 7.8.   Financial instruments in the formal system[a]

1972	USA	Canada	Japan	France	Germany	Nether-lands	UK
% of new borrowing during year in the form of:							
1. Bills and deposits	38	39	40	48	36	35	56
Cash and transferable deposits	7	38	13	21	8	16	50
Other deposits	27		26	29	29	22	7
Money market paper etc.	4	1	1	—2	—1	—3	—1
2. Loans	38	30	43	42	43	44	36
Short-term loans	17	14	43	20	11	1	23
Long-term loans	21	16		22	32	43	13
3. Securities	16	21	13	9	16	8	2
Bonds	13	20	9	5	12	5	—
Shares	3	1	4	4	4	3	2
4. Life funds: equity on life assurance and pension funds	8	10	4	1	5	13	6
5. Total of above[b]	100	100	100	100	100	100	100

[a] See notes to Table 7.7.
[b] Equals total in Table 7.7 less all 'other' instruments (group 5 in Table 7.7).

financial instruments used to perform borrowing and lending transactions. The role of various instruments in total borrowing and
lending in 1972 is shown in Table 7.7. The instruments are grouped
under the five main headings used earlier. Broadly speaking, transactions in groups 1, 2 and 4, that is bills and deposits, loans and life
funds, largely involve financial institutions, while many dealings in
group 3 go through a formal financial market. In contrast, the
instruments in the other group, 5, are those in which dealings take
place largely outside the formal financial system. Thus the figures
should, in principle, provide some indication of the role played by the
formal system of markets and institutions in the total of financial
dealings.

However, this approach has its own problems. The comparison
between countries is here greatly influenced by the difference in both
the degree of consolidation of dealings within the groups, and the
coverage given to such items as trade credit and dealings between
unincorporated businesses and their owners; for example, included

under the final 'other instruments' in the United States figures are significant changes in the net investment of proprietors' capital in their own businesses. In general terms, Canadian and Japanese data, being non-consolidated, give substantial coverage of dealings in group 5, while, as has already been seen, UK figures give very little on this. Thus it is impossible, in practice, to use the figures to show the role of the formal financial system. One can do no more than speculate whether full information on trade credit and other loans in the UK would show these instruments to be as important as in Japan or Canada.

To provide a better basis for comparison, Table 7.8 shows the shares for instruments in groups 1 to 4 in Table 7.7, recalculated on a total that excludes new borrowing in group 5; it thus concentrates on the formal financial system where transactions are generally identified to a similar degree. This analysis confirms the importance of banking-type transactions in the UK market. Even allowing for the effects of varying coverage, the shares of short-term deposits and loans in the UK total are unusually high. The role of securities in total borrowing was also notably low for the UK in 1972, though in 1971, a year of substantial net borrowing by the government, security issues were much more important. Abroad, time deposits and longer-term loans appear generally to be more important as channels for new borrowing and lending while life funds are, as has already been seen, of particular significance in the Netherlands.

7.4 WHO USES WHICH CHANNEL?

The final stage in this limited comparison between financial systems in the UK and other countries concerns how the various channels for borrowing and lending are used; who is allowing their transactions to flow through which channel? To some degree this also shows who is in fact dealing with whom, especially where one party is a financial institution borrowing or lending through instruments specific to the institution. But, because of the lack of detail in the classification of instruments, it is not possible to identify the full flow of funds through the system. In what follows, the sources and uses of funds employed by each of the main groups are presented with borrowing and lending broken down into the five main groups of instruments. The accompanying comments are based on the more detailed breakdown of instruments used in Table 7.7, p. 176.

To tie in with the previous section, the figures for financial companies are shown, first, in Tables 7.9 and 7.10. The main form of new funds employed by the banks is of course deposits; but loans, mainly from the government, are significant in Japan, while both there, and

Table 7.9. Banks: sources and uses of funds

1972	USA	Canada[b]	Japan[c]	Germany	Netherlands	UK
			Percentage share. Each item represents in group's sources and uses of funds in			
Sources of funds[a]						
Savings	5	5	—[c]	6	2	2
Bills and deposits	77	85	78	61	90	95
Loans	4	—	15	—	3	—
Securities	2	6	10	20	1	—
Life funds	—	—	—	—	—	—
Other instruments	11	4	—3	13	4	3
	100	100	100	100	100	100
Uses of funds[a]						
Investment	3	1	—[c]	2	—	—
Bills and deposits	5	8	3	—1	33	56
Loans	68	66	80	68	62	51
Securities	16	6	11	6	5	—6
Life funds	—	—	—	—	—	—
Other instruments	8	19[b]	6	25	—	—
	100	100	100	100	100	100

[a] Including transfers.
[b] Consumer credit is classified under other instruments.
[c] Saving and investment by banks are assumed to be nil.

even more in Germany, security issues have been a notable source of new funds in recent years. The major use of banks' funds is for loans, though in the UK deposits primarily with overseas financial institutions are particularly important. In the United States and Japan banks also purchased a substantial amount of securities in contrast to the sales by UK banks in 1972. The large 'other' uses for Germany relate to the foreign exchange holdings of the Bundesbank, while in Canada consumer credit granted by the banks is classified under 'other instruments'.

The pattern of sources of funds for other financial institutions reflects the varying importance of the different types of organization within this group, already examined in Table 7.7 and 7.8, pp. 176/7. The UK institutions are unusual in having an important part of their new borrowing in the form of loans, mainly from banks, which is

Table 7.10.   Other financial institutions: sources and uses of funds

1972	USA	Canada	Japan[b]	Germany	Netherlands	UK
Sources of funds[a]						
Savings	5	4	—[b]	7	10	8
Bills and deposits	44	2	66	30	18	36
Loans	7	9	6	2	3	16
Securities	12	—4	3	1	—	6
Life funds	22	53	11	49	68	34
Other instruments	11	36	14	11	1	—
	100	100	100	100	100	100
Uses of funds[a]						
Investment	2	3	—[b]	8	1	10
Bills and deposits	3	15	8	16	—	14
Loans	58	29	74	58	83	39
Securities	32	50	21	18	14	35
Life funds	—	—	—	—	—	—
Other instruments	6	3	—3	—	2	2
	100	100	100	100	100	100

Percentage share. Each item represents in group's sources and uses of funds in

[a] Including transfers.
[b] Saving and investment by OFIs are assumed to be nil.

paralleled by their increased holdings of deposits. Abroad, deposits predominate as a source of funds in the United States and Japan, while life funds are of much greater significance in the Netherlands and Canada; OECD classifies Canadian savings banks and trust companies as monetary institutions, leaving insurance companies and pensions funds as the main other financial groups. The 'other' sources are also important in the Canadian figures and these mainly comprise increased investment by associated companies; in Japan, most transactions with the overseas group are included under this heading.

Loans formed the main use of funds in 1972 for OFIs in all countries except Canada, where purchases of securities were larger. The latter were also important in the UK and the United States, reflecting the size of the insurance companies and pension funds. In the Netherlands, where pension funds are particularly important, a large part of new saving through funds was channelled into debt certificates, which are here classified as loans.

The figures for the sources and uses of funds for persons, given in Table 7.11, reflect the fact that neither bills and deposits, nor securities nor funds can form a source of funds to the group by OECD definitions. Loans are thus the main form of borrowing and are particularly important in the UK and Canada. In both Canada and Japan other sources are also a significant factor; these represent transactions in trade credit and dealings with associates. But for all countries except the UK, savings and transfers accounted for over half the total of new funds involved in capital transactions by persons in 1972.

Direct investment in physical assets formed around one-third to

Table 7.11. Persons: sources and uses of funds

1972	USA	Canada	Japan	Germany[c]	Netherlands[b]	UK
			Percentage share. Each item represents in group's sources and uses of funds in			
Sources of funds[a]						
Savings	74	57	55	69	n/a	45
Bills and deposits	—	—	—	—	n/a	—
Loans	24	41	20	30	n/a	53
Securities	—	—	—	—	n/a	—
Life funds	—	—	—	—	n/a	—
Other instruments	2	2	25	1	n/a	2
	100	100	100	100	—	100
Uses of funds[a]						
Investment	57	31	32	46	n/a	33
Bills and deposits	36	44	56	38	n/a	51
Loans	—1	—	—	—	n/a	4
Securities	—	—5	4	8	n/a	—13
Life funds	11	19	8	8	n/a	26
Other instruments	—7	11	—	—	n/a	—
	100	100	100	100	—	100

[a] Including transfers.
[b] No split is available between persons and companies.
[c] Includes all housing transactions some of which are actually carried out by other groups.

Table 7.12.   Industrial and commercial companies: sources and uses of funds

1972	USA	Canada	Japan	Germany	Netherlands[b]	UK
			Percentage share. Each item represents in group's sources and uses of funds in			
Sources of funds[a]						
Savings	56	59	34	58	n/a	46
Bills and deposits	—	—2	—	—	n/a	2
Loans	26	12	42	32	n/a	42
Securities	12	12	4	4	n/a	8
Life funds	—	—	—	—	n/a	—
Other instruments	5	19	20	6	n/a	12
	100	100	100	100	—	100
Use of funds[a]						
Investment	74	79	39	79	n/a	39
Bills and deposits	2	3	21	17	n/a	30
Loans	2	1	—	—	n/a	11
Securities	—	2	2	1	n/a	6
Life funds	—	—	—	—	n/a	—
Other instruments	22	15	38	3	n/a	15
	100	100	100	100	—	100

[a] Including transfers.
[b] No split is available between persons and companies.

one-half of personal uses of funds, with the United States figure being notably high. Deposits with banks and other financial institutions are normally the main form of personal lending, with the acquisition of life assurance and pension fund rights an important outlet in the UK and Canada; although precise figures are not available, this is also the case in the Netherlands. Private individuals in the UK are unique in being major sellers of securities, a situation that, as was seen above, has persisted for a long period; but persons have been net sellers of ordinary shares in both the United States and Canada in recent years.

Although companies can of course issue securities to provide themselves with a new source of funds, in none of the countries studied has this source been of major importance recently. Table 7.12 shows that, in 1972, security issues were most significant in the United States and Canada, but even there loans, mainly from banks, have been of greater weight. This is particularly so in the UK, where such loans form the only major type of borrowing identified; as usual in the

Canadian and Japanese figures, 'other' transactions in trade credit and the like are also important. UK companies' borrowing from the banks has been accompanied by increased holdings of deposits to a far greater extent than elsewhere. In addition, company purchases of securities are higher in the UK, as are loans made by them, which include both new local authority mortgages and direct investment overseas by UK companies. In most other countries, trade credit and loans to associates form the only major use of company funds other than direct investment.

Presentation of government sources and uses of funds is complicated by the inclusion of transactions between the main groups within government (Table 7.13). This accounts, in part, for the importance of loans as both a source and a use of funds, particularly in the case of the UK, Netherlands and Japan, where there are substantial intra-government transactions. It also shows up in the figures

Table 7.13.   Government: sources and uses of funds[b]

1972	USA[c]	Canada	Japan	Germany	Netherlands	UK
	Percentage share. Each item represents in group's sources and uses of funds in					
Sources of funds[a]						
Savings	—64[c]	37	37	72	59	55
Bills and deposits	66	4	19	—	—8	—3
Loans	1	3	10	18	38	50
Securities	75	46	20	7	6	—6
Life funds	15	—	3	—	—	—
Other instruments	5	10	11	3	5	4
	100	100	100	100	100	100
Uses of funds[a]						
Investment	—[c]	47	48	74	56	77
Bills and deposits	5	9	6	9	14	—8
Loans	12	6	16	—	37	29
Securities	—	15	7	3	—	—
Life funds	—	—	—	—	—	—
Other instruments	43	23	23	14	3	2
	100	100	100	100	100	100

[a] Including transfers.
[b] For all countries, the figures include some transactions between major government groups, mainly those between central and local government and social security funds.
[c] All spending by US government is classified as current expenditure.

Table 7.14.   Overseas: sources and uses of funds

1972	USA	Canada[c]	Japan[b]	Germany	Netherlands	UK
	Percentage share. Each item represents in group's sources and uses of funds in					
Sources of funds[a]						
Savings	52	76	—	4	3	—
Bills and deposits	4	7	—	—	49	83
Loans	24	44	—	6	15	10
Securities	4	—	—	—9	15	2
Life funds	—	—	—	—	—	—
Other instruments	17	—27[c]	100[b]	99	18	6
	100	100	100	100	100	100
Uses of funds[a]						
Investment	—	24	61	5	29	—
Bills and deposits	56	—8	—	10	35	87
Loans	6	22	—	—	2	13
Securities	35	139	6	55	5	—2
Life funds	—	—	—	—	—	—
Other instruments	4	—77[c]	32[b]	30	30	2
	100	100	100	100	100	100

[a] Including transfers.
[b] Nearly all foreign transactions are included under 'other instruments'.
[c] Transactions in foreign investments (other than currency) are included under 'other instruments'.

for Japan and Canada, where government financial institutions and social security funds respectively are major buyers of government securities. Securities were particularly important as a source of funds to the US government in 1972, whereas in the UK debt was being repaid; as has been mentioned, the situation in the UK was very different in 1971 with the government a major borrower, but Fig. 3.3, p. 76, shows that this has only infrequently been the case. Bank deposits represent an unusually high proportion of government uses of funds in Germany. The large 'other' uses of funds for both the United States and Japan reflect unidentified transactions of various kinds.

The transactions of the overseas group are summarized in Table 7.14. The great importance of two-way dealings in bills and deposits in the UK is immediately evident. The same situation exists, but on a lesser scale, in Canada and the Netherlands. Purchases of securities were an important outlet for foreign funds in the United States in 1972 and were significant in Canada and Germany. In contrast, in the

UK; there were small net sales of securities, and in Japan the sales were much larger; the latter represent a reversal of some of the substantial purchases in earlier years. For Germany the major 'other' items are foreign exchange holdings and export credits, while for the Netherlands direct investment transactions are included here. In the case of Japan, all transactions of the overseas group, apart from those in securities, are classified as 'other'.

7.5 HOW DOES THE UK DIFFER?

To summarize, the above analysis suggests that the financial system as a whole plays a larger part in the UK than it does in the other countries examined. Borrowing and lending activities are in total greater in relation to economic magnitudes, and the role of overseas dealings, particularly those with foreign financial institutions, is unusually important. In addition, UK persons and companies seem to do more borrowing and lending than is usually the case elsewhere, but companies are net borrowers to a much lesser extent than in most other countries. The government plays a relatively minor role in the UK financial markets.

Among the formal institutions and markets, the extent of bank activity in the UK is unusually high; this would be even more evident if intra-bank transactions were included in the figures. As a result, the role of the deposit and loan markets is generally more important here than abroad, while the securities market has in recent years been a much less significant channel for new borrowing and lending than in most other countries. The latter situation ties in, of course, with the lower net borrowing by companies, and the fact that the UK government has had only intermittent recourse to the securities market.

It appears that the UK market is also unique in the extent of the two-way transactions that take place between financial institutions and individual other groups. The circuit between banks and the overseas group is notable here; so also are the transactions in the UK between banks and companies in 1972 and 1973. In general, institutions abroad seem to be more involved in channelling funds from persons to other groups, especially companies, than is the case in the UK. Again this links up with, but is in no sense necessarily the cause of, the low level of net borrowing by companies. Naturally, there are some overseas institutions dealing primarily with one sector; savings and loan associations in the United States are an obvious example. But in the terms of Fig. 6.1, pp. 150/1, the general pattern of flows seems to have more of a downward, and right-hand, drift than in the UK. In addition, UK financial institutions appear to play a more important role in the system as net borrowers and lenders than do institutions elsewhere.

8. What determines financial structure

8.1 THE KEY INFLUENCES

The structure of the financial system can vary greatly from country to country and from time to time. The UK financial system differs in a number of important respects from that of other developed countries. It has also changed quite markedly over the last decade. Why is this the case? What determines the financial structure we have and the way it has developed?

The straightforward answer is that financial structure is determined by the nature of the financial transactions that the people and organizations in the country undertake. Financial instruments, markets and institutions exist in the form that they do because people and organizations choose to make a certain amount of financial dispositions and to do so in a particular way. Both the extent to which money is used for current and capital spending and the degree to which borrowing and lending take place are important. Above all, the character of the financial system will be influenced by how far both deficit and surplus units exist within the country, by whether there are many or few people with income over and above their current requirements, and by how far there are others with opportunities to spend that exceed their available resources.

However, this does not really explain why the UK, or any other, financial structure is as it is. It simply pushes the question one stage back. What then determines the nature of the financial transactions that people make? What persuades people to use their surplus funds for lending rather than for buying more goods and services or investing in physical assets? Why do some people choose to borrow to supplement their spending power while others do not? And what determines the particular borrowing and lending channels that are used?

Four types of influence are important here. First, there is the group of factors that determine fundamental attitudes to saving and investment, borrowing and lending; these include things such as individuals' standard of living and their view of risk-taking and provision for the future. A second set of influences derives from the economic and social structure that the financial system serves, the characteristics of those people or groups that are in surplus or deficit, the type of business organization that exists, the role of government

and the like. The nature of the social and economic policies prom-
ulgated by the government forms a third influence. Finally financial
structure will be determined to some degree by what has happened in
the past, the heritage of institutions, markets and financial habits that
influence the way people behave today. This is particularly the case if
the structure contains within itself rigidities of any kind that inhibit
the system from adapting to changing circumstances.

Each of these groups of influences is discussed in general terms
below. An attempt is also made to see how far they help to explain the
special features of the UK financial system.

8.2 THE NEED FOR SPARE INCOME

The most fundamental factor affecting decisions about borrowing
and lending is the basic economic situation or standard of living of
the individual person or organization. The key question is, is there
any income to spare over and above that required for day-to-day
survival? Without this surplus income, financial choice does not exist,
lending is clearly not possible, and some spare income either now or
in the future is a prerequisite for borrowing. To induce a potential
lender to part with his money, the borrower must be able to show at
least the possibility of repayment, and he will usually have to offer
some additional attraction in the form of interest or dividends paid
on the amount borrowed. For it is a basic characteristic of most
people that they require the prospect of more money in the future in
order to persuade them to give up the use of money now. Some of the
reasons for this are discussed below. But interest payments are a
fundamental fact of financial life.

The way in which the existence of spare income influences financial
structure becomes very obvious if one thinks of a subsistence-level
society. In this situation, most people have not got adequate funds
even to feed and clothe themselves properly, while the small businesses that exist have difficulty in maintaining their present equipment in working order. Apart from the exchange of money for goods,
the only form of financial transaction that is likely to be at all
common is straight money-lending, where borrowing is secured on
some non-perishable item already owned by the borrower. Even this
presupposes that the borrower both had and will have some spare
income; the item had to be purchased in the first place, and the
money-lender's charges must subsequently be paid. And the money-
lender himself must have a source of funds.

Very similar limitations on borrowing and lending can exist even
within our own affluent society. A particular example is the financing
of new business ventures. In many cases such ventures appear

sufficiently uncertain in their outcome to make potential lenders doubt whether the business will in fact have sufficient spare income to meet interest and repayment requirements. Hence, even with relatively promising ventures, few people are prepared to lend money on the security of future income alone, as is frequently done with loans to established companies or private individuals. Instead, lenders require some form of existing wealth, like a mortgage on the proprietor's house, as security in order to persuade them to part with their funds.

When people's standards of living rise, the potential for borrowing and lending increases. But the nature of the financial system that develops depends critically on exactly how this potential is exercised. As was mentioned in Chapter 1, the existence of surplus income does not in fact mean that this will be used for lending. The holder of the income may choose to acquire physical assets instead, or he may even decide not to accumulate wealth at all, but to enhance his current purchases of goods and services. Much will depend on how much surplus income he has and what he had in the past. In addition, the extent of borrowing will depend on the nature of the opportunities that exist to secure future income to service the borrowings. Either it must be possible for borrowers to invest the money in capital assets in a productive manner in order to obtain future surplus income, or they must be able in some other way to ensure that they can meet their future commitments; for example, the government can do this through its revenue raising powers.

Essentially both potential lenders and potential borrowers are faced with two decisions. First, how are they going to allocate their present and future income between current spending and the accumulation of wealth; more generally, how do they rate consumption now compared with that in the future? Secondly, in so far as they choose to accumulate either wealth or its converse in the form of liabilities, in what way will they do this? In particular, will those with surplus income choose to hold physical or financial assets?

As we have seen, in a subsistence level economy neither of these choices exists. The extent of surplus income both now and in the future will clearly have a key influence on how these decisions are taken. But even where holdings of surplus income are broadly similar and comparable opportunities exist for obtaining future income, financial behaviour may differ. For the way that financial choice is exercised will be determined also by people's attitudes to taking risks and their views about providing for the future.

8.3 THE UNCERTAIN FUTURE

The questions of risk and provision for the future are integrally linked. Risk enters into financial choice because borrowing and lending, saving and investing involve the exchange of money in the future with money in the present. Whatever the terms of the financial contract, or the nature of the physical assets purchased, there must be uncertainty about what will happen in the future, whether the loan will be repaid, whether the house or the security will reach the value hoped for, or what amount of goods and services money will buy in the future. It is this uncertainty that leads most people to demand an additional return in the form of interest if they are to give up consumption now for consumption in the future; this is over and above any extra money required to compensate them for any expected rise in price of goods and services over the period. And the greater the uncertainty about the future, the higher the return normally demanded.

Both individuals and the organizations that they set up and run differ in their views about uncertainty in the future. In part, these differences can be seen as the result of fairly objective factors. A married man with several children and little accumulated wealth obviously needs to take more thought about his future finances than does a young wealthy bachelor. He is likely to be more cautious about taking risks, though he has equally greater need to provide for future uncertainties. Similarly, a company with a strong bank balance, limited capital equipment and diversified markets needs worry less about the future for any given product than the specialist company that is already heavily in debt. Given the power to tax, most governments need have little concern about their ability to service borrowings in the future; unless, that is, their behaviour in the financial markets conflicts with other policy objectives (see below).

But superimposed on these objective needs to provide for the future are individual attitudes to taking risks. How far do people mind the possibility of finding themselves, or their company, in financial straits? How do they view the chance of possibly making a large sum of money in the future? Do they want to feel secure, to know that virtually whatever happens their way of life will not be disrupted, or do they enjoy 'taking risks', rating the pleasurable anticipation of a gain above the fear of a loss? Are those in charge of a company cautious people who like to feel the future cash position is secure, or are they more inclined to 'have a go' at backing a new idea?

How people view risk-taking is essentially a matter of personal and social psychology. Although uncertainty is a permanent part of our lives, and a certain amount of it can be a stimulus to creative activity, in financial choice most people behave generally as though they were averse to risk. That is, if asked to choose between a given sum of money for sure or an equal chance of a larger or a smaller amount, they will plump for the certain option. And a large number of people are prepared to pay out a small certain amount, in terms of an insurance premium, in order to make sure that they do not incur possible large losses. Not all financial transactions show this risk-averse character; when gambling or buying premium bonds, people behave as though they were positively seeking risk. But, in most cases they do this only when the sum staked is small in relation to their total resources, while the potential gain could be large.

Objective needs for the future and underlying attitudes to risk-taking combine to influence how an individual or organization distributes surplus income and which of the potential borrowing opportunities is taken up. They determine both the extra return wanted for bearing the risk arising from uncertainty about the future and the type of financial instrument used for borrowing and lending. The man who has heavy future commitments will probably aim to accumulate some wealth through saving the part of his income surplus to current requirements. If he is highly risk-averse, he is likely to look for a home for his savings that is relatively safe (at least in money terms), such as an assurance policy or a bank or building society deposit; he will probably be very reluctant to put his money into a small business or a speculative property venture, or to borrow heavily, except perhaps to acquire a house. But if risk is less of a worry to him he may be prepared to let the future look after itself to some degree and to spend some of his potential savings making life more pleasant now; he may even borrow to this end. What he saves may be lent out in relatively risky forms, which offer potentially higher returns, like the purchase of securities or deposits with lesser-known financial institutions.

Similar contrasts in behaviour can be readily seen among companies and even between governments. In all cases the person, or organization, is adjusting his financial transactions in the light of his basic financial position and his view of the future and of risk-taking. In doing so, the individual has normally to take the financial system as given. There is an existing set of financial institutions and markets and a selection of financial instruments and physical goods, each with certain risk characteristics and particular returns. The individual chooses, from what is available, the portfolio of assets and liabilities that best suits his requirements.

In making this choice, the individual or organization may try to follow what is regarded as financially rational behaviour; that is, he will carry out those financial transactions that maximize his expected financial return for the level of risk that he considers to be acceptable. Or he may simply lend or borrow to an extent required to bring him into what he considers to be in some way a satisfactory position. The two approaches need not necessarily produce the same answer in terms of financial transactions. And choice may be constrained for a number of reasons to be discussed below. But paradoxically, though most of us individually have to take the financial system as given, the nature of the system is moulded by the combined choices of individual people and organizations. However, as will be seen, some groups can have a greater influence in the process than others.

8.4 THE NATURE OF DEVELOPMENT

The characteristics of financial choice described above determine the fundamental nature of the financial system. They explain why lenders receive and borrowers pay interest, this extra return being in part related to the uncertainty associated with the transaction as well as to expected changes in the overall level of prices. The fact that all financial systems, from primitive to highly developed, are of this general form suggests that preference for money today rather than in the future and aversion to risk are fundamental human characteristics. But since financial systems differ greatly in other respects, in terms of both the structure of markets and institutions and the levels of interest rates, it is evident that the way in which financial choices create a financial system is influenced by other factors as well.

The most significant of these relate to the basic make-up of the country that the financial system serves. One aspect is the level of economic development which affects financial structure in two ways. It influences first the extent of surplus income or potential saving that is available in the country, and secondly the nature of the opportunities that exist for productive investment, that is capital spending that will produce surplus income in the future. The two effects are of course closely interrelated; there will normally be little surplus income unless productive investment is possible, either at home or abroad, while capital spending cannot take place unless some surplus income is turned into actual saving.

More saving and greater investment opportunities in principle encourage the development of the financial system. But the nature of the system will be greatly affected by the way the savings are distributed between the people and organizations in the country, and the characteristics of the investment opportunities. Some examples will help to clarify the effects.

If saving is concentrated in the hands of a few rich people, and if these people also undertake most of the capital spending, then there will be limited need for a financial system. And since rich people are better placed to take risks, channelling of funds may well be directly in the form of securities issued by the investors rather than via the risk-absorbing medium of a financial institution. However, as surplus income develops in the hands of a wider range of people, they are unlikely all to be able to undertake direct investment projects themselves. Instead, they will wish to keep their savings in more secure forms, and if potential borrowers are to tap these funds, they must offer a suitable type of financial instrument. Some of the less risk-averse lenders may be prepared to hold securities given suitable inducements; others are likely to seek much safer outlets, at which stage a role for the financial intermediary develops.

Thus the spread of savings from the few to the many is an important stimulus to the development of financial institutions and the introduction of new types of financial instruments. But much will depend on the precise nature of the investment opportunities that exist in a country. Scale is particularly important here. So long as productive investment can be made in small amounts, as in farming or with business based on simple technology, direct investment by savers is still possible. And direct lending to potential investors is probably less risky, since the borrowers are likely to be friends or relatives whose abilities are known and whose businesses can be easily observed and understood. But if large-scale investment is involved, it will be well beyond the limits of most individual lenders, both in amounts of money and apparent risk. Hence some form of intermediating body is required.

8.5 HOW THE COUNTRY IS ORGANIZED

The types of institutions and markets that grow up within the financial system also depend on the nature of the organizations that exist elsewhere within the country. The way in which people choose to organize themselves into groups for the purpose of carrying out various activities has an important effect on borrowing and lending transactions. Three types of organization are involved here: the basic forms of social organization—families, households and the like; the type of business organization adopted; the role played by the group of organizations collectively known as government.

The nature of social organization is important because of the effect it has on an individual's objective need to provide for the future. The existence of family responsibilities in principle involves more concern for the future. But where there is some kind of extended family structure, the need to provide financially for sickness or old age is lessened; it is replaced by a need to ensure a family group of sufficient size. It is interesting to speculate which way round causation works; whether it is the increased affluence that enables better financial provisions to be made that causes the breakdown of extended family arrangements or vice versa, or whether both are influenced by other common factors. Either way, the nature of borrowing and lending that occurs will change with social organization.

Similarly, the form of business organization that exists affects the character of financial transactions. It is also closely linked to the question of the scale of investment opportunities discussed above. The small business, owned and run by one person, tends to be limited in its borrowing capacity. As has been seen, lenders may be reluctant to put up money without extra security while the proprietor will be constrained by his need to take on personally all the risks of the business, including the liability to repay and service any borrowings. Hence, the business will be able to invest only on a small scale.

The wish to create larger enterprises, with greater continuity, has led to the development of other forms of business enterprise, notably the joint stock company. Here the organization is separate from the person who owns and finances it. The owners' liabilities are usually limited to their original investment, and instead of holding physical assets directly they have a financial instrument that is both marketable and offers a return for risk-taking. This has enabled a far larger amount of borrowing to be undertaken, so facilitating large-scale capital spending. It has also made its mark on the financial system, through the associated growth of securities markets and of specialized investing institutions.

The character of both social and business organization helps to explain many of the differences that exist between the financial structures of developed and undeveloped countries. Naturally, the types of organization are themselves closely linked with the level of economic development, and the above analysis illustrates something of the role that the financial system plays in the process of economic development. However, when comparing the UK with other developed countries, few broad differences in structure of this kind persist. A more important aspect in this context, and a significant factor in all situations, is the role played in economic and social life by the government.

Government activities can of course vary greatly, all the way from simply providing a limited number of essential common services like defence and the law to complete control of the provision of all types of goods and services, as in the communist countries. The authorities can also act as a major source of income in the form of welfare and pension payments and the like. In the UK, the government plays a major role in both spending and income redistribution. From the point of view of the financial system, both the size of government activities and how far these are financed through the tax system are important.

In a certain sense, the tax system represents an alternative to the financial system. Not for nothing do the economists describe taxation as 'forced savings'. The government has in principle two ways of obtaining the money it requires. It can borrow from savers, who voluntarily choose to use their money to buy instruments issued by the authorities either directly or indirectly through financial institutions, or it can forcibly extract the money needed by taxing the private sector, thus effectively reducing the latter's ability to save. The more the government chooses to finance itself by borrowing, and the greater its total need for finance, the more it will be encouraging the development of the financial system.

In practice, the government's choice is constrained in a number of ways. Its ability to use the tax system will be influenced by the private sector's willingness to bear the tax burdens, which can be at variance with their apparent wish for government spending in different forms. And the power to borrow will depend on how far lenders are prepared to hold government instruments of various kinds on the terms that the government issues them. This has been a real practical problem in the UK in recent years, and the analysis in the previous chapter suggests that the UK government relies to an exceptional extent on taxation rather than borrowing as a source of revenue. The government's behaviour has also been influenced by the requirements of economic management, which are discussed further in the next section.

A final aspect of economic and social organization that can influence financial structure concerns the extent to which dealings of various kinds take place with persons and organizations overseas. For, while financial transactions overseas may develop independently of other links, they will be much encouraged if the latter are also important.

In part this is a question of the nature of economic development. For example, the economic growth of the UK was historically closely associated with an expansion in international trade and investment. This was in turn fostered by the political and social links maintained with British territories overseas. Along with these links there grew an important set of financial flows, with institutions like the merchant banks specializing in facilitating trade credit and the organization of international securities issues.

This also illustrates how economic structure in the past can influence the current financial set up. For, while the underlying political and trading links between the UK and the old British Empire have been loosened, much of the accompanying financial structure has been retained. And because many UK financial institutions retained their international links, they were in a position to play a major role in the re-expansion of international money and issue markets that has taken place in the last fifteen years or so.

8.6 THE EFFECTS OF ECONOMIC MANAGEMENT

The general influence of the role of the government on financial structure has already been considered. But there are two additional ways in which the government affects the financial system. These are, first, through action designed to control the way in which the economy behaves, and, secondly, as a result of measures aimed at furthering other official policies, which may sometimes be indirectly linked with questions of economic management. Both appear to be of considerable importance in the UK context.

Most governments today accept a responsibility for the overall management of the economy, the conventional aim being to try to secure economic growth, stable prices, high employment and a balanced overseas payments position, or some acceptable compromise between these often conflicting goals. There are three main groups of measures available for this purpose; fiscal policy, which covers manipulation of tax rates and the level of government expenditure, thus influencing the Budget surplus or deficit; monetary policy, which includes all action affecting the supply of money in the economy and the general availability of credit; and direct controls of various kinds, of which the most important in recent years has been prices and incomes policy. All three types of measures have been extensively used in the UK in the postwar period.

Since the rate of economic growth can influence both the availability of surplus income that could be lent and the attractiveness of the investment opportunities, which encourage borrowing, all types of economic management have some effect on financial behaviour. But it is the first two groups of measures, fiscal and monetary policy, that have the main impact on the structure of the financial system. Their operation is in practice closely interwoven. But to clarify matters their effects will each be considered separately to start with. The way they operate is described in relation to the UK only, though the general principles are similar in most developed countries.

In making use of monetary policy, the government has a very direct impact on the financial system. The basic aim is normally to increase or decrease the spending power in the economy by changing either the supply of money available (the notes and coin and bank deposits that are outstanding in the hands of the public) or the price at which money can be obtained (the level of interest rates). One method, often used in the past, is to enlarge the amount of money available simply by printing more notes. Historically, this was done in order to finance increased government spending rather than to expand money per se, and the government got the new notes into circulation by spending them itself. Today the approach is rather more sophisticated. The government aims to alter the monetary base of the financial system by adjusting its own borrowing, especially that in short-term forms like treasury bills, or by making use of such instruments as the 'special deposits' of the banks with the Bank of England. Because of the way the system functions, this will normally lead to changes in the amount of bank deposits outstanding and the availability of borrowing facilities of various kinds. Assuming people's wishes to hold or borrow money do not change in corresponding fashion, interest rates and spending plans will be affected.

What the government, through the agency of the Bank of England, is doing is to change the availability of the assets like treasury bills that the banks are required to hold as part of their reserves. If banks are close to the official minimum reserve that must be held, any reduction in the total amount of reserve assets limits the extent to which banks can hold deposits and so lend. An increase in the amount of 'special deposits' that must be held has a similar effect. Equally, an increase in the availability of reserve assets makes it easier for banks to increase their deposits and lending. In the 1950s and 1960s the impact of such changes was primarily on the deposit banks, since these were the only group operating to a formal 'liquid' reserve, initially 30% of deposits but reduced to 28% in 1963. Since 1971, all banks have been required to keep a minimum reserve ratio of $12\frac{1}{2}\%$ of their 'eligible liabilities', exclusive of any special deposits.[69]

The effects of these changes spill over to other financial institutions. For while the initial effect of an increase in money supply is a rise in bank deposits and lending, this will in due course stimulate an increase in borrowing and lending of other kinds. Bank interest rates will tend to fall and other financial institutions will hope to enlarge their own business by attracting away some of the new bank deposits. By offering higher interest rates than the banks, they will encourage the holders of bank deposits to exchange them for, say, building society deposits or life assurance premiums; the newly created money will then be in the hands of the building society or insurance company, which can use this money to expand its lending. As the money moves from institution to institution, the speed with which it circulates increases and additional layers of intermediation are introduced into the financial structure. The process of expansion is, in principle, limited only by the way rising interest rates affect the ability of banks and others to continue to make profitable loans with the money for which they compete; ultimately this in turn depends on the willingness of people or organizations buying productive physical assets to increase their borrowing at the going rate of interest.

There is much dispute about the way in which monetary policy affects the behaviour of the economy; differing views are held about the mechanism by which changes in money supply flow through to incomes and spending, about the extent of any such effect and whether it results in changes in output or in the level of prices. It is not proposed to examine the, sometimes heated, arguments here.[64] What is of importance, for present purposes, is the way in which monetary policy affects the structure of the financial system. In general terms, an expansionary policy will directly encourage more borrowing and lending and a contractionary one, the reverse. The initial influence of changes in policy is evidently through the banking system, either stimulating or restricting the development of banks and the markets in which they are important, relative to other sections of the financial system. An example of this effect can be seen in the UK in the period 1971–73, where the very expansionary monetary policy followed during the period clearly helped to encourage the rapid expansion of the banking sector. Other factors were, however, also at work, notably a change in the competitive environment of the banks. The degree to which the initial shift to or from banking is subsequently offset depends on the extent of competition between the various parts of the system, including whether primary borrowers and lenders switch readily between alternative financial instruments in response to changes in interest rates.

In addition to operating on the reserve base of the financial system, monetary policy, or more precisely credit policy, can be effected by more direct means, notably by using direct controls over the lending by financial institutions. Such measures were much used in the UK during the 1950s and 1960s, owing to difficulties in ensuring that the banking system responded readily to reductions in the money base at a time when the authorities wished to reduce the availability of credit without causing an 'excessive' rise in interest rates. These problems arose because the banks held liquid assets in excess of the required minimum and also had holdings of other assets, notably government securities, that could be exchanged for loans to final borrowers. They could thus frustrate official policy by switching their holdings; the resulting changes in the distribution of bank assets were seen in Chapter 4.

The system of requiring the banks to make special deposits with the Bank of England was introduced in 1958, partly as a way of dealing with the problem of excess reserves without having recourse to direct controls over bank advances. However, ceilings continued to be imposed on bank lending throughout most of the 1960s; up to 1961 these applied to the main deposit banks only, but subsequently they were widened to include virtually the whole banking sector. And direct controls were imposed on hire purchase and other forms of instalment credit through manipulation of the terms under which such credit might be extended.

From the point of view of the structure of the UK financial system, the important feature of such direct controls is that they have operated on one part of the system only; those financial institutions not directly restricted were free to expand their business within the limitations imposed by control on the amount of reserve assets and the money supply. Assuming even a limited degree of competition within the financial system, one would expect this to lead to the growth of one set of institutions at the expense of the others. This was indeed the case with the banking sector in the UK, where restrictions on deposit bank lending helped merchant banks and others to expand their share of the business during the late 1950s and early 1960s. Once the controls were widened the effect was reduced, though discrimination still existed as a result of the reserve ratio to which the deposit banks had to adhere. But as the remaining banks were brought within the net of controls borrowers began to use yet other channels, leading to a revival in commercial bills and growth in leasing and second mortgage loans.

In theory at least, changes in fiscal policy have much less of an affect on financial structure, though they obviously influence the size of financial flows in any given period. Adjustment of tax rates or the level of government spending mean that persons or organizations have a different amount of income available to be saved or spent. As a result, they must adjust current purchases of goods and services, capital spending or savings, or all three to some extent; often the first adjustment is made through saving, changes in spending coming later. At the same time, the government's financial position has altered, and it has to borrow either more (if, say, taxes were reduced) or less (if its tax revenue has been increased or spending cut).

Given suitable adjustments in interest rates, the government can in principle borrow back any extra funds it needs from the increased saving of people who now have more income available; conversely, it can use higher revenue to repay borrowing. This does not nullify the effect of the policy changes on the economy, since these work through what is called the multiplier effect, the way in which increased spending by one group raises income in the hands of another which raises the latter's spending and so on. Changes in fiscal policy will produce fluctuations in the pattern of financial flows between the government and the rest of the economy, and an active fiscal policy requires that there be good established channels to facilitate government borrowing and lending. But, provided the borrowing does not involve changes in the monetary base, and so associated changes in monetary policy, financial structure will not otherwise by specially affected.

In practice, changes in fiscal policies are almost always accompanied by changes in monetary policy. This is often a matter of design, the two being intended to work in consort. It may also be forced on the government by problems of attracting sufficient finance from outside the banking system without raising interest rates to a level considered to be undesirable; in this situation, the government's only alternative is to borrow from the banks, which will lead to an expansion in money supply. In fact, problems of borrowing sufficient amounts at an acceptable level of interest rates have been a continuing factor in the UK government's policy in the postwar period, even in periods of fiscal restraint. This has sometimes led the authorities to expand the money base in periods when such action was contrary to the main aim of economic management. The use of direct controls over the availability of bank credit has been encouraged as a result.

8.7 OTHER OFFICIAL AIMS

Apart from questions of economic management, the government often influences financial behaviour in furtherance of other, usually longer-term, policies. Measures taken to redistribute income and wealth are important here; their effect can be seen in the changing pattern of personal financial transactions, notably the sale of security holdings. Modification of corporate structure, such as the introduction of workers' shareholdings on a substantial scale, would also have a significant effect.

Probably most important in the UK context to date have been the steps taken to encourage both saving and home ownership on a wider scale. The ways in which these have created 'privileged' circuits was discussed in Chapter 5. The tax advantages granted to certain types of lending, like life assurance or national savings, where a long-term contract is often involved, naturally encourage people to use their funds in this particular manner, and so stimulate the growth of the institutions concerned. Similarly, the desire to ensure the flow of funds into housing finance at a reasonable price has led to controls on other competing institutions. The UK is not alone in this type of action, since it was the wish to protect the savings and loan associations in the United States that led to the introduction of regulation 'Q', which was in turn an important stimulus to the growth of the Euro-currency market. The latter serves as a very good example of how government action can influence financial structure.

In furtherance of its economic or social aims, the government may itself choose to become involved in the financial system, setting up publicly owned financial institutions. This may be because private institutions of the kind wanted fail to develop as quickly as is thought desirable. In the UK, the private financial system was well established before the fashion for government intervention developed, so that the only government-owned institutions are those designed to encourage national savings like the National Savings Bank. But in other countries the government has stepped in to help create a financial system as a means of encouraging economic development. This has occurred both in less developed countries and at times of economic restructuring, for example, after major wars; the latter factor is responsible for the heavy involvement of the Japanese, French and Italian authorities in financial institutions, though interestingly it did not produce a comparable development in Germany.

More relevant to the UK today, the government may also be provoked to step in when it feels that, in some way, private financial institutions are not performing their functions properly. In this situation, the authorities have in fact three alternatives available: they can try to manipulate flows directly through tax changes and other types of control already discussed; they can set up special new institutions to channel funds in the way desired; or they can bring existing institutions more completely into public control and, by changing their objectives, try to alter the way in which funds flow through them. Throughout the postwar years, there has been a persistent call by left-wing politicians in the UK for more government intervention in the financial system; this has been directed particularly towards the nationalization of banks, building societies and parts of insurance. However, nationalization does not necessarily alter the way in which institutions function within the financial system, as the French experience bears witness. In practice, the UK government has to date placed more emphasis on manipulating the private system rather than getting directly involved itself. In addition to tax incentives and other controls already mentioned, it has encouraged the setting up or expansion of various specialized institutions; the boost given to Finance for Industry in 1974 is a case in point. It has also taken a variety of steps designed to protect the users of the financial system, through, for example, the various Companies Acts and special regulations relating to insurance business.

8.8 WHY HISTORY LIVES ON

The financial system of each country has its own particular historical heritage. It has a pattern of instruments, markets and institutions that have developed in response to financial needs over the years. But the structure of needs changes as the economy develops as forms of organizations alter, and in response to changes in government policy. In theory, the financial system should respond to these changes as they take place, and there is no fundamental reason why the shape of historical development need be a factor determining the financial structure that exists now. The evident continuity in financial institutions and markets can perfectly well be ascribed to the fact that financial needs change only gradually over time.

However, in practice historical influences can live on beyond their time. They can thus contribute to differences in the financial structure of individual countries. In part the effect is a cosmetic one, reflecting apparent rather than real differences. But for a variety of reasons, the historical influence can be a fundamental one as well.

Apparent differences between financial systems arise because, over the years, particular financial functions have been grouped in different ways. In one country certain types of borrowing and lending may be conducted by specialized institutions, and in another they may be part of a more general grouping. In the UK, discount houses perform a specialized role in the money market that is unparalleled anywhere else; in most other countries comparable functions are carried out by the banks. Similarly, UK merchant banks have had a specialized function in relation to corporate finance and investment advice that is frequently carried out by major groups abroad. In addition, essentially the same types of financial transactions may go under different names and comparable institutions may exist in disparate guises simply owing to the history of their development; the varying character of the housing finance institutions in different countries is an example of this.

The important point here is that the financial system can be providing basically the same services in all cases; it is just that they are organized in a different way in the various situations. If there are no special advantages or disadvantages in carrying out the particular activities in a certain grouping, the basic character of the financial systems is not altered.

One of the main problems in deciding whether historical development has in fact a significant influence on financial structure lies in trying to assess whether such advantages or disadvantages exist, whether grouping really matters. Do the merchant banks gain a real advantage from their specialized nature? Can they offer a better service than a broader-based banking group? Is the multi-purpose financial conglomerate more or less effective than more specialized institutions?

These questions would not arise if one could presume that the financial system operated in an ideal competitive world and was fully adjusted to people's current needs. In that situation all the effects of historical development would be apparent rather than real. It is because financial systems do not operate in this theoretically ideal world, do not adapt immediately to changing requirements, that the influence of history can be of real importance. Two main groups of factors impede such adjustments in practice. The first concerns the situation within the financial system itself, the second the attitudes and habits of those whom the system serves. The nature of each of these is summarized briefly here; they are examined in more detail in the next chapter.

Within the financial system, the factors inhibiting the adjustment process include the advantages gained from already operating in a particular field and the problems that a new entrant can face. These can be severe, even where, as in the UK, there are few formal limitations on new entry. In addition, agreements not to compete in particular ways, such as the cartel on bank interest rates that operated for so many years in the UK, alter the way in which the adjustment process takes place; the impact of the cartel on the deposit banks before and after its removal in 1971 has already been discussed.

Possibly even more important in the UK context is the subtle influence of habit, and the resulting antipathy to change within the financial system. For example, there is evidence that the Bank of England's wish to maintain the traditional demarcation lines between the UK financial institutions caused changes to be more gradual than would otherwise have been the case. Behind this policy undoubtedly lay a desire to preserve financial stability, though with hindsight it may be doubted whether the fears that change would be destabilizing were soundly based. Equally, agreements to limit competition in any way, like the bank cartel or the various agreements between insurance companies, tend to create attitudes in favour of preserving the *status quo*.

Comparable lags in the process of change arise from the way in which the financial choices of those outside the financial system are conditioned by past habits and patterns of behaviour. As discussed below, the choices made by individuals and organizations in the course of their financial transactions are not always strictly rational in a financial sense; people do not always provide themselves with the currently best portfolio of goods and services, assets and liabilities, maximizing return for a given level of risk. In part this may be because there are other aspects of financial transactions that are highly valued, like the pleasure of chatting with the bank manager or the insurance agent, the status of having a merchant bank or a stockbroker. But, more important, financial transactions may not be undertaken with the aim of attaining a best position in any sense. Financial decisions are often taken on a very *ad hoc* basis, influenced by what has been customary, what other people have done and so on. Obviously, if such behaviour is financially very disadvantageous, lessons are gradually learnt and habits changed. But once again, the process of adjustment of the financial system is slowed and the role of history in determining financial structure becomes more important.

There is strong reason to think that history has in fact played a particularly significant role in determining the structure of the UK financial system that exists today. In addition to the factors already mentioned, two other considerations are important. First, the UK has not suffered the kind of major reconstruction that occurred in continental Europe and Japan following wartime destruction, or in the United States after the 1929 crash. Secondly, the government has not so far chosen to intervene in a major way to mould the financial system in any particular pattern; as indicated, its actions have been largely confined to the incentives and the effects of monetary policy. Thus, the UK financial system has been relatively free to develop by a process of continuous evolution, the pace of adjustment to changing need being restrained by the various factors outlined above. How far this has produced the financial system best suited to the needs of the UK today is the subject of the final chapter.

9. An effective financial system

9.1 THE RIGHT BIT OF EQUIPMENT?

We have now seen how the UK financial system works, the way in which it differs from financial systems elsewhere and some of the factors that have made it the way it is. The final question that remains to be considered is, do we have the financial system we need? To return to the earlier analogy, we know what our bit of electrical equipment does, something about how it is made up and why the particular design has been adopted. We are also aware of the other models that are in existence. But is it the right piece of equipment for the job? Or could it in some way be improved?

This question is easy to ask, and extremely difficult to answer. It raises two kinds of problem. First, it is necessary to decide what the ideal financial system might consist of, to provide standards against which the actual system may be judged. An external measure is needed, for in a certain sense we always have the financial system we want, just as, in a democratic system, we get the government we deserve. The nature of the financial system is in practice determined by the combination of financial transactions that people choose to make. To question whether the system is entirely appropriate to current needs implies that, for some reason, the financial choices that people make are not those best suited to them. This may be because people are not fully aware of their true needs or because the way the system operates in some way constrains them from fulfilling these needs; or both may be the case. Either way, some separate indicator of 'true' needs is required.

A variety of needs that the financial system should be serving can be identified. There is, first, the basic economic requirement that resources should be used efficiently, that we should get the maximum benefit from what is available. From the point of view of the financial system, this implies two types of efficiency, the ability to channel resources from saver to investor in a manner likely to contribute best to efficiency elsewhere in the economy, and the use of a minimum amount of resources in the process of providing both this service and the associated payments facilities; these are known as allocating and operating efficiency respectively.

Few people would dispute, in principle, the need for economic efficiency, in the financial system as elsewhere. But on top of this requirement are superimposed various social needs that may at times conflict with the aim of economic efficiency narrowly defined. The most acceptable way of working is not always the most efficient, the socially responsible company is often not the most attractive short-term investment. Equally, there can be conflicts between different measures taken in furtherance of economic aims, and between economic efficiency in the short and the longer term. As has been seen, the operation of government policy can have an undesirable and distorting effect on the financial markets, while successful short-term speculation is not in all cases conducive to the best use of resources in the longer term.

It is thus difficult to obtain a clear unambiguous view of the standards against which the financial system should be assessed. And there is still a second problem to be solved, namely how to measure performance in practice. A proper evaluation of effectiveness requires much detailed information about financial behaviour and the way the financial markets and institutions operate. This type of data is not so far available on any scale for the UK. Although quite a lot is now known about the way money flows through the financial system, information on the way financial decisions are taken and their implications for performance is much more sparse.

For this reason, the analysis that follows is in the form of a discussion of various criteria for effective performance by the financial system, together with an essentially qualitative assessment of how the UK system stands in relation to these ideals. The problems of evaluating performance are also considered further, while some specific criticisms levelled at the financial system are briefly examined to see how far they appear to be well founded. The lack of hard data means that there can be no really firm conclusions from the analysis. But an idea of the adequacy of our financial markets and institutions emerges.

9.2 THE STANDARDS OF ECONOMIC EFFICIENCY

It was mentioned above that there are two sides to the economic efficiency of the financial system. They are whether the system is allocating funds in an efficient manner, and whether the markets and institutions that carry out this allocation themselves operate using a minimum of economic resources; these can be seen as the external and internal aspects of the efficiency of financial institutions and markets.

Taking the internal question of operating efficiency first, the ideal is that financial institutions and markets should be making the least possible use of land, labour and other scarce economic resources. If resources are correctly priced, this implies that institutions should be operating in a way that minimizes their costs. The problem is that in real life, where conditions are continually changing, it is extremely difficult to point to a particular way of doing business that is the best in the sense of being the least costly and the most efficient possible. Blatant inefficiencies may sometimes stand out. But the practical assessment of operating efficiency tends to be a rather messy and often inconclusive process, involving examinations both of trends in costs and productivity and of the conditions under which financial institutions operate.

In the UK, assessment is made more difficult by the great shortage of suitable data on the costs and productivity of financial institutions. There is little information publicly available for any of the main UK institutions, though the data are undoubtedly available within the individual companies. This contrasts with the situation in the United States, where much more cost data are made public and some extensive analysis of operating efficiency has been made.[68]

The situation is best in insurance, where companies normally provide some breakdown of cost figures. But the interpretation of this data is extremely difficult, and no real conclusions on efficiency can be drawn from the figures. [25, 26] In banking, one of the few published attempts to assess efficiency was by the Prices and Incomes Board in their report on bank charges in 1967.[9] This used specially collected data to examine the position for the main deposit banks but concluded that 'a rigorous analysis of the trend of costs with respect to output is impossible'. The general view of the report was that the banks could achieve further economies notably in branch distribution and in the organization of ancillary activities; some of these may have been achieved since then.

This being the situation, the UK investigator has to rely largely on looking at the conditions under which financial institutions and markets operate to see whether in practice these are likely to be conducive to efficient operation. The actual conditions are usually measured against the ideal of a competitive world in which there is free choice by all users of the financial system, no factors inhibiting competition between existing institutions and no bars to the entry of new institutions into the financial system. The argument behind this approach is that a free market system of this kind provides the greatest incentive towards minimum-cost operation. However, problems of interpretation can arise, for example where there are important economies of large-scale operation; in this situation minimum-cost operation may be incompatible with the existence of enough institutions to secure free competition in the market. Thus, failure to measure up to the standard of free competition does not necessarily imply that the system is not operating efficiently; but it is an indicator that the position *may* not be ideal.

The extent to which there is free choice and competition within the financial system is also important with regard to allocating efficiency. Here the ideal is that the available funds should be allocated to those projects that themselves represent the most efficient use of economic resources, those that offer the highest return for the risk involved. For this to happen, money should be flowing freely in response to differences in return with no arbitrary rules or methods of rationing to hinder its movement. Such differences in the cost of borrowing as persist should be accounted for by the varying levels of risk involved or related aspects such as the period to maturity of loans or the type of interest or dividend payment. This should be true of both the borrowing by ultimate investors and that by financial institutions, that is the terms of lending in the form of bank deposits, life assurance policies and the like. There should thus be no difference in the price of essentially comparable financial instruments and no evidence of borrowers who cannot obtain funds at a fair rate of interest or of lenders who obtain a patently raw deal.

To some extent, it is possible to assess directly whether the financial system in practice allocates funds efficiently. Where differences in risk and return can be fairly readily measured, as with securities quoted on the Stock Exchange, these can be examined to see whether comparable instruments are being valued on a similar basis. The evidence for both the UK and the United States suggests that this area of the financial system is in fact very efficient at allocating funds; the conclusion assumes that overall return on a security and its variability are good measures of the true profitability and risk associated with this type of borrowing. [56, 59]

In other areas of the financial system, it is much more difficult to see how the disparities in the return or cost of financial instruments are accounted for by differences in their risk and other conditions. There is a lack of published data on the terms on which most non-marketable instruments like loans and deposits are issued, and also on the true risk associated with various classes of business; as with operating costs, the main institutions must have historical data on the way their business has turned out. Some evidence is available on how certain groups of institutions actually determine the rates they pay and charge for the money they borrow and lend, and the implications for allocating efficiency within these areas are discussed in Section 9.5. But there is little to show whether the differences in return between main groups of instruments and the main types of financial markets represent an efficient disposition of funds.

The investigator is therefore thrown back to examining whether conditions in the financial system are likely to be conducive to allocating as well as operating efficiency. If there is free choice and a free market in financial instruments, this will encourage financial institutions to price different kinds of borrowing and lending in an efficient way and to take the correct degree of risk in channelling funds between lenders and borrowers. New financial institutions will be free to develop to take advantage of any unsatisfied borrowing or lending needs; the latter may exist because, for example, of arbitrary allocating rules used by established organizations. As with operating efficiency, the lack of competition does not necessarily mean that the financial system is not efficient in its allocation of money. But it is a possible warning sign.

The other indicator of the economic efficiency of the financial system is its profitability, the level of profits earned by the institutions relative to the risks they take. This is, however, not an easy indicator to interpret. If financial institutions appear to be earning excessive profits compared with takers of similar risks, this may be because they are acting as monopolists and restricting entry to the business. In this case, the system is not likely to be allocating funds efficiently; either the institutions' borrowing rates are too low or they are charging too much for their lending. New entrants would probably erode this situation by attracting business away through more competitive pricing. But excess profits could also be caused by the under-pricing (or exploitation) of the land or labour or other resources used by the institutions; this, if it persists, is an indicator either of some inefficiency elsewhere or of severe demarcation between the financial system and other parts of the economy. Equally, the lack of overly high profits does not of itself imply that the financial system is efficient. Costs may be unduly high, thus offsetting the extra profits from allocating inefficiencies; it will be seen that this can occur even in an apparently competitive market.

In what follows, some consideration is given to how far the apparent profitability of the UK financial institutions can be used as a key to the financial system's overall efficiency. But for the reasons discussed, attention is focussed primarily on the extent to which the financial system in the UK is freely competitive and the nature of the competition that exists. First of all, however, we need to look more closely at how the users of the UK financial system in practice determine the extent and nature of their financial transactions.

9.3 ARE FINANCIAL CHOICES EFFICIENT?

The basic factors underlying financial choice were examined in the previous chapter. Standards of living, the extent of investment opportunities, the need to provide for the future and attitudes to risk are all important determinants of how people and organizations borrow and lend. Assuming that people are averse to risk, the rational behaviour from a financial point of view is to order financial transactions so as to obtain as much money as possible given the risk to be taken; in other words, to maximize return for a given level of risk. In practice, other considerations may enter the decision-taking process. From the point of view of the economic efficiency of the financial system, the key question is whether these other factors mean that the resulting decisions are no longer financially rational.

The importance of this criterion of rationality lies in the fact that it is one of the conditions that needs to be satisfied if a competitive market is to produce both efficient operation among financial institutions and efficient allocation of funds among alternative users. If potential lenders do not put their money into the financial instruments that offer the highest return for the risk being taken, and if borrowers do not go to the cheapest source available to them, then the incentive to financial institutions to minimize their costs and allocate funds efficiently is reduced. Equally, the system will not allocate funds efficiently if lending and borrowing are not carried out up to the point at which the marginal gain in return or the additional cost are equivalent respectively to the value of present spending given up or the return on the purchase of physical assets.

There is a good deal of evidence to suggest that many private individuals do not take their financial decisions in an overtly rational way. Sometimes, as discussed below, this may be because people are pursuing particular social aims. But surveys also indicate that decisions to lend or borrow in a particular way are often taken because this is the form best known to the individual concerned, or because it is the one used by other people he knows or for a variety of similar reasons. Furthermore, as mentioned in Chapter 1, many people appear to be ignorant of the precise terms of the financial contracts that they have entered into, especially where these are long-term ones like life assurance policies and pension schemes.

None of these facts is incompatible with the possibility that the resulting decisions do approximately maximize return to the lender or minimize his borrowing costs. But the apparent lack of understanding and knowledge of financial matters raises suspicions that this is not the case. And there are some instances where people and their financial instruments seem very ill-matched; non-taxpayers buying national savings, or putting money in building society deposits or life assurance policies for the supposed tax benefits, are some obvious examples.

The efficiency of the financial decisions taken by companies and other organizations is more difficult to assess. Financial sophistication has clearly been growing in recent years as the behaviour of many companies in the money market bears witness. But among smaller companies there remains a considerable lack of knowledge about available sources of funds, which suggests that, at this level at least, all decisions may not be taken on a financially efficient basis, even if they are rational within the limits of existing knowledge.

Overall, there is some reason to suppose that the financial choices made by the users of the UK financial system are not always those best designed to promote the system's economic efficiency. The situation has been changing over the last couple of decades and it is probable that, even among private individuals, financial decisions are more fully understood than they were; this is partly a result, as well as a cause, of the growing attention paid to financial matters in the media. However, other factors still have a significant influence. As a result, the nature of the competition within UK financial markets is unusually important as a criterion of whether the financial system is acting in an economically efficient manner.

9.4 HOW FINANCIAL INSTITUTIONS COMPETE

To what extent and in what way do UK financial institutions compete with each other? In examining this question, two aspects are especially significant; these are the extent of actual or implicit collusion limiting competition between existing institutions, and the degree to which new or existing institutions are inhibited from entering certain areas of the financial markets.

On the first of these, there is no doubt that agreements limiting competition have existed extensively within the UK financial system. The cartel arrangements concerning the interest rates paid and charged by the major deposit banks have already been mentioned several times. Non-life insurance companies have operated agreements controlling premium levels (the so-called tariff agreements) and the life companies have jointly set the commission rates paid to agents. Building societies have had a system of recommended mortgage interest rates while the Stock Exchange has set the minimum commission levels to be charged by its members.

The feature of all these agreements is that they are primarily, though not exclusively, concerned with price; they limit the extent to which institutions compete through the level of interest rates or other charges associated with the financial service they sell. The agreements thus reduce the incentive any one institution has to minimize its costs in terms of resources used. Lower costs cannot be reflected in reduced charges or increased interest payments and so used to encourage new business. Furthermore, in so far as competition continues to exist between members of the agreement, it must take other forms, for example the provision of additional special services of various kinds.

This sort of competition on service can represent a very wasteful use of resources. The buyer of the basic financial service, the loan or the insurance policy has no chance to choose how much additional service he wants; he must pay the same basic price whether the supplements are few or many. In this situation, the person concerned to get the best value for money will naturally go for the product offering the most additional benefits, since these are effectively obtained free. This, in turn, encourages the provision of supplementary services to a level well beyond what people would choose to have if they had to pay directly for them. Where this occurs, the financial system is likely to be operating inefficiently, in that it is not meeting people's true needs, nor is it minimizing the costs of providing financial services. And financial choices are distorted by the fact that one type of service is being subsidized through unduly high charges for another.

The major financial institutions in the UK compete extensively in the provision of various ancillary services. Banks, building societies and insurance companies all offer the convenience of wide-ranging branch structures. They provide customers with a variety of other inducements, from free chequing facilities and newsletters to financial advice of various kinds, for some of which a charge is made. They also advertise extensively and compete in various ways for the attention of professional advisers like solicitors and accountants. Other groups such as unit trusts, spend large sums bringing their products to the attention of the consumers; while stockbrokers, who until recently were forbidden to advertise, have provided 'free' research and investment advisory services to their clients.

There is much to suggest that the scale on which some of these services are provided reflects, at least in part, the limitations imposed on price competition. However, the way in which individual financial choices are made is probably also a factor. Competition in terms of interest rates or charges is of little value to an individual institution if the people or organizations who use financial services do not respond; instead, competition in other ways is encouraged. If people do not know the charges they are paying to the bank or the hire purchase company or the true return on their life assurance policies, then changes in these will be no use as a means of attracting business; the availability of a strategically sited branch office or a well chosen advertising campaign may be much more effective.

Thus if financial choices are not responsive to changes in price, agreements to limit price competition are reinforced. There is no incentive for any one institution within the group to challenge the agreement since they stand to gain little from doing so. In this sense, something of a vicious circle leading to inefficient forms of competition has existed in major parts of the UK financial system in the period under review. To some degree it still persists. But the last few years have seen the abandonment of two of the most important agreements, the clearing bank cartel and the main insurance tariff arrangements, while the Stock Exchange has been faced with competition from Ariel. Price competition has clearly been stimulated as a result, which suggests that the institutions involved believe that many of their customers are in fact reasonably price-sensitive.

The breakdown of the two agreements mentioned is partly attributable to government intervention, notably the changing views of the Bank of England with regard to bank competition and the outcome of the Monopolies Commission investigations of certain insurance tariff agreements. But another factor that has throughout tended to check the operation of the vicious circle described above is the extent to which new financial institutions have been able to grow up within the UK financial system and existing institutions to expand into new areas of business.

There have been some limits to the process. The Stock Exchange controls new entry into broking and jobbing, while the Bank of England's attitudes have been important in determining how far certain groups moved beyond their traditional boundaries, particularly where acquisitions were involved. Government monetary policy has limited the ability of deposit banks to expand their lending business, and in certain fields, like deposit banking and insurance, new entry has been made more difficult by the established branch structure and large reserves of existing institutions. New entrants in these areas have also been required to have a minimum capital in order to protect the public from undue risk. But in other respects, few limits have been placed on new developments within the financial system. Many new institutions have been established during the period while the new opportunities exploited by existing groups, such as the merchant banks, were examined in Chapter 4.

However, the lack of major constraints on new entry does not of itself ensure that efficiency within the financial system is encouraged. It makes for continued competition, but, unless there is response to changes in cost or interest rates, the competition provoked will be on other grounds, and the result is then just bigger and better frills. A look at the UK experience suggests that, where the new entrants have competed for the business of the more sophisticated users of the financial system, such as the larger industrial companies, competition has been very much in terms of price. But in other areas the result has been more mixed. Much effort has been devoted to accentuating product differentiation that is often somewhat artificial, particularly within life assurance and unit trust investment. And, where attention has been drawn to competitive charges or interest rates, the emphasis has often been on limited aspects of the total financial choice involved. In particular, the risks associated with higher interest rates or lower charges have frequently been ignored, both by those providing the financial service involved and those using it; the initial growth and subsequent failures among both secondary banks and some new insurance companies bear witness to this.

Overall, therefore, it is doubtful how far the competition that exists within the UK financial system is sufficient to stimulate either allocating or operating efficiency to the full. Overt limitations on price competition and new entry still exist, though their coverage and effectiveness has been much reduced in recent years. The growing understanding of the economic aspects of financial choice has helped to provoke a more efficient form of competition, but it appears that there is a good way to go before all competitive activity is of this form.

However, this is as much a problem of the way financial choices are made as the responsibility of the financial institutions and markets; unless, that is, the latter are seen as having responsibility to educate the buyers of their services as well as to sell to them. A number of institutional groups have indeed taken this general view. But it is certainly not ubiquitous, since some institutional practices clearly make financial decisions more complicated than they need be. The continuing attempts of some lending groups to disguise the true rate of interest being charged and the lack of publicity given to surrender values on life assurance policies are two notable examples.

9.5 ARBITRARY RULES AND RISK-TAKING

For individual financial institutions to channel funds efficiently from lender to borrower, their own financial choices must be economically efficient. This means the institution must determine the interest rates and associated charges that they make to borrowers and the return that they give to lenders in a manner that correctly allows for the risk characteristics of the business. And the relationship between the terms on which they lend and borrow must be such that the capital they employ is producing the 'right' amount of risk-changing; capital must be earning an adequate but not excessive return for the risks the institution is taking. To what extent is this the case within the UK financial system?

The problems associated with direct examination of the relationships between risk and return on different financial instruments and the profitability of financial institutions were discussed earlier. Here, the concern is primarily to see whether there are any indications from the practice of financial institutions that suggest the above conditions may not be satisfied.

Many financial institutions employ rule of thumb methods, both for arriving at the level of interest rates charged and paid and for deciding whether or not to lend to a particular borrower, or, in the case of insurance companies, to take on a particular risk. The key question is how far these arbitrary rules reflect the underlying risk characteristics of the business being undertaken. Obviously, they are intended to do so in a general way, but there is some reason to think that they may result in a distortion of allocation, particularly where the higher risk type of businesses are concerned. For example, building societies normally refuse to lend to people who do not fulfil their conditions, rather than charging a higher rate for higher risks. The Bolton Committee has suggested that banks are also unwilling to charge the full price for high risks, preferring instead not to lend at all to smaller risky ventures.[33] Non-life insurance premiums were for many years calculated on a somewhat unscientific basis, though lately attempts have been made to relate premiums more precisely to the risks associated with different categories of insured; this is something that has in fact been done for many years in life assurance business.

How far these practices have led to inefficiencies in the pattern of fund flows is difficult to say. Where competition has ensured that there are alternative sources of the financial services in question, the problem is less serious. It may thus have been more significant in the case of building societies than for banks, since the former are the major providers of house loans while many alternative suppliers of ordinary bank loans have arisen. For insurance companies, new entrants into the business have also helped to offset the effect of traditional methods of operation.

Any distortions are, however, clearly reinforced where tax concessions give the institutions special privileges, as with the two groups just mentioned. Such concessions themselves represent another form of arbitrary rule that can distort the pattern of allocation in a manner that may not be economically efficient, for example encouraging house ownership where people might in principle prefer to rent. And the tax structure and government intervention generally can have a similar effect; differential tax rates between income and capital gain and limits to interest rates on small deposits are both possible causes of inefficient allocation of funds, however desirable they may perhaps be for other reasons.

It is probable that arbitrary rules of various kinds do introduce a degree of inefficiency in the allocation of funds by the UK financial system. There is little evidence that potential borrowers or lenders frequently go unsatisfied. But, to the extent that higher risk takers are forced to deal solely with new specialized institutions like secondary banks or venture capital companies, they may well be paying more or getting less for their money per unit of risk than efficient allocation suggests that they should. Much depends on the extent to which real economies of large scale or of specialization exist, something that is difficult to establish. But marginal ventures or additional saving that should in theory be carried out may be inhibited.

There is the further question of whether financial institutions are, overall, taking the correct amount of risk. Arbitrary cut-off points beyond which risks will not be taken at any price could imply that risk-taking has been inadequate. In addition, because it is difficult to assess the high risks properly, managers, whose rewards are not related to risk-taking, have a strong incentive not to take on very risky business. And competitive pressure may not have ensured that institutions were, none the less, pushed to their risk-taking limits. In theory, this should show up through the institutions concerned earning too high a level of profits relatively to the risk they take. It is possible that this could in fact be established in the case of stockbroking, where margins have been protected by minimum commission rates, and in deposit banking, where profits have benefited from the agreement that current accounts do not earn interest. But in general terms, the extent to which institutions compete on service means that operating inefficiencies or extravagances may well serve to offset any extra profit earned as a result of limited risk-taking.

In many ways, the UK experience with regard to risk-taking is a paradoxical one. On the one hand, it can be argued that the major lending institutions in the UK have been more restrained in their risky lending than they might have been. Similarly, the large investing institutions have been criticized for being slow to move into equity-type investment despite the long-term nature of their liabilities. But, as the experience of some secondary banks and life assurance companies has shown, there are severe dangers in the opposite extremes of over-rapid expansion in risky lending and too great a degree of disparity between the types of borrowing and lending undertaken. It is interesting to speculate, though virtually impossible to show, how far recent developments are the direct result of earlier restraint. Whatever the cause, neither extreme represents a fully efficient allocation of funds by the financial system.

9.6 SOME CRITICISMS EXAMINED

The above analysis suggests that, for a variety of reasons, the UK financial system may not always either operate with minimum use of economic resources or allocate funds in the manner most conducive to economic efficiency. The conclusion can be put no more, or less, strongly than that; much detailed investigation will be needed before the 'may' can be turned into a more definite 'yes' or 'no' about the financial system's economic efficiency.

However, even if the overall verdict is one of the 'doubtful but not proven' type, this brief study of the various aspects of economic efficiency, together with the earlier exposition, does shed light on the validity of some of the criticisms made of the financial system and the way it operates. It also points to some changes that might help the system to become closer to what is needed from the point of view of economic efficiency. The latter are considered in the concluding section of this chapter. Here two basic types of criticisms levelled at the financial system in recent years are examined in more detail.

The first of these criticisms relates to the general issue of whether the UK financial system is too big. Do we really need all these financial institutions and markets, which seem to some to have little or no relevance to what goes on in the 'real' world? At times this criticism reflects ignorance of the real function of the financial system, something that should not be true of any reader who has come thus far through this book. It can also derive from an ethical standpoint which views too much financial dealing as wrong; this we are not concerned with here. But behind the confusion that can exist, there is a real question to be answered. To the extent that we need a financial system to channel funds from lenders to borrowers, do we get this at too great a cost? Is the allocating function fulfilled with an inefficient proliferation of financial markets and institutions and with an unnecessary degree of layering of financial instruments?

It was indicated above that the financial system does not seem to operate at maximum efficiency. A variety of frills is provided with financial services that may not really be wanted, and the proliferation of new institutions has been in part the result of the inadequacies of existing groups. To the extent that there are economies of scale in the operation of financial institutions, the latter development was not necessarily an efficient one; it might well have been better if the newer developments had taken place within existing groups.

The rationalization moves of recent years, particularly by the major banking and insurance groups, suggest that some of the resulting inefficiencies may now have been removed. How much further the move to wider financial groupings can effectively be taken is more difficult to say. Economies in branch rationalization and other operating advantages have to be weighed against the difficulty of selling a wide variety of services simultaneously and the loss of personal touch that a large grouping can involve. Clearly the smaller specialist institution has a continuing role to play. But it is perhaps doubtful whether this is as widespread as was the case for much of the period under review.

This implies that there is perhaps some justification in the view that the financial system has used too many resources to perform its channelling function. But there is also another aspect of this question, which concerns the role of secondary markets, like the Stock Exchange and that in certificates of deposits, and the increase in layering that has been associated with the rise of the inter-bank money market. Activity in secondary markets, particularly the Stock Exchange, is often seen as epitomizing the irrelevance of much that goes on within the financial system. The market is viewed as an area for speculative transactions that have nothing to do with the process of channelling funds from lenders to borrowers and is therefore unnecessary and a waste of resources. Similar comments are made about the great growth in dealings between banking institutions.

As was discussed in Chapter 1, the value of secondary markets is that they allow longer-term borrowing (in the case of ordinary shares, effectively permanent borrowing) to be financed with shorter-term funds. They thus assist the allocation of funds by bridging the gap between potential lenders, who want to be able to regain their money when needed, and borrowers, who have long-term investment projects to finance. The gap between lenders and borrowers can of course partly be bridged in other ways. Chapter 4 showed how financial institutions perform a comparable function, and inter-bank dealings have grown for a similar reason. But it is doubtful whether, in the absence of a secondary market, any institutions could safely provide much permanent capital without comparable borrowings. And, provided there are no distortions forcing funds to flow through the channels associated with marketable instruments or affecting the costs involved, there is no reason why markets where they exist should not be as efficient a way of allocating funds as any other.

What many critics of the secondary markets imply is that such distortions do exist in practice within the UK financial system. Some fairly obvious problems arise from the method of operation of the Stock Exchange. Agreements limiting price competition in various ways and controlling entry may well have led to costs of dealing and new issues being higher than is economically desirable. Other requirements, such as extensive public disclosure of information, may, however desirable in themselves, affect the willingness of borrowers to use particular sources of funds. But the more fundamental issue is whether the existence of secondary markets encourages too great a degree of short-term speculation in existing marketable securities. The critics suggest that speculative activity causes sharp fluctuations in both market values and the availability of new long-term funds, making it difficult for borrowers to obtain adequate funds at reasonable prices. Thus, secondary markets are seen as being not only irrelevant but an actual obstacle to the efficient allocation of funds.

This question is best examined in the context of the second main group of popular criticisms of the financial system, which can be summarized in the statement that the City does not provide enough money for industry. It is the supply of long-term capital that is really at issue here, and the question came particularly to the fore in 1974, owing to the fall-off in new security issues and the growing financial problems of a number of companies. Suggestions have been made both that financial institutions have devoted too much effort to overseas business to the exclusion of domestic activities and that, in their domestic activities, institutions have paid too much attention to short-term opportunities in the stock market and in the property investment and not enough to long-term industrial investment; the investing institutions have been especially pilloried in this regard.

The role of overseas versus domestic business is the easier of these two allegations to assess. As was seen earlier, the bulk of overseas dealings relates to banking business, and flows from the UK are very largely balanced by corresponding inflows. This business in the Euro-currency markets is highly competitive, but there is no evidence that the capital involved in it does not earn an adequate return for the risks taken. The initial involvement of UK banks in this field was undoubtedly in part stimulated by their inability to expand business at home. But this was essentially the consequence of government monetary policy rather than of arbitrary rules established by the institutions themselves.

Foreign currency earnings from overseas business have been substantial, and there seems little reason to believe that overseas activity has in any way hampered developments at home. More probably the reverse is true, since the experience gained has been applied subsequently at home. This occurred, for example, with the introduction of sterling certificates of deposits. Only in so far as there has been excessive risk-taking abroad, with too great a degree of pyramiding of deposits, could this activity endanger the domestic activities of the institutions concerned. As with domestic inter-bank dealings, it is extremely difficult to say whether or not this has been the case; but the strength of Euro-currency markets in the face of recent international financial problems is encouraging.

The question of whether financial institutions have misallocated funds between alternative domestic uses is much more difficult to answer. Undoubtedly funds have flowed heavily into property investment at times, long-term borrowing by industry has been low and the stock market has been volatile. But part of the reason for these trends lies outside the financial system.

First, for a variety of reasons, associated partly with other aspects of government policy, property investment offered unusually high rates of return to investors in the 1960s and early 1970s. As the demarcation between the property and the financial markets was broken down, so funds flowed into property, thus evening up the returns on different types of assets. In this sense, allocation of funds has become more, not less, efficient, though the effects of government policy can be seen as an underlying distorting factor.

Secondly, a low level of longer-term borrowing by industry can in principle be as much because companies do not wish to borrow as because funds are not available; the level of fund flows that takes place is after all determined by demand as well as supply. The analysis in Chapters 2 and 7 has shown that UK companies have been unusually dependent on their own saving for the finance of invest- ment. They have been substantial borrowers, but much of this bor- rowing has been offset by their lending activities. Companies have thus chosen to invest substantial sums in financial rather than physi- cal assets, implying that it may be more a lack of profitable invest- ment opportunities than a lack of funds that has inhibited borrowing. Furthermore, as far as long-term funds are concerned, the scope for higher gearing plus the increased availability of bank loans has meant that there was little need for companies to have recourse to the stock market in the early 1970s.

However, the situation was undoubtedly very different in 1974, with a number of companies short of funds but unable to borrow more from the banks. Yet new borrowing in longer-term forms remained low. How far was this a justified and efficient situation reflecting low profitability on new industrial investment? Could it in any sense be attributed to short-term bias on the part of lenders?

Different issues are involved depending on whether one is talking about banks or investing institutions. With regard to the banks, the question is whether they could undertake more longer-term lending than they do already, effectively are they doing the degree of risk- changing that they ideally should? This may not have been true some years ago, particularly where the deposit banks are concerned. But with the increase in longer-term lending and growth in competition seen recently, it seems doubtful whether the banks could undertake more longer-term lending, without using longer-term sources of funds than at present.

Investing institutions have been the traditional providers of long- term funds. They have substantial holdings of all types of securities and this type of lending is fully compatible with the long-term nature of most of their liabilities. But if their financial behaviour is to be efficient, they need to allocate their lending in a manner that maximizes their return relative to the risk they are taking. Theoretical work suggests that, provided secondary markets are efficient, in that all the available information is fully reflected in today's price, and dealing costs are not too high, performance may be improved by concentrating on the short term; the long term can in a sense be left to look after itself.[61] Since the Stock Exchange appears to be an efficient market in this respect, investing institutions have naturally tended to put more weight on short-term developments, adjusting their holdings of securities and the extent of their new investment frequently to changing conditions.

In principle there is no reason why this emphasis on the short term should in any way distort the overall allocation of funds. Indeed, provided other people and organizations are free to take their decisions in a financially efficient way, the financial system should operate in the most effective way from an economic standpoint. But there are some practical consequences that may not be altogether desirable.

In the first place, where economic conditions change sharply, as in the last few years, thus leading to fluctuation in the expected return on capital spending, there will inevitably be sharp movements in the market values of both financial and physical assets. If financial choices are made efficiently, there will in consequence be sharp swings in the level of capital spending. While this is efficient in an economic sense, it will probably conflict with other policy aims such as the maintenance of full employment or a steady growth in the productive potential of the economy.

Such conflicts underlie much of the criticism of recent conditions in the stock market. The government has wanted to maintain a steady level of investment in a situation where the underlying return on capital spending has probably been below the market cost of funds. Industrialists prepared to follow government exhortations have thus found themselves unable to obtain long-term funds at what they felt was a reasonable price. It should be stressed that, in the absence of formal rationing, it is never correct to say that a market cannot in an absolute sense provide adequate funds. The money is available, but at a price; the question is whether the price is acceptable or not. In 1974 there was no absolute shortage of funds in the hands of investing institutions, and those companies prepared to pay the going rate had no difficulty in obtaining money.

The most satisfactory answer to this problem is avoidance of the sharp fluctuations in economic conditions that lead to volatility in both return on investment and prices in financial markets. This would remove much of the disparity between short-term and long-term rates of return that is essentially the cause of differences of view. But not all the problems associated with short-term return maximization can be removed in this way. For, in so far as efficient behaviour in financial markets pushes industrialists into taking a short-term view of their own investments, it will encourage more dealings in physical assets. Companies may also be pushed into more active involvement in financial markets, a trend noted in Chapter 2. Economic efficiency may be improved thereby, but there can be social problems, as discussed in the next section. And, where capital spending relates to highly specific assets that are difficult to value and to sell when financial conditions change, industrialists may be unable to avoid taking a longer-term view than the institutions, who deal in highly marketable assets, would take.

Justified differences of opinion about what is the most desirable pattern of fund flows can thus arise owing to the different priorities given to various economic and social aims. But in terms both of their own priorities, and of those of economic efficiency narrowly defined, the behaviour of the institutions cannot really be held responsible for the low level of long-term borrowing by industry in 1973 and 1974. Corroboration for this view comes from the fact that no new institutional channels, other than the officially sponsored Finance for Industry, have arisen to fill the supposed gap, something that would have been expected in a competitive market if there were a genuine shortage of long-term funds for profitable investment projects.

Furthermore, in so far as outside pressure may, in the future, lead institutions to provide long-term funds when the return on investment is below the current market rate for the risk involved, it is the people who lend to those institutions, the depositors, policy-holders, prospective pensioners or shareholders, who will suffer. Their interests are being subordinated to those of the various participants in the businesses receiving funds. Put in more general terms, allocative efficiency in the financial system, and the benefits that flow therefrom, will then be to some degree sacrificed in favour of security of employment, longer-term economic growth or other benefits expected from additional industrial investment.

9.7 WHERE SOCIAL NEEDS CONFLICT WITH EFFICIENCY

The financial system is part of the economic mechanism that we use to allocate scarce resources in the most efficient way possible. It has developed because there were economic and financial advantages to be gained from transferring funds between surplus and deficit units.

The factors determining financial choice are essentially economic in character, relating to present and future financial needs.

But the financial markets and institutions are also social organizations, just as we are social as well as economic beings. The two parts of life can be split only in theory; in practice every economic action has its social consequence and vice versa. Financial institutions are themselves employers, and the way in which they organize themselves affects how these people live. The way institutions take financial decisions affects the activities of other organizations like companies and so has an influence on other people's lives. Financial decisions themselves may be influenced by non-economic factors; this is especially so for individual people, while fundamental attitudes to risk-taking are probably formed as much by personal and social factors as by economic circumstances.

The social aspects of the financial system are, however, frequently neglected. Indeed, it is sometimes suggested that the market mechanism is the best way of allowing social as well as economic choices to be freely expressed. The individual chooses his job for social as well as economic reasons, weighing up the income offered against other factors. Similarly, the lender or borrower has to balance out the social implications of his decision against the financial return and risk involved. The two aspects may or may not conflict; if they do a decision must be made as to which is given priority. And, the argument goes on, if all choices are freely taken in efficient markets, the best of all possible worlds will occur in a social as well as an economic sense.

But, as is now widely recognized, this does not always happen in practice. Economic needs in terms of the efficient use of resources can be at variance with social aims of better working conditions or a pleasant environment. Certain social costs, like pollution, are not fully reflected in the costs taken into account by private industry. Equally, financial decisions that represent efficient behaviour by the individual taking them can have undesirable social consequences.

One area where this can be so has already been mentioned. This concerns the effects of short-term time horizons in financial decisions. An emphasis on the short term encourages companies to buy and sell physical assets, or the businesses that control them, more vigorously; such activity in its more extreme form has been called in a pejorative manner 'asset-stripping'. From a narrowly economic standpoint, this may be an efficient process, but it can produce severe social disruption for the employees, customers and suppliers involved. The effect is aggravated where there are sharp changes in economic conditions, which undermine the financial viability of existing asset dispositions.

Conflicts relating to wider social considerations can also enter into borrowing and lending decisions. In providing money in a particular way to a particular organization or individual, the lender is implicitly taking a view not only about the adequacy of the return being obtained but also about the social desirability of the project financed by the borrowing. If finance is provided, it may be because the project is believed to be desirable as well as rewarding, or because withholding finance is not necessarily the most effective way of improving an undesirable situation; since views of what is socially desirable vary, other people may readily provide the funds that one lender withholds. None the less, if a polluting company or an oppressive regime can obtain funds on acceptable terms, the financial system is in some sense condoning this type of behaviour. This is especially true of ordinary shareholders, who technically control as well as finance the companies whose equity they hold.

Issues relating to the social desirability of the projects financed are particularly complex for the financial institutions. At law, institutions are responsible to their 'owners', whether shareholders, policy-holders or others. Their aim should be to act in the manner most likely to meet the owners' needs; in economic terms, this is seen as maximizing the return to the owners. Where social considerations conflict with this aim, in for example lending to finance highly commendable but not fully viable projects, what should the institution do? How is it to interpret its owners' wishes, where there is often no mechanism for ascertaining these? Furthermore, since the institutions are themselves social organizations, other parties are affected by their decisions. For example, if institutions maximize return to the owners, how will this affect employees or customers? More generally, in any decision, whose interests should be taken into account and how are they to be assessed?

UK financial institutions have in the past seen themselves as being primarily concerned with efficient behaviour in a narrowly economic sense, and they have tended to ignore most of the social aspects of financial decisions. Some potential conflicts have been recognized, as shown, for example, in the setting up of the takeover panel to protect users of the financial markets from the extreme effects of short-term profit-maximization by some operators, and the general acceptance of the need for action on 'insider' dealing. Employee interests have also been given increasing prominence. And where public opinion has been strongly behind them, as on the question of compensation payments by Distillers to the thalidomide victims, major institutional investors have used their power directly to further social aims.

But in general, the institutions have been reluctant to take any initiative in giving social issues, or even wider economic aims, priority over financially efficient decision-making. In part, this reflects their concern about the adequacy of their expertise in areas other than financial decision-making. But there is also much uncertainty as to how, with any change in priorities, the conflicting objectives between different interest groups should be reconciled.

9.8 A FINANCIAL SYSTEM FOR THE FUTURE

It is always easier to analyse and criticize a system than to prescribe how the situation might be improved; it can be even more difficult to put the prescription into effect. None the less, our study of the way the UK financial system works indicates some possible areas for improvements.

First, it is helpful to consider how what is required of the financial system may change in the future. The contribution made towards an efficient allocation of economic resources will almost certainly remain paramount. But, with rising standards of living and increasing awareness of social and environmental conditions, the social consequences of economic activity will probably bear more weight in decision-taking in the future than they have in the past. And in an era of demands for ever greater disclosure, the major participants in the financial system are likely more and more to be called to public account for their actions and the reasoning behind them.

There are four main ways in which it appears that the major organizations in the formal financial system could adapt their own behaviour so as to help ensure that these future demands are met. First, the restrictions on competition and free entry that still persist should be removed; this applies particularly to the Stock Exchange, which has been notably slow to recognize the changing climate of opinion within which it operates. Secondly, institutions could do much more to improve the flow of information about their activities. Here, data on actual operating experience are especially important; as discussed, information on costs, business outcome and related matters is sadly lacking in the UK. But information on fund flows and holdings could also with advantage be improved, notably that concerning the term structure of borrowing and lending and the true value of outstanding holdings.

These data would enable people both within and outside the formal financial system to judge more clearly the effectiveness with which institutions and markets operate. Such judgements may, of course, not be an attractive idea to the organizations concerned. But the third area for improvement is one that would assist the latter directly in their day-to-day activities. It concerns the question of risk assessment. The arbitrary rules adopted by a number of institutions for dealing with risk and the consequences that follow from this were considered in Section 9.5. In so far as these rules can be replaced by a more accurate means of measuring risk and relating it to required return, both the institutions concerned and the financial system as a whole should benefit. Over the last twenty years, the thinking about handling financial risks has been revolutionized by the work of Markovitz,[67] Sharp,[70] Lintner[66] and others, and this thinking has gradually been used to improve the techniques that can be used in the real world. However, use of such techniques in practice depends on the willingness of financial institutions to adopt new methods of approach in this area and on how far managers are prepared to innovate, and to adapt the way in which they carry out their business.

The other main way by which financial institutions could themselves help to improve the financial system relates to the problem of social choice discussed in the last section. Where economic and social aims are potentially in conflict, or where the interests of different groups like employees and shareholders are seriously at variance, the institutions have no real mechanism for deciding how the dispute should be resolved. Technically, an appeal to the owners of the organization is possible, but this is a route seldom used except in takeovers; in practice, decisions are taken by management. In part, the question of how social choices should be exercised is a problem shared by all private-sector organizations, and its solution may lie in legislative changes. But the financial institutions could help by considering ways in which the views of key groups like customers, employees and shareholders can be more clearly and openly expressed and the issues that are involved more fully debated.

However, by no means all the factors that inhibit the effective operation of the financial system are under the control of the organizations in the formal system. The way in which the government behaves in relation to the financial system is also an important influence. Just as economic and social aims can conflict, so can the different aims of government policy. How this conflict is resolved is again a question of social choice; the control of inflation may weigh more highly than efficient allocation in the financial markets. But the government can greatly assist the effectiveness of the financial system by avoiding the use of policy weapons that either distort financial choice or affect the competitive situation of certain financial institutions. The history of UK monetary policy shows how influential government action can be, while the continued existence of tax advantages for certain types of saving remains a major distorting factor at the present time. And an approach to economic management which avoids major fluctuations in financial conditions would greatly help to lessen the potential conflict between short- and long-term attitudes to investment and financing decisions discussed in Section 9.6.

Government action could help to improve the financial system in other ways. If financial organizations fail to measure up to the standards of competition and disclosure that are ideally required, then it is in the government's power to ensure that changes occur. Most of the improvement in financial data that has taken place in the last decade has come this way, but more could be done. Equally, the government has done something to stimulate greater competition in financial markets. In this context, it is important that there should be a clear official view of the type of financial system that is wanted in the light of basic economic and social priorities, something that has not been very evident in recent years. In its absence there is a danger of piecemeal intervention and action in one area which runs counter to aims in another.

But in the last analysis, it is the people and organizations that use the financial system that determine its structure and the way it operates, both now and in the future. Even the government's actions in this sphere are ultimately based on public choice. Thus *we* all have to choose whether we really want an effective financial system and how we want to balance economic efficiency against social aims. The way in which each individual makes his own financial choice will help to determine what happens in the system as a whole. If the system is to be effective in meeting needs, the choices made must reflect these needs.

This does not mean that individuals *need* be financially rational, in the sense of maximizing return for a given level of risk. Everyone is perfectly at liberty to say 'I can't be bothered to take too much time over financial decisions', or 'I don't understand the alternatives, so I'll just do what you say'. But we all have to take the consequences of our financial decisions, both individually and as a society. And one of the best ways of ensuring that consequences are in fact acceptable is to understand what financial decisions really involve and how the financial system relates to other economic and social activities. It is with the aim of furthering such understanding that this book has been written.

Appendix: the statistical data used

A1. INTRODUCTION

The nature of the statistical data used as a basis for analysing the UK financial system and comparing it with financial markets and institutions abroad was outlined briefly above. Section 1.11 deals with the UK alone and Section 7.1 with the comparison between the UK and elsewhere. The purpose of this appendix is to give more precise details of the actual sources used, to discuss certain special aspects of the way the data have been used and to indicate how the estimated figures for group holdings of assets and liabilities were derived.

A2. DATA ON THE UK

(a) *Precise sources*

As indicated in Chapter 1, the basic sources for the data on the UK used in Section 7.1 were the official statistics as published in the *Blue Book on National Income and Expenditure, Financial Statistics* and the *Bank of England Quarterly Bulletin*. Most of the figures used were derived from the first two of these sources. Since much of the analysis was prepared prior to full publication of the 1973 national accounts, the actual issues mainly used were the *Blue Book* for 1973 (with figures up to 1972) and *Financial Statistics* for April 1974 (the first issue to include details of financial transactions in 1973).

Virtually all the detailed figures in Chapter 3 and the figures for all 1963 transactions and 1973 sources and uses of funds in Chapter 2 were derived from these issues. But, as full details of the income and expenditure of the main groups are available only in the *Blue Book*, the figures for 1973 in parts A and B of Tables 2.2 and 2.4 to 2.7 are from the 1974 *Blue Book*. As a result of revisions to the figures between April and August, the saving and investment figures shown in these tables are not entirely consistent with those used in the sources and uses calculations. The data on unidentified transactions in Figure 4.17 are also from the 1974 *Blue Book*, this being the only source to show a split between banks and OFIs. Most of the detailed figures for 1973 used in Chapters 4 and 5 were from the June 1974 issue of *Financial Statistics*. For details of the sources of information on holdings of assets and liabilities, see Section A2(c), p. 229.

(b) *The funds flow data*

Three aspects of the funds flow data used here to describe current financial transactions call for further comment. These are the way net flows have been used to derive an analysis of sources and uses of funds, the treatment of unidentified items and the approach adopted towards direct investment transactions with the overseas group.

Sections 1.10 and 1.11 explain the 'net' character of the UK flow of funds data and some of the reasons for this, as well as the differences between the OECD treatment of sources and uses of funds and that adopted in Chapters 2 to 6. The OECD approach is the one more conventionally used in flow of funds analysis and has the advantage that one can quickly tell from it whether a group is building up its holdings of financial assets and liabilities or running them down. However, where there are frequent transactions in both directions, this presentation makes it difficult to see the exact pattern of the actual sources and uses of funds in any given period. The presentation adopted in Chapters 2 to 6 is designed to provide such an analysis. Both approaches clearly have their uses.

The problems associated with unidentified types of financial transactions and the ways these have been handled have been discussed at various stages in the text, notably in Sections 1.11 and 3.8. In the analysis of group borrowing and lending, the net balance of unidentified items has been treated as an 'other' financial instrument. This can be justified on the basis that the main transactions not shown are those in direct trade credit and the like, which come under this heading, though clearly the true flows would be two-way ones. The fund flow figures do not, however, allow at all for imputed items like unfunded pension rights, though an allowance has been included in the estimate of holdings (see opposite).

In the official figures, direct investment flows between the UK and overseas are treated as financial transactions, investment overseas by UK companies being a form of lending by them while investment in the UK by the overseas group is a way they lend to UK companies. This treatment arises from the concentration in the national income accounts on investment within the UK and the way this is financed. However, when examining the financial transactions of the main groups, it seemed helpful to treat these direct investment flows as a form of capital spending, thus separating them from transactions in financial instruments conventionally defined. This has been done in Tables 2.4, 2.5 and 2.7. As a result, the figures for net borrowing and lending shown in these tables differ slightly from the surplus and deficits shown in Fig. 2.8, where the normal national income account definition is used.

(c) *Estimates of holdings*

The starting point for the estimates of holdings of assets and liabilities was the work done at the Department of Applied Economics in Cambridge for the years up to 1966.[48–50] The general method employed to update these to 1973 was as follows. The 1966 data were first aggregated into the six main groups and major types of financial instruments used in the official flow of funds figures. The resulting holdings of assets and liabilities were then adjusted for the net transactions that took place during the years 1967–73 with an allowance for changes in market values where relevant. The resulting estimates of each group's holdings were then aggregated, and the totals for the holdings of different instruments as assets and liabilities were checked both with each other for consistency and against any published data on the outstanding amounts of the instruments at end 1973. Where discrepancies existed, adjustments were made to the figures for the individual groups.

The major problems related to the allowance for changes in market values and the areas where transactions are not fully identified in the flow of funds figures, as with trade credit and unfunded pension rights. For securities, published indices were used to estimate how the value of both outstanding holdings and new transactions accumulated; transactions were assumed to take place at mid-year. Since transactions by each group in different types of company securities could not be separately identified, combined indices for debentures, preference and ordinary shares were used, weighted by the distribution of each group's holdings at end 1966. Indices of short- and long-term British government securities were used for government debt, the choice between them depending on some rather arbitrary assumptions about the distribution of the group's holdings.

For holdings of physical assets, the estimates of the increases since 1966 were based largely on the changes shown in the official figures for net capital stock and stocks and work in progress contained in the *Blue Book*. These figures are not exactly comparable with the Cambridge estimates; for example, the total *Blue Book* figures for 1966 are well below the Cambridge total for all physical assets. However, it seemed reasonable to assume that the two sets of estimates had moved broadly in line. The figures for each group were checked against the gross increase implied by the total of capital spending during the period.

The treatment of trade and similar credit in the estimate was very inadequate owing to the very limited data available on transactions taking place since 1966. The estimates were made on a net (credit granted less received) basis, using a rough figure for the net increase during 1967–73 based on the published data, which are for certain types of credit only. However, the implications of fuller, though still very rough, estimates were discussed in Section 3.7. For unfunded pension rights, the other main item not identified in the official figures, it was assumed that the value of holdings had increased in line with the outstanding book value of life assurance and pension funds.

The nature of the estimating process means that the 1973 figures can give only a broad view of the pattern of asset and liability holdings in that year. This was all that the estimates were intended to provide. In fact, where market values are not involved, that is everywhere but for securities and physical assets, the estimates are felt to be reasonably accurate. As far as the overall pattern is concerned, it is interesting to compare the figures with some estimates published subsequently for 31 March 1974.[51] These figures examined physical assets in much more detail and show a rather higher value for them in total; holdings by persons are relatively higher and those by government lower than in the estimates used above. But the general picture is very similar, and the significance of both companies and the government as net holders of wealth is confirmed.

A3. THE COMPARISON BETWEEN THE UK AND OVERSEAS

(a) *Precise sources*
The figures used in Chapter 7 were derived from the OECD publication, *Financial Statistics*. Most of them came from volume 7, 1973.

(b) *Treatment of the data*
Apart from the question of the classification of sources and uses of funds discussed in Section 1.10, the major problem in the use of the OECD data lies in the differing definitions employed by the various countries, both for the division of people and organizations into groups and for the aggregation of financial instruments. OECD attempts to standardize the presentation, but some significant variations remain. The most important of these were indicated in Chapter 7, but a more complete comparison of the definitions used is given in the following table. This also shows how the various types of instrument have been grouped for the purposes of analysis of sources and uses of funds. The classification for the UK is broadly in line with that used in Chapters 2 to 6 with the exception of the treatment of bank loans overseas.

The classifications for different countries compared

General classification	1. United States
1. Main groups	
Persons	Private individuals, personal trusts and non-profit organizations
Companies	All non-financial enterprises, including unincorporated business
Government	Federal, state and local government, social security funds, Post Office savings
Overseas	Rest of the world
Banks	Monetary authorities and commercial banks
Other financial institutions	Savings and loan associations, savings banks, insurance companies and pension funds, mutual funds, etc., plus federally sponsored credit agencies
2. Extent of consolidation	Persons and other financial institutions and state and local government are not consolidated; companies are only so within corporate groups
3. Instruments	
(a) Bills and deposits	
Cash and transferable deposits	Includes foreign exchange held by monetary authorities
Other deposits	Time deposits and CDs with banks and share accounts at savings and loan associations, etc.
Money market paper, etc.	Includes government securities of maturity one year or less and savings bonds
(b) Loans	
Short-term loans	Consumer credit, bank loans, open market paper, etc.
Long-term loans	Mainly mortgages
(c) Securities	
Bonds	Includes government bonds with maturity over one year
Shares	Includes mutual fund shares
(d) Life funds	Equity on life assurance and pension funds
(e) Other	
Monetary gold and SDRs	—
Trade credits	—
Other instruments	Includes proprietor's equity in unincorporated business, net direct investment abroad and banking transactions with monetary authorities and government

General classification	2. Canada
1. Main groups	
Persons	Includes unincorporated businesses and residual
Companies	Non-financial companies and non-financial government enterprises
Government	Federal, provincial and municipal government and social security funds
Overseas	Rest of the world
Banks	Central bank and other monetary institutions including chartered banks, savings banks, trust companies, mortgage loan companies and sales finance companies
Other financial institutions	Insurance companies and pension funds, mutual funds, etc., plus government financial institutions
2. Extent of consolidation	Not consolidated
3. Instruments	
(a) Bills and deposits	
Cash and transferable deposits	Includes official holdings of foreign exchange
Other deposits	—
Money market paper, etc.	Treasury bills, finance company and commercial paper
(b) Loans	
Short-term loans	Bank and other loans, including some longer-term
Long-term loans	Mortgages
(c) Securities	
Bonds	—
Shares	Includes share issues by subsidiaries
(d) Life funds	Equity on life assurance and pension funds
(e) Other	
Monetary gold and SDRs	—
Trade credits	Includes consumer credit
Other instruments	Includes all foreign investment (except currency) and claims on associated enterprises

General classification	3. Japan

1. Main groups

Persons	Includes unincorporated businesses and non-profit-making organizations
Companies	Private non-financial companies
Government	Central government administration, local authorities and non-financial public corporations, government financial institutions (postal savings etc.)
Overseas	Rest of the world
Banks	Central bank, city and local banks, long-term credit banks and banking departments of trust banks
Other financial institutions	Insurance companies, trust departments of trust banks and various specialized institutions

2. Extent of consolidation

	Not consolidated except for transactions in deposits, loans, etc., by both banks and OFIs and in loans and shares by central government

3. Instruments

(a) Bills and deposits	
Cash and transferable deposits	—
Other deposits	Time deposits, instalment savings deposits, postal savings, etc.
Money market paper, etc.	Short-term government securities
(b) Loans	
Short-term loans ⎫ Long-term loans ⎬	No split available; housing loans ? less important than elsewhere
(c) Securities	
Bonds	Includes long-term government bonds
Shares	—
(d) Life funds	Operating assets of life insurance companies, etc.
(e) Other	
Monetary gold and SDRs	Includes official foreign exchange reserves
Trade credits	Personal transactions are net
Other instruments	Includes some miscellaneous money market and security transactions and most foreign transactions

General classification	4. France
1. Main groups	
Persons	Includes unincorporated businesses and private non-profit institutions
Companies	Private non-financial companies
Government	Central, state and local government, social security funds (including certain pension funds) and public enterprises
Overseas	Rest of the world including non-metropolitan France
Banks	Central bank and other monetary institutions including general banks and 'popular' credit banks
Other financial institutions	Insurance companies, savings banks, mutual funds and investment trusts and various specialized institutions
2. Extent of consolidation	Some consolidation in financial and government groups
3. Instruments	
(a) Bills and deposits	
Cash and transferable deposits	—
Other deposits	Time and savings deposits, certain non-negotiable short-term bonds
Money market paper, etc.	Treasury bills and certificates of certain financial institutions
(b) Loans	
Short-term loans	Loans up to two years by financial institutions and trade and finance bills discounted
Long-term loans	Loans over two years by financial institutions and one year by others
(c) Securities	
Bonds	—
Shares	Includes provision of capital by Treasury to public enterprises
(d) Life funds	Change in reserves of life insurance companies
(e) Other	
Monetary gold and SDRs	—
Trade credits	Credits up to one year
Other instruments	Certain reserves of insurance companies

General classification	5. West Germany
1. Main groups	
Persons	Personal transactions only (but in Chapter 7 includes all housing transactions classified in a separate group)
Companies	All private and public non-financial enterprises including unincorporated business but excluding housing
Government	Central, regional and local government and social security funds but excluding housing and public enterprises
Overseas	Rest of the world including East Germany
Banks	Central bank, commercial banks, savings banks, central giro institutions, private and public mortgage banks and post office savings bank
Other financial institutions	Insurance companies and pension funds, building and loan associations
2. Extent of consolidation	n/a
3. Instruments	
(a) Bills and deposits	
Cash and transferable deposits	Deposits with banks by non-banking groups
Other deposits	Time deposits, savings deposits, saving certificates, funds with building and loan associations, etc.
Money market paper, etc.	Treasury bills, discountable government bonds, etc.
(b) Loans	
Short-term loans	Bank loans up to one year
Long-term loans	Bank loans over one year plus loans by building and loan associations, etc.
(c) Securities	
Bonds	—
Shares	Includes investment fund units
(d) Life funds	Funds placed by persons with insurance companies and pension funds
(e) Other	
Monetary gold and SDRs	Includes official foreign exchange holdings
Trade credits	Not identified
Other instruments	Includes various direct loans and credits and some intra-group dealings, also net unidentified items

General classification	6. The Netherlands
1. Main groups	
Persons } Companies }	Financial transactions of persons and companies are not separately identified
Government	Central, state and local government and social security funds
Overseas	Rest of the world
Banks	Central bank, commercial banks, giros and agricultural credit banks
Other financial institutions	Savings banks including postal savings bank, life insurance companies and pension funds
2. Extent of consolidation	Financial groups are consolidated and government partly so, but persons and companies are not
3. Instruments	
(a) Bills and deposits	
Cash and transferable deposits	—
Other deposits	Time deposits, savings deposits and foreign currency deposits of non-bank groups
Money market paper, etc.	Includes treasury paper and commercial bills
(b) Loans	
Short-term loans	Short-term bank loans, government debt, etc.
Long-term loans	Long-term bank loans, etc.; here includes debt certificates
(c) Securities	
Bonds	—
Shares	—
(d) Life funds	Equity on life assurance and pension funds
(e) Other	
Monetary gold and SDRs	—
Trade credits	—
Other instruments	Includes direct investment abroad and certain security transactions

General classification	7. UK

1. Main groups

Persons	Includes unincorporated businesses and private non-profit-making bodies
Companies	Private non-financial companies
Government	Central government, local authorities and nationalized industries
Overseas	Rest of the world
Banks	Central bank and all UK banks including discount houses
Other financial institutions	Building societies, part of savings banks, finance houses, insurance companies and pension funds, unit trusts, etc.

2. Extent of consolidation

	All consolidated as far as possible

3. Instruments

(a) Bills and deposits

Cash and transferable deposits	Includes official foreign exchange and all bank transactions in foreign currencies with foreign residents; also all bank deposits and CDs
Other deposits	Deposits with building societies, finance houses, savings banks, etc.
Money market paper, etc.	Treasury and commercial bills and tax reserve certificates

(b) Loans

Short-term loans	All bank loans, hire purchase credit, local authority short-term debt, etc., also government borrowing from the Bank of England.
Long-term loans	House purchase loans, local authority borrowing, etc.

(c) Securities

Bonds Shares	Split is estimated

(d) Life funds

	Equity on life assurance and pension funds

(e) Other

Monetary gold and SDRs	—
Trade credits	Public sector and overseas (net) only
Other instruments	Accruals, etc.

Bibliography

The publications listed below represent some of the background reading used in writing the book. They have been selected as those most suitable as further reading on the topics covered. In addition some detailed publications, to which specific reference is made in the text, are included.

1. GENERAL STUDIES OF THE UK FINANCIAL SYSTEM

1. Central Office of Information, *British Financial Institutions* (Reference Pamphlet 24), HMSO, 1971.
2. Inter-Bank Research Organization, *The Future of London as an International Financial Centre,* HMSO, 1973.
3. N. Macrae, *The London Capital Market*, Staples Press, 1964.
4. H. McCrae and F. Cairncross, *Capital City*, Eyre Methuen, 1973.
5. J. R. S. Revell, *The British Financial System*, Macmillan, 1973.
6. J. R. S. Revell, *Financial Structure and Government Regulation in the UK, 1952–1980* (IBRO Occasional Paper No. 1), Inter-Bank Research Organization, 1972.
7. J. Robertson, 'Honest Money, Open Government and a Fair Society', *Banker*, December 1973.
8. Committee on the working of the Monetary System (Radcliffe Committee), *Report and Evidence*, HMSO, 1959.

2. PARTICULAR INSTITUTIONS AND MARKETS IN THE UK

(a) *Banking*

9. National Board for Prices and Incomes, *Bank Charges* (Report No. 34), HMSO, 1967.
10. E. Nevin and E. W. Davis, *The London Clearing Banks*, Elek, 1970.
11. J. R. S. Revell, *Changes in British Banking* (Hill Samuel Occasional Paper No. 3), Hill Samuel, 1968.
12. *British Banking: Changes and Challenges*, Institute of Bankers, 1968.
13. P. Einzig, *Parallel Money Markets*, Macmillan, 1971.
14. 'Recent Developments in London's Money Markets' (2 parts), *Midland Bank Review*, August and November 1969.
15. 'The Inter-bank Markets in Sterling', *Midland Bank Review*, August 1973.
16. R. Kellet, *The Merchant Banking Arena*, Macmillan, 1967.
17. S. Mason, 'Merchant Banking Today and in the Future', *Journal of Business Finance*, Winter 1971.

18. E. Reid, *The Role of the Merchant Banks Today*, Institute of Bankers, 1963.
19. G. Young, *Merchant Banking: Practice and Prospects*, Weidenfeld & Nicolson, 1966.
20. W. M. Scammell, *The London Discount Market*, Elek, 1968.

(b) *Other institutions and markets*
21. *Consumer Credit. Report of the Committee* (Crowther Committee), HMSO, 1971.
22. E. J. Cleary, *The Building Society Movement*, Elek, 1965.
23. H. B. Rose, *Building Societies and the Changing Capital Market* (The Bellman Lecture), Abbey National Building Society, 1974.
24. *Committee to Review National Savings* (Page Committee) *Report*, HMSO, 1973.
25. R. L. Carter, *Economics and Insurance*, P. H. Press, 1973.
26. G. Clayton, *British Insurance*, Elek, 1971.
27. J. H. Dunning, *Insurance in the Economy* (Occasional Paper No. 34), Institute of Economic Affairs, 1971.
28. *Linked Life Assurance* (Report of the Committee on Property Bonds and Equity-linked Life Assurance—Scott Committee), HMSO, 1973.
29. E. Victor Morgan and W. A. Thomas, *The Stock Exchange: Its History and Functions*, Elek, 1962.
30. P. K. Woolley, 'The Economics of the UK Stock Exchange', *Moorgate & Wall Street Review*, Spring 1974.
31. *Institutional Investors and the London Stock Exchange* (Occasional Paper No. 1), British Finance & Accounting Association, 1972.
32. H. Burton and D. C. Corner, *Investment and Unit Trusts in Britain and America*, Elek, 1968.
33. *The Committee of Enquiry on Small Firms* (Bolton Committee) *Report* and *Research Reports* 4 and 5, HMSO, 1971.
34. S. Mason, 'The Role of the Capital Market in Financing Small Business' (unpublished paper), 1973.

3. FINANCIAL MARKETS OVERSEAS

35. *Capital Markets Study*, OECD, 1968.
36. P. Readman *et al.*, *The European Money Puzzle*, Michael Joseph, 1973.
37. *A Description and Analysis of Certain European Capital Markets* (Paper prepared for the Joint Economic Committee of Congress of the US), US Govt Printing Office, 1964.
38. *The Development of a European Capital Market* (Report of a Group of Experts), EEC Commission, 1966.

4. STATISTICAL SOURCES AND ANALYSES

39. *Financial Statistics*, HMSO (monthly).
40. *Notes and Definitions to Financial Statistics*, HMSO (annually).

41. *National Income and Expenditure (Blue Book)*, HMSO (annually).
42. Rita Maurice (ed.), *National Accounts Statistics Sources and Methods*, HMSO, 1968.
43. *Bank of England Quarterly Bulletin*, Bank of England (quarterly).
44. *Bank of England Statistical Abstract No. 1*, Bank of England, 1970.
45. *An Introduction to Flow of Funds Accounting 1952–70*, Bank of England, 1972.
46. *Statistics relating to quoted securities*, Stock Exchange (quarterly).
47. J. Moyle, *The Pattern of Ordinary Share Ownership 1957–1970* (University of Cambridge Department of Applied Economics Occasional Paper No. 31), Cambridge University Press, 1971.
48. J. R. S. Revell, *The Wealth of the Nation* (University of Cambridge Department of Applied Economics Monograph 14), Cambridge University Press, 1967.
49. J. R. S. Revell and A. R. Roe, 'National Balance Sheets and National Accounting—a Progress Report', *Economic Trends*, May 1971.
50. A. R. Roe, *The Financial Interdependence of the Economy 1957–1966 (A Programme for Growth No. 11)*, Chapman & Hall, 1971.
51. J. Rothman, *The Wealth of the United Kingdom*, Sandelson & Co. Ltd, 1974.
52. 'National Balance Sheets: a new analytical tool', *Bank of England Quarterly Bulletin*, December 1972.
53. 'Banking Sector Balance Sheets', *Bank of England Quarterly Bulletin*, December 1973.

5. MORE THEORETICAL ANALYSES

54. A. D. Bain, 'Flow of Funds Analysis: A Survey', *Economic Journal*, December 1973.
55. W. J. Baumol, *The Stock Market and Economic Efficiency*, Fordham University Press, 1965.
56. R. A. Brealey, *An Introduction to Risk and Return from Common Stocks*, MIT Press, 1969.
57. G. Clayton, 'British Financial Intermediaries in Theory and Practice', *Economic Journal*, December 1962.
58. J. C. R. Dow, *The Management of the British Economy 1945–60*, Cambridge University Press, 1964.
59. M. Dryden, 'A Statistical Study of UK Share Prices', *Scottish Journal of Political Economy*, November 1970
60. J. Duesenberry, 'Criteria for Judging the Performance of Capital Markets' in H. K. Wu and A. J. Zakon (eds), *Elements of Investment*, Holt Reinhart, 1965.
61. E. F. Fama, 'Multi-period Consumption–Investment Decisions', *American Economic Review*, November 1970.
62. N. J. Gibson, *Financial Intermediaries in Monetary Policy*, Institute of Economic Affairs, 1967.
63. R. W. Goldsmith, *Financial Structure and Development*, Yale University Press, 1969.

64. C. A. E. Goodhart and A. D. Crockett, 'The Importance of Money', *Bank of England Quarterly Bulletin*, June 1970.
65. J. G. Gurley and C. S. Shaw, 'Financial Intermediaries in the Saving and Investment Process', *Journal of Finance*, May 1956.
66. J. Lintner, 'Security Prices, Risk and Maximal Gains from Diversification', *Journal of Finance*, December 1965.
67. H. M. Markovitz, *Portfolio Selection: Efficient Diversification of Investments*, John Wiley, 1959.
68. M. E. Poliakoff *et al.*, *Financial Institutions and Markets*, Houghton Mifflin, 1970.
69. H. B. Rose, 'Competition and Credit Control—The New Framework', *Three Banks Review*, March 1972.
70. W. F. Sharp, 'Capital Asset Prices and the Theory of Market Equilibrium under Conditions of Risk', *Journal of Finance*, September 1964.
71. P. E. Smith, *The Economics of Financial Institutions and Markets*, R. D. Irwin, 1971.

Index

Bold type indicates main references